WHAT TO CONSIDER IF YOU'RE CONSIDERING COLLEGE

WHAT TO CONSIDER
IF YOU'RE
CONSIDERING
COLLEGE

New Rules for Education and Employment

KEN S. COATES
BILL MORRISON

DUNDURN
TORONTO

Copy Editor: Tara Tovell
Interior Design: Janette Thompson (Jansom)
Cover Design: Laura Boyle
Cover Image: Lunamaria/istock.com
Printer: Webcom

Library and Archives Canada Cataloguing in Publication

Coates, Kenneth, 1956-, author
  What to consider if you're considering college : new rules for education and employment /
  Ken S. Coates and Bill Morrison

Issued in print and electronic format.
ISBN 978-1-4597-2372-6 (pbk.) -- ISBN 978-1-4597-2373-3 (pdf). -- ISBN 978-1-4597-2374-0 (epub)

  1. Career education. 2. Vocational guidance. 3. Postsecondary education. 4. Education, Higher.
5. High school students--Vocational guidance. 6. High school students--Vocational education. I. Coates,
Kenneth, 1956-, author II. Title. III. Title: What to consider if you are considering college.
  LC1037.C63 2015   370.113   C2015-900584-1
                                          C2015-900585-X

1 2 3 4 5   19 18 17 16 15

We acknowledge the support of the **Canada Council for the Arts** and the **Ontario Arts Council** for our publishing program. We also acknowledge the financial support of the **Government of Canada** through the **Canada Book Fund** and **Livres Canada Books**, and the **Government of Ontario** through the **Ontario Book Publishing Tax Credit** and the **Ontario Media Development Corporation**.

VISIT US AT
Dundurn.com | *@dundurnpress* | *Facebook.com/dundurnpress* | *Pinterest.com/dundurnpress*

Dundurn
3 Church Street, Suite 500
Toronto, Ontario, Canada
M5E 1M2

CONTENTS

For our grandchildren:

William Griffin, Spencer Griffin, Victoria Griffin,
Katie Coates, Christopher Coates, Hazel Coates

Graeme Gibbons, Ella Gibbons, James Tosoff, Henry Tosoff,
Quinn Morrison, John Morrison, George Morrison

In the hope that they will make the choices that serve them best.

ACKNOWLEDGEMENTS

This book emerged out of the interest and controversy that surrounded the release of a previous book, *Campus Confidential*, a work that explored the Canadian university system from the inside. As we wrote the book, we were asked repeatedly, "What should we advise our kids to do?" or, from younger people, "What should I do with my life?" and specifically, "Should I go to college?" This book is our answer to hundreds of such questions. Following the endless debate about this same topic in the United States — which typically focused more on "Which college?" than on "Is college the right choice?" — convinced us that we had something to say to American students as well.

We greatly appreciate the invitation from Dundurn Press to prepare an edition for the American market. We have been close observers of the American scene for many years, having visited dozens of U.S. colleges, spending extended periods of time at various campuses, from Duke University in North Carolina and Florida State in Tallahassee to the University of Alaska in Fairbanks and Washington State in Pulman, Washington, and we have visited a great many others, from Qatar to New Zealand to Singapore, where we have felt the power and influence of the American college system. We thoroughly enjoy exploring campuses simply to get a sense of the place and to imagine what is like to study, teach and work in such settings. We greatly appreciate the welcome we received from faculty, staff, and students alike; their comments on their college experiences shaped our understanding of America's remarkable — and remarkably diverse — postsecondary system.

Our work has benefited from endless conversations with faculty members, students, administrators, parents, and employers. We apologize to them for our obsession with the subject. We also wish to thank Kaiti Hannah, Lorien Hughes, and Amanda Sampson, who read a draft of the book and offered valuable comments. What you see here, however, is the result of thousands of conversations, seemingly endless reading, and a great deal of discussion between the two of us.

We know that we have sampled only a small percentage of the thousands of community colleges, colleges, universities, and technical institutes in the United States, but we have, we think, developed a strong affinity for this remarkable system. Our work has been added to over the years by many conversations with faculty and administrative colleagues from American schools, attendance at conferences where speakers discussed the strengths and challenges of the U.S. system, and from the rich and highly professional reporting in the *Chronicle of Higher Education* and the Internet-based *Inside Higher Ed*. America's colleges and universities (but not yet its community colleges and technical schools) attract a great deal of scholarly and journalistic attention. Our e-readers are full of the detailed books, analytical and often polemical, written about this highly contested topic. We have benefited enormously from the insights and controversies that surround postsecondary education in the United States and gratefully acknowledge, collectively, the work of these writers and scholars.

The U.S. edition of *What to Consider* began with a conversation with our then-editor at Dundurn, Diane Young. Her enthusiasm for the project overcame our reluctance to pontificate about matters American. Carrie Gleason, her successor at Dundurn, did an excellent job of keeping our project on track and maintaining our enthusiasm for this undertaking. The production team at Dundurn was up to its usual prompt and professional standard. We are particularly grateful to Tara Tovell for her careful copy-editing of our draft. That this project was completed in a timely fashion owes a great deal to Sherilee Diebold-Cooze, Ken's executive assistant, who managed to keep him on track through some very busy months.

As always, we owe an enormous debt of gratitude to our wives and partners, Linda Morrison and Carin Holroyd, whose support for our writings clearly knows no bounds, for we have tested every reasonable boundary in a literary collaboration that has now stretched over thirty years! We are blessed with nine children (Bill has four, Ken has five) and thirteen grandchildren (Bill seven and Ken six, with a seventh due in May 2015). We have written this book with the futures of our children and grandchildren very much in mind.

The writing of this book was shaped, in significant ways, by conservations with Ken's daughter Hana. She is fourteen years old, a wonderful and talented young woman who is deeply obsessed with American universities. (Thank you, *Gilmore Girls*, for setting up an intense competition in her mind between Yale and Harvard.) Hana's constant enthusiasm for colleges and universities has kept this topic fresh and relevant; our discussions with her have focused her teenage mind on what lies ahead. If current thinking holds, she will be applying to Reed College, along with Yale, thanks to Rory Gilmore!

It was thirty years ago, in the fall of 1983, that we first met as college teachers and started to write together. Although we also write books on our own, and have other collaborations, this book is the fourteenth we have written or edited together. We hope that this book, like the others, will find its audience, and we earnestly wish that young Americans will find in it much good advice that will help them navigate what looks to be, for people starting out in life, an increasingly difficult future.

Ken Coates, B.A., M.A., Ph.D., Johnson-Shoyama School of Public Policy, University of Saskatchewan

Bill Morrison, B.A., M.A., Ph.D., DLit. (Hon.), Professor Emeritus of History, University of Northern British Columbia

INTRODUCTION

SO YOU'RE THINKING OF GOING TO COLLEGE.

STOP! Stop right now before reading any further. Ask yourself three crucial questions:

- Why?

- Why?

- Why?

If you are wondering why we ask this question three times, it's because it is so vital for your future.

For those of you just finishing your secondary education, choosing your path after high school is one of the most important decisions you will ever make, perhaps *the* most important. It's crazy to make it without giving it serious thought. It's equally foolish to make it based solely on what other people want you to do, or think you should do. For better or worse, your decision will shape your future in dramatic ways. You need to think long and hard about it. That's what we want to talk to you about.

Going to college can be a good choice. But it's not a good choice for all high school graduates. For some, it can be disastrous — leading to debt, disillusionment, and failure. College is not the only good option open to you. Have you considered

- Technical college?

- Two-year colleges?

- Starting a business?

- Working for a year or two?

- Traveling or volunteering?

- An apprenticeship?

If you're listening to the general chatter — particularly from parents, guidance counselors, and politicians — you may believe that college is your only option. It isn't. For some of you, going to college will be a terrific choice that launches you on a path to happiness and prosperity. For others, it will be an absolutely wrong choice. Many students find out too late that they've made a bad decision, and end up back home by Christmas or the spring, poorer and sadder for the experience. Others will slog unhappily to the graduation finish line — only then to discover that they are ill-prepared for the world of work.

Of course your parents are ambitious for you. They want you to get a job indoors in a comfy office. Their Google and Apple fantasy is as strong as yours, unless you are Ivy League material, in which case they dream of you pulling down a six-figure starting salary from a Wall Street financial institution. Appreciate what your parents have in mind. They don't want you to end up working outside an office doing a job that involves physical labor — unless, of course, you are working on some climate change, artistic, environmental, or similarly prestigious project. And, let's be honest, your parents also want you out of the house, preferably before you are thirty, with the money you need to launch yourself into a good life.

For those of you who already have an undergraduate degree or who find yourselves feeling insecure about your current situation, you may be wondering what to do next. Perhaps the job you were dreaming of hasn't materialized. You fought through to graduate with a law degree and can't find a job. Not what you planned for, right? You wanted to be a teacher, but there are so many unemployed teachers in their twenties that it's impossible to find a teaching job. And if you find a position in one of the country's cash-starved schools, you find yourself with a low-paying job in difficult conditions. Perhaps you are working in a Starbucks, not a high school. This wasn't why you borrowed $100,000, why your parents saved for years and fought hard to get you into a prestigious college, or why you spent four years there.

Should you return to college to get a different, or advanced, degree? Should you go to a technical institution or a community college and qualify for working in a trade? Something must be done: you are on the good side of thirty (but not by much) and your parents are hinting that they'd like to downsize their house. The choices you made after high school have not worked out as you'd hoped. Obviously, you cannot unmake them, but you are young enough to make a new choice.

Regardless of how you've come to this decision point, now is the time to make smart, informed choices. This book will help you make the choice that best suits you; it also will help you prepare to meet the demands of the workforce of today and the next twenty-five years.

AN UNCERTAIN FUTURE

The future is as uncertain as it has been at any time in the last 150 years. People do not have a clue about what's to come, though many make money pretending they do. Twenty years ago, the main things that now define your life — smartphones, Facebook, Twitter, instant messaging, sexting, on-demand videos, iTunes, eBay, and illegal downloads — simply did not exist. Twenty years from now, who knows? Right now, China is on track to become the world's largest economy. The United States, the world's greatest economic power for the entire lifetime of your grandparents and parents, finds itself on shaky ground. You can still see signs of the American dream around you — but don't for a second believe that Donald Trump is much more than a public relations illusion. Realize too, that despite the self-image of a country that fancies every person can be a billionaire, people such as Steve Jobs, Bill Gates, and Michael Zuckerman are very few in number. You might end up like them, but then you might win the lottery too — the odds are about the same.

The challenges are everywhere. India is on the rise, and the Philippines and Vietnam may not be far behind. Europe, once solid and reliable, is torn by financial crises and social tension. If you think the American job market for young adults is tough these days, you should see how limited the prospects are for your contemporaries in countries such as Spain and Greece.

In this unstable environment, how do you prepare for a successful future? Join the knowledge economy? Those who talk about it don't really know if a college degree will give you a good career. That huge demand for skilled trades in the supposedly revitalized manufacturing economy? Don't count on it. Most of the manufacturing coming back to the United States is either high technology–based or non-union or both. The coming flood of retirements that will create hundreds of openings for young people? Not with middle-class jobs disappearing so fast and the value of pensions collapsing. Far too many grandparents are heading back into the workforce instead of enjoying the leisurely retirement they had planned. At least, the experts say, the service economy will remain strong — but will it? And if it does, how many high-paying jobs do you expect to find in the restaurant, hotel, car rental, and tourism industries? Look at the minimum wages in the different states. Yes, Seattle is talking about $15 an hour, but the federal minimum wage as of this writing is $7.25 an hour, and many service jobs don't pay much more than that. Many young people think it's cool to be a barista, and perhaps it is: we aren't experts on cool. Starbucks pays $9 to $12 an hour, depending on location. You want a career as a barista? We don't knock the job; someone has to do it, but will it be you? Can you live on your own for $10 an hour? Look at house prices and imagine how far $20,000 a year will take you. Things are worse in other sectors — read up on what it's like to work for Walmart. You might say all these wages should be raised, and wouldn't it be nice if they were, but that's not what this book is about. This book isn't about political policy and it isn't about everyone; it's about you, specifically, and your future.

We live in a time of constant and dramatic change. No one really knows what lies ahead — not us, not your parents or teachers, not politicians or governments, not the people who make their living forecasting the future, and not the college recruiters. Indeed, the only piece of wisdom about which we have absolute confidence is this: no one knows how the next ten to forty years will unfold.

And yet, here you stand — ready to make the choices that will determine your future, and you have some tough decisions to make. If you are about to graduate from high school, you need to determine how you will make your way into the confusing, high-stakes world of life. Your parents and guidance counselors urge you to go to college — but they are telling almost everyone else the same thing. If you live out west or in Alaska, or are willing to travel to the remote wildernesses of northern Canada, you might land a well-paid, low-skill job in the resource sector. There's good money to be made in the Bakken oil field in North Dakota and in the oil sands of northern Alberta. You may be planning to leave home. (Be honest: don't all young adults want to be fully independent of their parents?)

If you really do want to go to college, though, which one do you pick? America has the world's best higher education system, offering a tremendous variety of opportunities for high school graduates. Some of these schools set the global gold standard, and there are thousands of young Americans fighting to get into them. Others are so desperate for students that almost anyone who is walking and breathing can get in — although the dropout rate can be high. If, on the other hand, you've already gone to college, did you make the right choice? Which program has the best potential? Why not a technical institute or community college? How about an apprenticeship program? Or the military? Or a year of travel or international work, or even volunteering? So many options, so many expensive choices, and so little guidance.

PREPARING YOURSELF: HOW WE CAN HELP

This is where we come in. We want to help you make a careful choice about your future. Whatever you choose to do will have upsides and downsides. It can cost a small fortune to go to college (and the prices for the top colleges are the highest in the world). That money is poorly spent if you drop out after a year (or sooner), if you are not really interested in what the place has to offer, or if you cannot find a decent job for years after graduation. And if you have not heard about the student debt crisis, open your eyes. American law is such that you cannot really escape student debt, even if you are flat broke and declaring bankruptcy. Money you borrowed so easily at the age of eighteen and spent so cheerfully during your college years could be dragging you down for the rest of your life. Total student debt in the United States passed $1.2 trillion in June 2014, with over 7 million debtors in default, which means their credit is probably ruined.

The average student debt in 2014 was $28,000, which isn't too high, but a very small percentage owed more than $200,000! And a small percentage means 167,000 people. Read the Wikipedia article on "Student Debt" and be very afraid. We have watched too many students make too many bad choices over the years. We want to help you figure out what is best for you — for now and for the future. Time spent thinking and planning your future may well be the best investment you ever make.

As we proceed here, we will try to maintain an avuncular tone — we'll give you the advice a friendly uncle would. We adore colleges and we like students. We wish both of them well, though we recognize that both have their faults. We also are fond of community colleges and really keen about technical institutes, and we like well-planned travel, work, and volunteering. We offer ourselves as guides — two veteran university teachers and administrators who have been working with young adults for, well, a very long time.

Preparing for life after high school and college is a difficult and confusing task, for parents as much as for the young adults heading off to advanced education or the world of work. We want to help. We have seen thousands of new students make their way, nervous and uncertain, onto campuses. We have welcomed them to their first class at college, and have sat with them and their parents when their dreams exploded in a welter of failed examinations, skipped classes, and poor essays. As parents ourselves, we have watched our children work their way through their studies and make their difficult way into the paid workforce. We know that there is nothing easy about what lies ahead. We have seen many students fail — and then succeed elsewhere in life. We have watched young adults make foolish decisions that hounded them all their lives. We have seen people underestimate the value of a community college diploma and misunderstand the importance of work experience. We think we have some wisdom to share.

We should, however, confess: we are both old. One of us is moderately old; the other is really old. One of us got his B.A. in 1978 and the other in (shudder) 1963. So, why should you listen to a couple of seniors? Let us ask you this: Do you want advice from some newcomer who just got out of college the day before yesterday, the ink on the diploma still damp, some dude who hasn't got over his last beer bust and beer pong (or Beirut) match? Or would you rather listen to two guys who've been in and around colleges and universities all over the world (first as students, and then as teachers and administrators) for a total of nearly ninety years? There's not much we haven't seen and done in the field — and here we are giving you the benefit of all this hard-won experience. Go ahead: listen to this newbie next door, or to a couple of veterans. Your life, your choice.

We have another confession to make, which you will have figured out for yourselves if you've read the Acknowledgements: we aren't Americans. We are Canadians, and have spent most of our lives in the Canadian system, which is quite like the U.S. system, except that our colleges (Canadians usually call them universities) are almost all public, and the tuition fees are therefore far lower than they are in your country. No one in Canada pays anything like the sixty thousand dollars a year that the top U.S. schools charge; the average tuition fee for an arts degree in Canada is about five thousand dollars a year. However, we know the American system pretty well. We have spent time at American universities: Florida State, the University of Alaska, and others. One of us taught two semesters as a Distinguished Visiting Professor at Duke, and got to sample the high end of the college spectrum. Another of us taught for a couple of years in New Zealand, which further broadened our experience. Of more value to you is probably the fact that we have no political axe to grind. We aren't Republicans or Democrats. We don't belong to the Occupy Movement or the Tea Party. We are simply keenly interested in postsecondary education, and in the welfare of students. We think that's worth a good deal to you.

We are not insiders in the American system, but for decades we have observed, admired, and criticized U.S. colleges. We have visited the elite institutions and marvelled at their intellectual depth and their facilities. Thomas Jefferson's University of Virginia is a particular favorite, and so is Middlebury College. We have spent time at run-of-the-mill state universities and toured several private colleges on the verge of being shut down. We have monitored, with alarm, the ever-escalating tuition fees at the top schools — amazed at the willingness of American parents to pay so much for their children's education. We have made great friendships with scholars and teachers from across the United States, envious at the salaries and working conditions of faculty members in the elite institutions and dismayed by those of the poorer colleges.

We don't presume to tell you what to do, since the life trajectory of each family and every student is different. If you do choose to go to college, we can offer our insights into how they operate, what typically happens to families and students in their first year, and how to get the most from a college career. But if you decide — as many of you should — to choose one of the various non-college options available to you, we can help you to be clear about your rationale and your prospects. Even those of you who have already completed a degree or diploma can, we think, benefit from what we have to offer.

Let us make this crystal clear: we believe that, for the right student, with the right attitude, a college education is an unbeatable experience and a fully worthwhile investment. If you are that student, your college experience will help you to develop valuable skills, gain insights into the human condition and the natural world, make great friends and lifelong contacts, and emerge at graduation as a profoundly changed person. However, we also know that community colleges, technical institutes, and apprenticeships are brilliant options for just as many students — and that time spent traveling, working, or volunteering can equally set you up for a very successful life.

In the chapters that follow, we are going to encourage you to consider all options — college, apprenticeship programs, community colleges, technical institutes, entrepreneurships, religious and military colleges, volunteering, travel, and work — before making a decision about what comes next. Whether you are a soon-to-be high school graduate who can draw upon your parents to support you in this process or a young adult who needs to make a change, we are going to help you to think long and hard about the match (or mismatch) between your skills and interests and the choices you are considering. We will ask you to look deep into yourselves to identify — honestly — your desires, abilities, and work ethic to succeed in the demanding and largely unsupervised world that you're about to enter.

We have written this book to challenge you to look at the wide variety of options available to you — and not simply default to the institution closest to home. For some of you, this process may affirm the choice that was already at the top of your list; for others, the outcome may be very different from what you expected. In either case, we'll have done our job, you'll have done your homework, and we believe that you'll be better prepared for what lies ahead.

POSTSCRIPT

The week we finished this book, we listened in on President Obama's Summit on College Opportunity. The president was surrounded by fans of his college and university policies, interrupting his speech regularly to applaud declarations of support for college education, funding commitments, and the strong encouragement that marks his sincere commitment to advanced education. Community college and college executives, along with student representatives and parents celebrated a president who understood their concerns about growing tuition rates, the high cost of student debt, and the need to prepare young people for the world of work. The country, it seems, has a real strategy for responding to the needs of young Americans: send them to college.

But the talk made us feel uneasy. The reality is that the relentless expansion of community college and college enrollment has, on the whole, failed in its goal of helping young Americans adjust to the realities of the modern economy. While there is a lot of talk of successful graduates — the ones who get career-launching jobs at Google or Apple — there are three groups of young people whose experiences were largely ignored until the last few years: the large number of students who fail to complete their academic programs (almost half at some places), those who graduate but cannot find a job, and graduates who find a job that does not require a college degree. The last of these — the underemployed — are the symbols of the disconnect between ambition, training, ability, and the realities of the workforce.

Expanding the community college and college systems is not, in our opinion, the right response to the challenges of the twenty-first century. President Obama, in working with the advanced educational institutions that benefit from his policies, has gone too far in promoting college education as the best route to individual success and prosperity. Going to a community college or college is unquestionably the right choice for some students. It is equally clear that this option is the wrong choice for an almost equal number of students, including many who are currently studying in these institutions. President Obama compares college education in the twenty-first century to public elementary and high school education in the twentieth century. We think this is a false comparison. Public school is for everyone; college is not. There is evidence that the United States has significant shortages of graduates in selected fields; there is equal evidence that the system is over-producing graduates in other fields. The American strategy of sending as many as possible to postsecondary institutions is too simplistic, too narrowly focused, and disconnected from the reality of individuals' lives and the needs of an evolving workforce.

Be careful! Politicians tell people what they want to hear. President Obama's message implies that all students are capable of success at community college or college — something that is simply not true. The Summit on College Opportunity implies that there are great career-type jobs waiting for all diploma and degree holders. Also not true. The rhetoric suggests that there are only a few paths — through community colleges or colleges — to middle-class success or personal achievement. This is also untrue. You face complex life choices as you prepare for a very uncertain world. Listen to yourself — prepare yourself. Do not be overwhelmed by political commentary, even when it comes from the president. President Obama's heart is in the right place. But like too many people in contemporary America, his commitment to expanding the postsecondary sector is likely also to continue the process of weakening the entering classes of colleges, increasing unhappy experiences in postsecondary education, over-producing graduates for the modern economy, and creating the impression that America's time as the land of opportunity is coming to an end.

1

THE CROSSROADS:
MAKING CHOICES THAT MATTER

You are likely reading this book because you have reached a significant crossroads in your life. Now is the time for you to decide what you will do next — and the options are many. Chances are, as an American youth or young adult, you've heard that going to college is the only responsible choice you can make. After all, President Obama, governors by the dozen, high school principals, and probably your parents are all singing the same song. The college case is like a One Direction song — one of those monotonous, uninspired, and vapid pieces that you find yourself humming without remembering where it came from, part of the cultural fabric of the country. That "Go to college, young person" message — which filters into your consciousness from family members, television and movies, business leaders, and government advice — may have been fine advice for your parents' and grandparents' generations, but things have changed. If you're going to make the choice that is right for you, you need — first and foremost — to consider not only where we, as a society, are, but also where we are going. In this chapter, we'll do our best to guide you through that consideration.

More than ever before, it must now seem as if everybody wants something of you. Your parents, of course, want you to be happy — but they also want you to be independent, employed (ideally established in a prestigious and rewarding career), and out of the house. Employers want you to be well-trained (for the jobs of the present and future) and ready to work — hard and with real commitment. And governments want you contributing to society and paying lots of taxes (mostly to support your parents and grandparents in their retirement, for which they will probably forget to thank you).

In much of the modern world — certainly in our part of the world — achievement has become the exception rather than the norm. Ours is increasingly the world that Malcolm Gladwell describes in *Outliers*, in which he argues that the most talented individuals in any field must spend ten thousand hours practicing to hone their skills to the highest possible level. How many do this? How many become masters of the football field, or the operating theater, or the concert hall? People such as Yo-Yo Ma and Serena Williams, maybe — but not many. But, of course, this was always true: there were never many masters. If you are one of those truly stellar individuals, you are special — and as long as you continue to challenge yourself, you may be destined for a successful life.

But a caveat here, one of many you will make along the road to self-awareness. There is a strange belief in our culture that high academic performance and basic intelligence automatically translate into true career success. Unfortunately, this isn't always true. Everyone knows people whose quirky personalities, mediocre work ethic, and other shortcomings kept them from finding and keeping great jobs and achieving their full potential. There is growing evidence that character, integrity, and pure grit are more important determinants of future success than natural ability and intelligence. Let's put it simply. Being smart is not enough. Nor is getting into an elite college an assurance of career success. In *Crisis on Campus: A Bold Plan for Reforming Our Colleges and Universities*, Mark Taylor took a close look at the experiences of graduates from Yale University. While the institution is deservedly famous and sends a high percentage of its graduates into the financial industry — itself something of a moral train wreck in recent years — the reality is that most of the graduates that he followed led average lives, with few superstars or multi-millionaires among them.

Fifty years ago a great many people in the United States worked hard at an early age to master difficult skills and meet a tough standard: studying Latin and preparing for the examinations which were a prerequisite for high school graduation and college entrance. Now, however, we live in an age where the pressure has been torqued back, at least in the public school system, where children are allowed to perform at their own level; if they think the task facing them is stupid or too tough, they are excused from trying.

Young people in the United States, especially those from privileged backgrounds, have the luxury of a more leisurely transition into adulthood than their grandparents had. High school graduates are spared the high-profile, high-stress, "study for years until final examination hell" system that East Asian high school graduates endure. They are not pushed hard by their teachers, unless they are in one of the high-pressure high schools that pride themselves on getting their graduates into elite schools. America's high schools are a source of endless battles, between parents and teachers, teachers and school boards, governments and the school system. Once the envy of the world, the American public education system has become aggressively mediocre, well back from the best in the world — places such as Finland, Taiwan, Singapore, Japan, and South Korea. A distressingly high percentage of American parents see it as their duty to insulate their teenage children from the challenges of adulthood, seeking instead to launch them gently into a world that is not insulated but confusing, complex, and surprisingly unwelcoming.

That being said, we fully recognize that not all of you have arrived at this moment easily. Those of you who come from families living in poverty or crisis, who come from rural and remote areas, who have suffered from racial or other discrimination, who have coped with physical or mental challenges, or who are continuing the transitions of immigration, have had very different experiences from the mainstream population. Across the United States, many African American and Hispanic students live in poverty, have little family or community support, and have grown up in stressful environments that can suck the vitality out of the most promising lives. Those of you raised in hardship know only too well the realities of contemporary American life; at least, then, you will head into adulthood with your eyes wide open.

So, young person, why is everyone so worried about you? You are eighteen years old or nearly so, in the final semester of high school. You might be able to vote, enlist in the army, drive a car, drink (legally or otherwise), and in general act like an adult. You and your friends are tired of your parents, teachers, and guidance counselors lecturing endlessly about colleges and jobs. Although you don't like to admit it, you are nervous too. If you aren't, you should be. It is hard to miss all the talk about the collapsing middle class, youth unemployment and underemployment, student and government debt, climate change, and all the other things that just make you want to stay in high school forever.

THE WORLD AROUND YOU

It seems unfair, doesn't it? You are heading into adulthood at a difficult time. Life may not be easy. Demographers claim you may have a lower life expectancy than your parents — the main causes are too much junk food and too little exercise; America has one of the highest rates of obesity of any major country in the world (at the top of the list are little Pacific nations such as Nauru). The financial misdeeds of your parents' generation and their governments, compounded by the spending habits of the baby boomers, mean that you are inheriting huge obligations that will dog you for the rest of your lives. The American national debt is now nearly $18 trillion, a sum that is simply incomprehensible. Perhaps you've seen the graphics trying to illustrate it: pallets on football fields stacked with thousand dollar bills. The national debt — your debt. And those wonderful technological innovations — the ones that put a smartphone in your hands, that allow you to share movies and music for free (but not, we hope, this book) — are also transforming the world of work by eliminating more jobs than they create. And all of the talk about climate change and impending ecological disaster is hardly designed to make you confident about the future.

It wasn't so long ago that the rewards of graduating from high school were more or less guaranteed. Even those who didn't finish twelfth grade could do reasonably well. As recently as the 1970s, a good deal of decently paid work could be found in the nation's auto factories, manufacturing plants, major retail stores, construction sites, fisheries, mines, and farms. An even easier route was through an unskilled or semi-skilled job with a unionized company — and again, the nation's automobile factories provided hundreds of thousands of high-paid positions with excellent benefits. Your grandfather went to work for General Motors, stuck it out for thirty years, and retired to Florida with a decent pension. A college degree was an even better ticket. Some of the country's major employers — major retail chains, the banks and stockbrokers, governments at all levels, the armed forces — hired for potential as much as skill and offered training and career progression for graduates from our universities.

America is a great place to live. There are many reasons that millions of people around the world fantasize about migrating to the United States. A number of countries are richer — Qatar, Luxembourg, Norway, and a few others — but America has traditionally been viewed as the land of opportunity. Is this likely to change? There are some ominous trends. The United States is great at producing wealthy people, but in other areas that matter, including life expectancy, infant mortality, literacy, educational attainment, inequality, safety, and the like, America's performance has been declining relative to the other top twenty-five nations. The country took a real hit during the 2007–2008 global financial crisis, and the subprime loans controversy damaged America's reputation for business integrity and competence. The combination of expensive — and largely unproductive — overseas military entanglements combined with desperate attempts to pull the national economy out of a potentially devastating tailspin tarnished America's global standing and left the country with massive debts and considerable uncertainty about the future. You don't have to be a socialist (we aren't) to be worried about the amazing increase in income inequality that's occurred over the past generation.

So, is there reason for you to worry? Quick answer: sorry, but yes. Bear with us for a short economics lecture on matters of vital concern to you. The United States has an enviable standard of living and quality of life, a superb entrepreneurial environment, several of the most dynamic cities in the world, and abundant opportunity for personal growth. Despite issues that sometimes dominate media attention, such as political logjams in Congress, growing distress about America's money-driven political culture, resurgent racial tensions and frustrations with President Obama and both political parties, the United States remains an impressive place. Whatever the country's shortcomings, and these are obvious and not few, you are coming into adulthood into one of the richest, most dynamic and, dare we say it out loud, greatest nations on the planet.

But there are some gloomy spots. The country's indebtedness is a problem (or not, depending on your political and economic viewpoint). Far too many African Americans suffer from poverty and social dysfunction. Illegal immigrants, who number in the millions, struggle to find their piece of the American dream. Native Americans do not share in the nation's prosperity, particularly if they live on isolated reservations. Pockets of real economic hardship can be found across the country: one-industry towns without an industry, farming regions in sustained decline, rural and remote communities that offer few economic opportunities and that are losing young people in droves, once-thriving fishing communities destroyed by the decline of coastal fisheries, and working-class segments of industrial cities that are now pockmarked by abandoned factories. Many immigrants, including thousands with diplomas and advanced degrees that are not recognized by American employers, struggle to find secure and decent jobs. All countries have sectors of economic distress and the United States is no different, but the nation does offer various government support programs to ensure that even people without work have some measure of support, although these programs are not comparable to those of other prosperous countries.

Another part of the problem rests with American companies. In recent years, firms in the United States have made impressive gains in productivity and competitiveness, primarily through major investments in labor-saving technologies. Simply put, Americans produce more per unit of work or input than most of their industrial competitors, although at a higher cost than low-wage countries such as China, the Philippines, and Mexico. U.S. companies struggle, as they do in other nations, to use new labor-saving and labor-enhancing equipment to keep up with the robotics-obsessed Japanese and East Asians. This is one of the classic double-edged swords of the twenty-first century: on the one hand, to stay competitive and hold on to market share in the hotly contested global market, firms have no choice but to invest heavily in new cost-reducing technologies; on the other hand, these investments will cut substantially into jobs for the vast army of low-skilled, high-waged American workers who have been central to the country's economic fortunes for decades. It will likely mean fewer jobs for the college graduate middle-management group — the kind of job you may well be thinking about.

The automotive sector is the best example of the industrial transition underway in the United States. On the positive side, foreign car companies have invested massively in new plants, although mostly in southern states that do not favour trade unions. At the same time, the large American-owned car companies have cut back substantially on their workforce, rewriting union contracts, laying off tens of thousands of workers, and taking whole communities, such as Detroit, down with them. For most of the twentieth century, the auto sector led America's manufacturing prosperity; in the twenty-first century, the same operations symbolize the daunting and painful transitions and downsizing in the country. This shift has not had huge implications for college graduates, though layoffs of white-collar employees certainly has, but it has stripped away a traditional route to middle-class prosperity for tens of thousands of people with a high school diploma or less.

Much the same trend is occurring inside the country's professional offices. Firms are changing in dramatic ways: more compact corporate structures with fewer middle-management positions, much less emphasis on developing professional staff over time, a sharper focus on staff with specialized technical or management skills, greater reliance on contract workers, fewer employees, and a willingness to outsource portions of work to other countries. Two decades ago, the American stock market operated through human interaction on the Exchange floor. Now, high-frequency trading has replaced thousands of financial workers with high-speed computers and complex algorithms. Tax forms, medical charts, diagnostic x-rays, scientific results, and many other functions are increasingly being handled outside the country. Government, however, has remained a steady employer, largely due to the continued growth of Homeland Security and related fields, such as borderlands management.

Your grandparents and, to a lesser extent, your parents lived in a world of loyalty — of employers to employees and of workers to their company. That sense of loyalty rarely exists today. The contingent workforce — a fancy term for people (often with advanced skills) who move around between companies in the same sector — is growing fast. When your grandparents and parents talk about the world of work, they are often referring to a time when career-long employment was the norm — rather than the exception — and when employers focused on developing the potential of individuals over the long term. This is not your world. Companies and employees no longer mate for life.

For the last decade or more, political leaders have been touting what they call the "knowledge economy." The world of work, they thought, was going to require at least fourteen years of education (elementary school, high school, and at least two years of postsecondary education). It made sense, on the surface, and it was so much cooler to talk about than what we might call the old "sweat economy." This was the world of Microsoft, Apple, BlackBerry, Cisco, Sun Computer Systems, Disney animation, eBay, Facebook, Google, and the like. With this in mind, the message pushed aggressively by President Obama makes intuitive sense — and parents and young people have responded to the simple and compelling directive: go to college!

But the knowledge economy has turned out to be largely an illusion. True, the high-technology sector needed skilled personnel. People with credentials in computer science, electrical engineering, and animation found ample opportunities. Those without specialist skills found themselves with fewer job offers, lower incomes, and much less job security. As it turned out, the United States has ended up with a combination of the knowledge economy and the old economy (construction, resource development, and old-style manufacturing — each one going through wild fluctuations over the past two decades). The real so-called new economy turned out to involve a rapid expansion of the service economy — as opposed to the anticipated economy of fancy and highly paid high-tech work. New jobs did emerge in the finance sector — with high-paying work with banks and insurance companies re-emerging from the wreckage of the collapse of Enron, WorldCom, Bear Stearns, and Arthur Anderson — creating excellent opportunities for economics, accounting, finance, and commerce graduates. Yale and Princeton send 40 percent of their graduates into the finance sector. But the real growth in employment came in the service industries: health care, restaurants, hotels, travel, recreation, fitness clubs, and personal and seniors' care. Most of these jobs, in contrast to the lofty promises of the knowledge economy, required little specialist education or training, offered little job security, and provided only modest incomes.

HOW THIS AFFECTS YOU

So how does all of this affect you? You aren't reading this book to learn about the work environment of the past twenty years. You want to get information that will help you make choices that will serve you well throughout the rest of the twenty-first century. So, let's bring it closer to home. It helps to start with the tough bit. America's young adults have been raised with extremely high expectations. Many have built up these expectations about work, education, and lifestyle and view them as a guarantee about their future — despite growing evidence to the contrary.

Expectations and realities, however, will not necessarily match. Many warning signs suggest that the future is not likely to be as easy as most young Americans have been led to expect. Although there is a great debate about the probable trajectory of American life, certain things seem evident:

- for the first time in the country's history a great many young people will not be more prosperous than their parents, and may well be poorer;

- technological innovation has made major inroads into the world of work and will continue to do so over the next three decades;

- the high cost of real estate will postpone home ownership for many in major cities;

- college debt will hang like a financial albatross over an entire generation;

- the public debt run up by your parents and grandparents, a debt that is still growing by an astonishing amount annually, will shackle governments for decades to come; and

- health care costs — their extent is a highly politicized question — will add to the taxes that today's teenagers will pay down the line.

Thanks to the globalization of our economy, combined with technological innovations, mechanization, and corporate restructuring, there is even more bad news:

- many of the jobs everyone thought would be waiting for today's youth have been outsourced to other countries;

- many young people struggle to find decent-paying, stable work, and the situation is not likely to get better in the near future;

- readily available, secure, decently paid blue-collar jobs, widespread unionization, and middle-management opportunities have given way to a world with fewer middle-management and more part-time jobs, largely union-free workforces in the private sector, and heightened workforce specialization;

- major national firms such as Best Buy, Toys "R" Us, Staples, Office Depot, Barnes & Noble, Radio Shack, Abercrombie & Fitch, Sears/Kmart, and Quiznos have recently announced major store closures. Even high-tech stars are cutting jobs, with Microsoft and Hewlett-Packard eliminating jobs en masse (eighteen thousand and twenty thousand positions respectively);

- companies at the low end of the cost chain, including Walmart and Target, dominate the retail sector, generally providing low-wage and low-benefit work; and

- those super-high-tech firms worth billions of dollars are most notable for the small size of their workforce. Instagram had only twelve employees when Facebook bought it for $1 billion. Much the same was true of Snapchat and many other digital startups. The new digital economy is great at producing wealth and billionaires, and much less accomplished at creating jobs. Even Apple, America's favorite corporation, creates many more jobs through outsourcing in China than it does in the United States, although embarrassment about the small size of the American workforce convinced the company to announce the opening of a manufacturing plant in Mesa, Arizona, in 2013. Of the company's eighty thousand direct employees, over half work in the retail side of the operation.

The crucial difference between the prospects facing today's youth and the world of their parents is that easy avenues for advancement and prosperity are becoming much rarer. Two generations ago, high-wage, low-skill work abounded in the country's factories, construction sites, and mining and logging camps. University graduates, regardless of field of study, attracted good salaries in a welcoming employment market. Skilled professionals — doctors, dentists, optometrists, engineers, and architects — typically had the choice of a variety of good career options. A vast range of middle-class work defined the country, permitting young Americans to start families on a single income, buy a decent house in the suburbs, launch small businesses in prosperous small towns and emerging cities, or find a place in rapidly growing federal, state, and municipal civil services.

The situation is far from hopeless, as we will show later. There are good opportunities for talented, motivated, and hardworking young adults. The coming retirement of the baby boomers should create thousands of openings for the ambitious, or so the young generation has been promised. (Let's face it: if they refuse to retire, they can't refuse to die — much as they might want to.) The world has shrunk in ways previously unimaginable. Many of today's young people will find themselves working in Asia, Europe, or other parts of the world — or working for companies based in those countries or for firms selling to or working well outside North America. But we also think that there will never in your lifetime be the same number of good opportunities that there were fifty years ago, so it is vital that you distinguish yourself from what we will later call "the swarm." Our advice isn't for everyone — it's directed at you.

Opportunities for entrepreneurship abound; digital technologies enable anyone to build a business and to sell products or provide services to customers the world over. Resource companies working in the western United States offer high wages and benefits. Entire new sectors — such as digital animation, social media, and e-commerce — have emerged in the past twenty years, creating great career prospects for the technologically proficient and creative. These opportunities are terrific but limited, for the number of such positions is small compared to the size of the national workforce. However, many more new avenues for personal and career growth will likely arise in the future; our favorite potential growth area is digital visualization, which we will discuss later.

But the sad truth is that, unlike the situation two generations ago, not enough of these jobs will be created to keep everyone in the middle class. The situation won't be exactly like contemporary China — where the choice seems to be between a good education and the rice paddy — but it's heading somewhat in that direction. Some of you will find berths in the middle class, and some will not. Getting there will be harder than it was for your parents and grandparents. For hundreds of thousands, a good inheritance is the key to long-term financial stability, although financial and workforce crises have forced many families to take large bites out of their retirement nest egg. Once you arrive, your hold on the spot may be uncertain. But, of course, if it was as easy now as it was fifty years ago, you wouldn't need us, would you?

LEARNING EQUALS EARNING – OR AT LEAST IT ONCE DID

For most young people in the United States, attending college used to be like winning an express ticket to the middle class. Everyone knew what the prizes were: white-collar work, a decent salary, and good benefits. With those prizes came the opportunities connected to financial security: marriage, children, a house, a car or two, and an occasional holiday in the sun. This, after all, is still what passes for the good life in America. Some aspire to become part of the "1 percent" — the truly wealthy — but most would be satisfied with a secure job providing a stable salary of at least seventy thousand dollars, proper health insurance, and a benefits package. This is still what young people want, and what their parents want for them. You will note that these aspirations tend not to include blue-collar work. Survey after survey of North Americans demonstrate the current preoccupation with escaping from working outdoors or making a living through physical and technical labor.

There was a time when a college degree delivered on its promise. Through the 1950s, 1960s, and 1970s, a degree took a young adult to within reach of the brass ring — largely because there were far fewer graduates per capita than there are today. In 1950, 34 percent of Americans aged twenty-five and over had graduated from high school, and about

5 percent had a college degree. By 2000, those figures were 80 percent and 25 percent. In that latter year, just over half of all adult Americans had completed at least some postsecondary education. Other studies give different figures: a U.S. Department of Education survey of fifteen thousand high school students in 2002, and of the same group again in 2012 at age twenty-seven, found that 84 percent of the twenty-seven-year-olds had some college education, but only 34 percent had achieved a bachelor's degree or higher.[1]

The high school graduates who headed for university in 1950 were a small minority of the population, were generally prepared to earn their degrees, and then, having done so, had a good chance of finding middle-class opportunities. The strong demand for government workers, lawyers, teachers, college professors, middle managers, and the like ensured that the vast majority of university graduates could, with comparatively little effort, find their way into a decent career.

Governments naturally thought that if the system worked for 5 percent of the population, why not for more? Or, as has been suggested, why not for everybody? Why should a minority of the population get all the good jobs? Flushed with the success of college education for the postwar generation, and believing wholeheartedly in the knowledge economy, governments throughout the Western world launched a huge expansion of the postsecondary system: new institutions opened; women and minority students were recruited to campuses; immigrants and children from working-class backgrounds attended in large numbers.

The message was simple, and in those days it was largely true: learning equals earning. For decades, the college system promoted that equation, with an equally simple point: college graduates earn substantially more than high school graduates over the course of their careers. The most recent data, shared enthusiastically by colleges, is that their graduates earn considerably more than high school graduates between graduation and retirement. Here's a table[2] that gives some interesting figures, showing that a man with a bachelor's degree earns twenty-six thousand dollars a year more than a man with only a high school diploma. Over a thirty-year working life (ignoring raises and inflation — this is a rough approximation), that difference comes to just under eight hundred thousand dollars.

Type of Degree	Annual Median Salary (2011)	Gender
High school diploma	$40,050	Men
High school diploma	$30,010	Women
College with no degree	$47,070	Men
College with no degree	$34,590	Women
Associate degree	$50,930	Men
Associate degree	$39,290	Women
Bachelor's degree	$66,200	Men
Bachelor's degree	$49,110	Women
Master's degree	$83,030	Men
Master's degree	$60,300	Women
Professional degree	$119,470	Men
Professional degree	$80,720	Women
Doctorate degree	$100,770	Men
Doctorate degree	$77,460	Women

The claim, though statistically true (though other sources give other figures), was always deceptive: it reflects average earnings across many occupations and is far short of a guarantee. Graduates in some fields earn a great deal more than high school graduates; other college graduates earn considerably less. So, an electrical engineer with a bachelor's degree will earn a great deal more than a film studies major, but the average eliminates the variation. There's more to it than that, however. Wealthy people are far more likely to go to college than poor people. And, no surprise, they carry that advantage into their adulthood. Also — and here things get sensitive — the students who finish college tend to have other characteristics that prepare them for lifelong success: a strong work ethic, good learning skills, and on the whole more intelligence than the average high school student. So, is it that successful people go to college and have greater success in their careers, or that people who go to college are, because of their studies, more successful in their careers? The answer lies somewhere in between, but there is growing evidence that personal characteristics contribute a great deal to college achievement AND career success. It's the personal qualities, not the credential, that produce the high income.

Indeed, somewhere between a quarter and a third of American college graduates earn less than the average income of those with only a high school diploma. Still, going to college makes for a powerful and simple plan, and it certainly works on parents. Go to college, regardless of the field of study, they say, and you will make a lot more money than those who do not (more if you're a guy — don't miss the gender disparities). Yeah? How about if you are a schoolteacher in Los Angeles living next door to a firefighter. Who has the degree? Who makes the higher salary? And there are many similar comparisons.

NARROWING THE FIELD

Colleges like to brag about the high employment rate of their graduates, using this as a major selling point, but they can be downright dishonest about this information. At least one law school was caught hiring its own graduates on short-term contracts after graduation so that the graduating class would demonstrate a high overall employment rate. Classy! And even if degree holders on average do have higher employment rates than those with community college diplomas and high school diplomas, there are two things to remember here. First, the graduate surveys exclude those people who started college and did not complete their studies; the numbers would be far less impressive if the colleges compared the employment experiences of all those who started college. Second, many companies, faced with a deluge of applicants for entry-level positions, routinely interview and select only college graduates for jobs that do not require any advanced study. The overproduction of college graduates is so substantial that firms use the college credential as a means of limiting the stack of resumés that they have to review. Do you need a degree to work at Starbucks? Of course not, but if you are a manager going through a stack of five hundred applications for ten barista-training jobs, why not limit the interviews to college graduates? They don't cost any more to employ than non-graduates. And remember, in order to get that extra eight hundred thousand dollars over your working lifetime, you have to forgo the four years (or five or six if you don't finish on time) of earned income that you missed by going to college. Worth it financially if you are a doctor or a Wall Street analyst; not so much if you are a barista.

CREDENTIALS MATTER

Credentials do matter — although not necessarily for the reasons that institutions, parents, and guidance counselors think. The first benefit of a college degree or diploma, sad as it is to say, is the simple fact that it separates an individual from the crowd. As one cartoon caption said, "The easier it is to get a college degree, the dumber you look for not having one."[3] At one time, a degree was a mark of high distinction and spoke directly to motivation, ability, determination, and the development of specific skills (and, if you want to be cynical, the presence of inherited wealth and privilege). Now, in a situation where well over half of all American high school graduates continue on to some form of postsecondary education (they don't all complete it), the primary advantage of a diploma or degree is that it indicates you are not one of those simply not able or willing to go to college or university.

So, a diploma or degree, if it does nothing else, can keep you on the list of candidates under consideration for entry-level, unskilled jobs. This won't make your heart beat faster. University or college recruiters don't share this information with prospective students, but it makes sense from the company's perspective. After all, diploma or degree holders have invested two or more years and a good deal of money in their own development, and have shown a certain level of motivation. Most of them can read and write at a fairly high level. This helps explain why 35 percent of all retail employees in the United States have a university degree (the other explanation is that they can't get better jobs).

A good illustration of this phenomenon occurred during the 2014 NCAA Basketball Tournament. Enterprise Rent-A-Car ran a series of advertisements during the tournament, featuring college students who had joined the company after graduation. Their proud boast was that Enterprise hired more college graduates than any similar company in the United States. Now, Enterprise is a fine company and there is absolutely nothing wrong about working for a rental car firm. The firm advertises the positions as management trainee posts, in the grand tradition of the American companies that offered entry-level workers an opportunity to move their way up over time. Some no doubt do precisely that, although many more, one suspects, leave the company within a year or two. Our point is this: precious few high school graduates and their parents fill out college application forms and write checks worth thousands of dollars for tuition in the hope that four years of expensive study will lead to a job at a car rental counter. This, however, is a key part of the current reality for college graduates.

This, then, is our first message: a diploma or a degree serves, at a minimum, as a means of separating people from the 30 percent of American high school graduates who do not continue their studies, and from those who do not complete high school at all (still 13 percent of the adult population). It is a barrier over which the really unqualified cannot pass. That doesn't say much, though. A four-year degree is a pretty expensive way to distinguish yourself from a group that includes many underachievers of various kinds.

THE EMPLOYMENT PARADOX

Many regions of the United States face a curious paradox: they have people without jobs and jobs without people. Studies reveal a large and growing number of unemployed people — including many thousands who are African American, are new to the United States, live with disabilities, or lack an adequate education and such basic employment skills as English language ability — who simply cannot find easy entry into the workforce and thus face years of unemployment, temporary positions, and low incomes. The situation is exacerbated by the large number of illegal immigrants seeking work in the United States, for those undocumented workers take many of the low-end, casual jobs and depress wages for others. At the same time, and this is the surprise, American businesses have many thousands of unfilled and unfillable jobs.

Some of these positions are in blue-collar work, while others require a high level of skill[4]: Microsoft imported over four thousand workers in 2013 and paid them an average salary of just over one hundred thousand dollars. Close to half of the trades workers in the United States are over fifty years of age, while the number of young people entering the field is stagnant. The construction industry, rebounding after years of recession, is already facing shortages of carpenters, project managers, construction supervisors, and even laborers. Across the economy, many of the other vacant positions are in highly skilled, high-technology positions, including electrical engineering, computer science, and related fields. In both cases, a severe shortage of people with critical skills has slowed corporate expansion and interfered with economic growth generally. Ironically, having hundreds of thousands of young adults coming out of colleges and universities with diplomas and degrees has not helped many companies find the people to meet their needs. Many countries are facing this paradox: Mongolia, a formerly Communist country that is joining the democratic and capitalist world, expanded its university system rapidly. Its resource economy has taken off. Its current problem? A shortage of skilled tradespeople and too many arts and science university graduates!

You can take an important lesson from this paradox: not all credentials are equally valuable in today's economy. Some degrees or diplomas provide the holder with only a minor boost in employment possibilities; the most promising opportunities (present and future) go primarily to people with specialized skills. In terms of job openings, income, and career security, accountants have a greater range of prospects than do generalists in biology or sociology. Nurses and doctors, in general, find opportunities that outstrip those holding degrees in business administration. The credentials do not reflect how hard it is to get the degree — getting a degree in philosophy is every bit as challenging intellectually as getting one in electrical engineering or marketing or speech communication — but rather reflect the connection between the skills learned and the marketplace. Leading-edge companies, from digital economy firms such as Google to fracking companies operating in North Dakota, require workers with targeted and very specific abilities — most of whom need specialized certificates, diplomas, or degrees — followed by practical experience.

Unfortunately, this is the raw truth about all credentials: they come with no guarantees. Even the most carefully crafted life — one based on the right selection of high school courses, a thorough evaluation of degree or diploma options, successful graduation, and an aggressive approach to job-hunting — is no assurance that a job, career, and high income will follow in due course. The best opportunities will go, now and in the future, to people with the right credentials and who exhibit the right personal qualities, at the right time, in the right place. Be off by a year or two, and the prospects could evaporate or at least decline. Right now, career possibilities for lawyers are in the tank across America, in part because of a massive, some would say outrageous, expansion of for-profit legal education in the United States. Anticipate the market — such as being a graduate from a top university or college in gas- and oil-related technologies at a time of huge demand — and discover a world of opportunity. Make a bad choice, and you may be in trouble.

TEACHERS: A TALE OF TWO COUNTRIES

Teachers are fundamental to the success of the education system and the national economy. America has a strange approach to education, paying its teachers subprofessional wages, disgracefully underfunding its education system, and being consistently entangled in unproductive and efficiency-destroying union contracts. In Finland, teachers are selected from the upper echelons of the university population, and are highly paid. America, in contrast, generally recruits teachers from the bottom third of the graduate classes of colleges. Finland produces some of the best educational outcomes in the world. America's performance is stagnant at best and declining in comparative terms. What does this mean for prospective college students and would-be teachers? Canada and the United States provide an excellent point of comparison.

Canadian teachers are, in our opinion, a good example of the fact that, even with careful planning, there are no guarantees that things will work out as planned. These young adults took the courses and did the work they needed to: they completed an undergraduate degree, made it through the highly competitive admission process to teacher education programs, and finished the education degree. They were recruited by the promise of jobs made available by large-scale retirements among the existing teaching force, high incomes, good benefits and, by no means least important, three months a year off work. But now, the declining number of students in most of the country has resulted in school closings and — thanks to an overproduction of teachers (i.e., teacher training programs graduating more teachers than needed) — a huge mismatch between the large and growing pool of candidates and the smaller number of available teaching positions. These hardworking, newly minted teachers, carrying high expectations, suddenly find themselves without a job or, in an increasingly common and frustrating situation, with part-time substitute teaching positions that can last for years.

America is dramatically different. Though many jobs are available, teaching is an undervalued profession, promoted more like missionary work than as a serious field of intellectual endeavor. Even the stories of great personal accomplishment — those teachers (think of *Mr. Holland's Opus*) who work with the poor and disadvantaged and deliver them to the nirvana of college admission — emphasize how difficult and unappealing the school environment has become. There are wonderful schools in the United States — the elite private schools and public schools in the wealthiest communities — that recruit master's- and Ph.D.-qualified teachers and provide them with the best possible resources. In contrast, the inner-city schools, lacking resources, parental engagement, and motivated students, are often inadequate and, in many instances, dangerous.

The United States has difficulty recruiting top people into the education field. The pay is often lousy and the work environment stifling. Parental support is mixed; too much engagement is often as serious a problem as not enough. Standards are low in international terms, and outcomes uncertain and uneven. On top of this, union–government relations are typically strained (Google "rubber room" for a real eye-opener), leading to a nation-wide debate over charter schools (those funded by government but independent of state and union control). American education graduates can usually find work, but the combination of low status, mediocre pay, harsh working conditions, and little public support makes for an unappealing profession.

The same profession, in two different countries and with different working environments, produces completely different outcomes. American teachers are poorly paid, it is easy to get a teaching degree or certificate, and many jobs are available. There is one striking similarity between the experiences of the teachers in both Canada and the United States: the dropout rate from the profession is sky-high. Working with you in high school and before, it turns out, is not everyone's idea of a dream job!

Lawyers are by no means the only group of professionals who have found themselves in a position where there is a severe disconnect between student aspirations and the workforce. In the past, similar things have happened to young adults with degrees in engineering (during the downturn in the oil and gas industry), architecture (when computer-assisted drawing came along), and other targeted and highly specialized fields of study. Indeed, governments and institutions have not been very successful at matching graduate rates with job opportunities, a sobering reminder to you of the difficulties involved in getting this right for yourself. If neither government officials who spend years studying employment patterns nor colleges charged with preparing young adults for the modern economy can identify the right mix of students, graduates, and job vacancies, how easy is it for a solitary student to make the right choices? We did not say this was going to be easy.

As these examples illustrate, there is no way to ensure success. We would, however, recommend that you try to avoid following the crowd. Students who gravitate toward fields that have high demand at the point when they leave high school sometimes find that by the time they have earned a diploma or degree (two to four or more years later) the market conditions have changed. Even worse, large numbers of high school graduates will likely have headed in that direction, resulting in too many people scrambling for the available positions. There is comfort in numbers. Heading where others are going seems, on the surface, to be a safe thing to do. You may feel that the fact that many others are doing the same thing that you have opted to do validates your choice. Wrong. Overproduction of diploma and degree holders is a key characteristic of the modern training and education system. You really need to find your own way.

A great deal rides on the ability of individuals, families, educational institutions, corporations, and governments to bridge the gap between ambition, talent, and need. It's more than sad that so little thought, effort, and honest talk is involved in young adults' decisions about their educational and career future. In the United States, enormous effort and a great deal of money is spent on getting young adults into the "right college," with precious little thought about whether or not this field of study makes long-term career sense. Getting a credential can be a wise move or a foolish one. Knowing which it is requires far more thought than most people give to the process.

You may be thinking at this point that we are contradicting ourselves. We keep saying that you need to make careful plans; but, at the same time, we tell you that nothing is permanent and guaranteed in the world of work. If the latter is true, what's the point of planning? Why not just get a generalist degree and hope for the best? The answer is that nothing is black and white. Some parts of the labor market are stable: there will always be a demand for doctors, accountants, and some other professionals, although even these sectors are unlikely to stay at a high level indefinitely. (But there may not, it turns out, always be a high demand for lawyers — that field is overcrowded, facing technological challenges, and coping with outsourcing. Jobs for lawyers are evaporating, and so are applications to law school. The market does figure these things out.) There will always be jobs for those in the skilled trades, but that's a different point, which we will make later. Jobs may change somewhat, but skills can often be transferrable: if you are great at math, you can use your skills in many fields, some of which may not have developed yet.

But you have to stand out from the crowd. You have to be good at something, though not necessarily a college something. The people at greatest career and income risk are those with low-quality generalist degrees (a B.A. majoring in nothing in particular) — which, however personally fulfilling, may not demonstrate any particular skills and, accordingly, may leave you largely unemployable in the ever-evolving economy.

PREPARING YOURSELF FOR A CONFUSING WORLD

As a young adult moving into the world beyond high school or looking to improve your current situation, you need to be prepared. Be aware, though, that

- well-meant advice based on the experiences of parents and grand-parents does not necessarily apply to current circumstances;

- it is a tough world out there, and the employment situation is going to get more confusing in the near future;

- global forces, corporate structures, and a rapidly changing economy are transforming opportunities for young adults, not always for the better; and,

- opportunities will exist, but they might not match your particular expectations and desires.

The easy way of saying all of this is that it's a rough-and-tumble world and it will likely get more so in the years to come. There is a chance that circumstances will improve dramatically, that jobs will appear when and as wanted by young adults emerging from a self-selected field of study at college or university. And if you believe that, we have some Enron stocks and a few dot-com specials we want to sell you. So many factors are at play — from demographics to international economics, from the market demand for college graduates to the fate of the American industrial sector — that it is impossible to say with confidence precisely how young Americans should prepare themselves for adulthood and the world of work.

There is, however, a way forward. It involves careful planning and preparation and a clear and thoughtful assessment of possibilities and options. It requires that you seek out the best possible means of testing and proving yourself, for there is much less space at the top than people currently believe, and tens of thousands of people who want the same opportunities. You need to be careful, methodical, and systematic in your approach. You need to be both realistic about yourself and knowledgeable about how the world of work and employment actually operates. Right now — and we say this based on years of working in postsecondary education — far too few young Americans approach life after high school with the single-mindedness of purpose that is required.

2

KNOW YOURSELF

THE IMPORTANCE OF SELF-AWARENESS

There is a myth in contemporary America that the only way to achieve financial and social success is with at least one degree. This "cult of college" has a hold on the American psyche that is hard to overstate, so pervasive is it across the country. Whether you're a teen about to graduate from high school or a young adult looking to improve your current situation, you undoubtedly have heard endless talk about the importance of going on to college. Thirty-five years ago, when our children were very young, we wondered about the television advertisements aimed at parents of newborn babies that urged families to start saving for their children's college education. In retrospect, these ads were right on the mark, for the cost of going to college has soared since that time. No country in the world is more college-obsessed than the United States and nowhere are the issues of status, tuition fees, recreation, family history, career aspirations, and institutional character more intertwined and tangled than in this country. Ironically, in a nation where going to college is directly tied to career and income expectations, there is remarkably little frank and honest talk about the relationship between tuition costs, institutional choice, career prospects, and long-term return on investment from postsecondary education. It's strange to see an obsession that's so uninformed.

Studies show that the vast majority of American parents want their children (that's you) to get a degree and to get one of the middle-class careers that you supposedly deserve. Wealthy and university-educated parents typically assume that their children will go to college. People from working-class, poor, and immigrant backgrounds have bought into the idea — long since disproven — that college is the great American leveler, producing real equality of opportunity for all based on getting the right kind of credential. When researchers ask high school students what they plan and want to do, the majority say the same thing: go to college. For some of you, this is an ideal choice; for others, it will be a costly and demoralizing mistake — you may hate it, and you may well not succeed.

If we have learned nothing else from our years of experience with our students and with our children, it's this: the best possible decisions in planning for the future are made by people who take the time to carefully and honestly know themselves. Let's start with the most basic question: How do you know if you are one of the people who would enjoy and benefit from a college education? To give an honest and useful answer, you have to know yourself. You must have a frank conversation with yourself about what you like and dislike, your strengths and weaknesses, your values, and your aspirations. This is not easy, especially for seventeen-year-olds. It's sad but unfortunately true that American society has avoided asking you these questions. Many of you have been told, repeatedly, that you can be anything you want to be — a dangerously misleading piece of advice that, in most cases, is simply not true.

WISHING DOESN'T MAKE IT SO

Thousands of high school graduates go to college intending to be medical doctors. They pick their high school courses accordingly and study hard to get good grades. Filled with optimism and dreams of a rewarding medical career and an impressive income, they submit their applications for college, planning to get a degree and then move on to medical school. Of these hopefuls, some drop out of undergraduate studies, while quite a few do not get grades high enough to make applying to medical school worthwhile. One of us served for several years on the admissions panel for a medical school. The students who made the shortlist (about a quarter to a third of those who applied) were amazing — brilliant marks, volunteer activities that would have overwhelmed Albert Schweitzer, a strong character, and a killer work ethic. However, only one in four of those amazing short-listed candidates was accepted into medical school; for the rest, the dream of being a doctor turned to disappointment.

But Americans are nothing if not stubborn. The university market expands to try to meet available demand. Medical schools are not like law schools and have not yet attracted for-profit institutions in the United States. But outside the country? There are many universities in Mexico (the University of Guadalajara has a large and successful program) and in the Caribbean that attract students from the United States. During the Reagan presidency, one of the strangest international maneuvers involved the invasion of Grenada, a tiny island in the Caribbean. One of the military units attached to the invasion had an unusual assignment: to find and protect the largely American student body studying medicine on the island. Other American students pay the high international fees to study in Australia or other countries. The main point holds, however. Even with these other expensive alternatives, the vast majority of young adults who go to university intending to become doctors end up disappointed.

In this chapter, we are going to ask you why, in light in all of the other excellent direct-from-high-school options worth considering, you think that you want to go to college. Getting into college is surprisingly easy. While it is hard (but not impossible) to get into a top school, the reality is that almost any student over the age of eighteen who really wants to go to college will likely to have hundreds — yes, hundreds — of options, such is the urgent need of many American institutions for butts, paying ones, in seats. There's a list in the Appendix of colleges that accept every person who bothers to apply. Many of the for-profit institutions, in particular, are completely shameless about bringing unqualified students into their programs; many private colleges and state-run institutions, counting on high enrollments to pay the bills, admit many students whom they know will likely fail. You may have seen that some of these places have been sending recruiters into Veterans Administration hospitals to sign up vets for admission (and big student loans). If getting into college is no great feat, getting out with a degree can, on the other hand, be quite difficult. So we'll lead you through a process of self-evaluation designed to show you whether you are ready to go to college and, equally important, whether you are likely to succeed.

Remember this point: Most colleges and universities will not be fully honest with you about the likelihood of your succeeding in your studies. The best schools select from the top 4 to 5 percent of applicants, which generally represents the top 1 percent of high school graduates. Unless you are an affirmative action admission or a legacy application, where many colleges relax the rules, if they let you in they know you are able to succeed. At the weaker schools, they are going to rush to cash your check within minutes of your applying; whether or not you are going to succeed is of less concern to them. Parents and guidance counselors aren't much help. They have generally bought into the cult of self-esteem and they exaggerate your abilities in the mistaken belief that encouraging you to set your sights high is better than telling you truthfully what you can and cannot do. And, of course, Oprah and her ilk will tell you that you can be whatever you want to be. If this were true, there'd be many more billionaires and brain surgeons than there are, wouldn't there?

The only one who is going to be truly honest with you ... is you! We want to make sure that you understand the issues, challenges, and possibilities — and that you make good decisions based on a full awareness of your skills, abilities, and motivation. You are likely to find this a bit unnerving, and you might not like what we have to say. Please remember that we have no vested interest in your final decision. But we aren't here to boost your self-esteem; instead, we strongly believe that making informed decisions about your post–high school career will stand you in good stead for the rest of your life.

DO YOU REALLY WANT TO GO TO COLLEGE?

First question, and we ask it again: why are you considering college? Have your parents talked about it for years and always assumed that you'd go? Did they make annual contributions to a college fund — new parents routinely brag about how quickly they set up the college fund, and grandparents are often eager contributors — and regularly remind you of your destiny, already paid for through a 529 plan? Do your teachers and guidance counselors (if you meet with them) tell you that you are college material? Are your friends all going? Or is it just the background noise of the modern world — from TV shows and movies (*Legally Blonde, Animal House,* and the rest), from politicians' speeches, newspaper stories, and hallway conversations? Did the college recruiters descend on your high school with tales of an exciting social life, enthusiastic teachers, great programs, excellent career opportunities, and, of course, the highly deceptive statistics that college graduates make much more money over their careers than the lowly minions who give up on themselves after graduating from high school?

Regardless of where the pressure comes from — and it comes from all these places and more — the reality is that the importance of going to college is probably hardwired in your brain. Understandably so, because in the 2013–2014 academic year, just under 66 percent of all high school graduates enrolled in college (two- and four-year programs), 68.4 percent of females and 63.5 percent of males. And the figure has been even higher: five years earlier, in 2009, it was 70 percent, the ensuing decline probably caused by the worsening situation of lower-income families.[1] This doesn't mean that 66 percent of people in your age group are going to college, because it doesn't include the 7 percent who have dropped out of high school.[2] It also doesn't mean that all of these college registrants graduate, since the dropout rate is considerable. Still, it's a substantial majority, and it's understandable that you would think that going to college is the natural and logical thing to do. But it doesn't mean that it's the right thing for you.

Back to the main question: do you really want to go to college? College-level studies are difficult. If you do attend college, you are committing yourself to an additional four years of schooling — and that is the minimum, since many students take five or more years to graduate. This means four or more extra years of being in the classroom for eight months of the year with four-month breaks to try to raise enough money to keep going, unless your family is wealthy enough to finance a summer holiday. It is a major commitment of time, money, and effort. Have you really given careful thought to whether or not you are ready for this substantial challenge?

There are some very good reasons for going to college. Note that we do not list among them such socially important things as "Because my friends are going," "Because I don't know what to do with my life and I need time to think about it," "Because I want to make lots of money," or "Because my parents want me to go." These reasons actually factor prominently into students' decisions, but have to be considered separately. Your parents may well be right, and you should give careful thought to their ideas and rationale. There will be more about this later.

College is an expensive place to get your head together and, while it works for some young people, most find it difficult to resolve their career and life ambitions while writing essays and cramming for examinations. Your friends, on the other hand, could easily lead you astray. Not many high school friendships — romantic or otherwise — survive the undergraduate years. To put it more gently, they are likely to be replaced by new friendships and partnerships. For now, in no particular order of importance, here are our top-four reasons why you should consider going to college:

- **Because you are curious about the world and you love learning.** This is the traditional reason, the one college professors like to think motivate most of their students. Those who approach college from this perspective and who have the requisite skills make the best college students and, because curiosity often comes with a strong work ethic, these people typically do well after their degree is finished.

- **Because you are academically well-prepared and talented, and you wish to test yourself, intellectually and skill-wise, at a higher level.** There is nothing wrong with being competitive and wanting to find out just how good you can be. The greatest benefits from a college education typically go to the best and hardest-working students; if you think you are one of these, then heading to campus can be a fine idea. Note the pattern here. It is the skills and abilities — not the credentials — that are key to future success. You can earn the best degree from the best institutions, but if you lack integrity, are lazy about work, have weak motivation, and lack the ability to pick yourself up off the floor, your credential will primarily serve as a wall hanging and a reminder of your lost youth.

- **Because you are truly interested in making the world a better place.** In the 1960s and 1970s, many students who attended college gave up good job opportunities because they were idealistic and hopeful about creating an improved world. College is a great place to find similar thinkers and to confront the ideas and realities that have shaped the human condition over time. Many leaders of social movements, politicians, commercial innovators, revolutionaries, environmentalists, journalists, and artists found their inspiration and guidance in college classrooms, study lounges, and seminar sessions.

- **Because you want to pursue a specific professional career** — engineering, registered nursing, medicine, and accounting are good examples — and you need a degree to do so. We have a strong caveat here: a large number of students change their plans mid-degree, based on weaker-than-expected performance or the discovery of new academic and career possibilities. But, if you have a firm sense that you want to try a specific occupational path and you have the skills to compete at the highest level, college may well be the only way to go.

This list is not long — and it is not complete — but it is a good place to start your self-evaluation. We could add less idealistic motives — finding a marriage partner from your own social class, getting a leg up for your NBA career, testing your tolerance for alcohol, and so on, but we won't. Do you fit into one of these categories? If not, ask yourself the same question we started with: Why do you want to go to college? If you do not have a clear and decisive answer to this question, you really would be well advised to give careful thought to alternatives. The happy news, as you will see later, is that there are plenty of good ones. Remember that the number-one predictor of young people's likelihood of going to college is whether their parents have college degrees. The second predictor is family income. There is not a lot of "you" in either of these criteria — yet you are the one who is going to have to attend classes, study hard, and complete all of the assignments. It must feel, at times, as though the fix is in.

HUMAN CURIOSITY

As you make your plans for going forward, one question hangs over everything else: Are you curious? This seems like an odd question. College, like high school, is a technical and academic challenge. It is supposed to be about study habits, proofreading essays, concentrating on examinations, meeting deadlines, and avoiding long hours at the student pub. And yes, it's about all of those things, and more, but it's much more fundamental — it's about basic curiosity.

Well yes, you say, of course I'm curious. Isn't everyone? What we mean by this question, though, is not whether you are curious about the Chicago Cubs' chances of winning the World Series in your lifetime (not good) or whether the next version of Starcraft Warrior will be as challenging as the last one (who cares, really?), but whether you are curious about intellectual questions — the things of the mind. Do you care about the science and politics of climate change? Analyzing the political contributions of Henry Kissinger? The history of Middle Eastern conflicts? The potential of quantum computing? Best practices in African American job creation and social policy? The right moral and political response to the arrival of thousands of Central American children at American border crossings? Colleges have courses and experts in all of these areas and many others. Look at the course calendar at any university. There are hundreds of faculty members, each with his or her area of interest and expertise. Check them out. This one is an expert on particle physics, that one on Etruscan tomb paintings, another one on the diseases of freshwater fish. Do any of them make your intellectual heart beat faster? Do you say "boooooring?" Remember, you will be studying this stuff. Do you really want to? Be honest.

You should be excited about the prospect of venturing into this environment. You should be keen to learn more about subjects you have sampled in high school and intrigued with areas of study that you have never attempted. College is tailor-made for intellectual discovery, for chasing down pathways of deep personal interest and for finding academic fields, thinkers, methods, and concepts that you have never even considered.

INTRODUCING THE SWARM

Many college students — more than in the past, we think, though it's impossible to prove — are not very curious. Influenced by the overselling of the financial benefits of a college education, they march directly from high school to university, having no clear idea why are they are doing so. In this book, we call these students — those who aren't much interested in reading, aren't intellectually curious, and don't engage with what the university has to offer — the swarm. They don't find the fact that synchro-tron science is unlocking the mysteries of the building blocks of nature very interesting. They are not really keen to learn about the economic foundations of the Civil War or the religious roots of contemporary ter-rorism. Very few of them find the nuances of advanced calculus riveting. College professors are deeply — sometimes bizarrely — fascinated by the ins and outs of scholarship, but all too often find themselves staring at stu-dents, members of the dreaded swarm, who make no effort to mask their indifference to book learning and to the specifics of a particular course.

Do you know what interests you? This is more than a scholarly question. We live in an age of mass information — with more informed analysis, factual information, inaccurate data, and partisan commentary available at your fingertips than at any previous time in human history. It dismays us to say so, but a great many students show no interest in any of this information. As a group, college-aged students rarely read news-papers. They dropped reading the paper edition long ago (so did we); but few of them even read the digital editions available on their computers, phones, or tablets. They do, interestingly, show an interest in their college newspapers. Book sales among young people have dropped precipitously — where would youth publishers be without the Twilight series?

There is a great debate about what has happened to your generation. Don Tapscott, a digital guru, argues in *Grown Up Digital: How the Net Generation Is Changing Your World* that the Internet age has made young people smarter, more critical, and better with information. You would like him. On the other hand there is Mark Bauerlein, whose wonderfully named book says it all: *The Dumbest Generation: How the Digital Age Stupefies Young Americans and Jeopardizes Our Future (Or, Don't Trust Anyone Under 30)*. He's not your pal. We want Tapscott to be right — and there are sure signs of growing youth confidence. But, so far, our vote is with Bauerlein. And, in any case, it's not a matter of your intelligence — it's about your approach to learning. You don't need to be Einstein, but you do need to be curious.

The problem is that too large a percentage of the students in most programs and at most colleges are not much interested in the world and, therefore, not very inspired by their studies. At the elite schools, where they recruit students because of their book learning and engagement with the world, the situation is quite different, of course; if you are at Harvard, you are by definition intellectually engaged. We are speaking here of the other 95 percent of the institutions and about 80 percent of the students at these institutions — both numbers are guesses — where engagement with the contemporary world is depressingly thin. If you don't follow politics on a regular basis, it's hard to find political science exciting. If you are not genuinely interested in the ordering of the natural world, then biology and geography will simply be abstractions — as bewildering as scientifically illiterate young people find theoretical physics. Ultimately, if you do not enjoy intellectual discovery and enlightenment, then college will be a tedious and completely unsatisfying place.

OUR CURIOSITY TEST

All young people thinking of going to college should give themselves this simple five-point test. It's easy — the easiest of your postsecondary career, with no studying, no pain, and no wrong answers. It is also one of the most important that you will ever take, and we won't be looking over your shoulder. Be honest with yourself (and with your parents, who, after all, you are probably counting on to help fund your college studies).

CURIOSITY TEST

1. **Do I like to read?** More precisely, have I read many works of serious fiction other than what some teacher has forced me to read as a course requirement in high school? Everyone who graduates from high school can read and write, more or less, but many have not read anything serious beyond course requirements. By "serious," we mean nothing with zombies in it or crazy nonsense about the Catholic Church (we're looking at you, Dan Brown), and at least something about the human condition past Oprah's self-help books.

2. **Do I read high quality non-fiction?** Not a biography of the boys of One Direction, but at least Malcolm Gladwell if not Naomi Klein or Niall Ferguson, or Jared Diamond. Do I read the newspaper or major magazines (*The Onion, Mother Jones, Rolling Stone,* or *Harper's, The Economist, The New York Times Review of Books,* and *The Atlantic* if I want to see what literate adults find intriguing) on a regular basis? It is okay to include the online versions of these publications or even exclusively online news sources, like the *Huffington Post* or, for political junkies, the *Drudge Report* or sophisticated aggregator sites like *Arts and Letters Daily*?

3. **Do I watch foreign films,** art films, or thoughtful PBS programs or series? If I watch horror films or films starring Adam Sandler, that doesn't make me a bad person (well, perhaps Sandler is going a bit too far). No one can deal with important and serious stuff all the time. But if I watch reality TV regularly and have never watched a PBS program or a film in a language other than English, then my answer to this question will be "no."

4. **Am I troubled or excited about world affairs?** Tensions in the Middle East, American presidential elections, developments in stem cell technologies, or the economic rise of China. When I heard about the bombing at the Boston Marathon, did I know where Chechnya was? Did the Russian engagement with Crimea and the Ukraine draw me to read up on President Vladimir Putin's background and Russia's complex relationship with Eastern Europe? Has the rise of the Islamic State of Iraq and the Levant drawn me to the newspapers or television news on a regular basis?

The point of this test is this: if you don't find learning about the physical world, the past and present of humanity, politics, the environment, and the fine arts interesting when you are in high school, why do you think you will find them interesting in college, which involves learning about all of these sorts of things?

So, how did you do? If you answered yes to most, if not all, of these questions, there is an above-average chance that you will enjoy college and do well. Curious students succeed in college, assuming that their basic skills (writing, reading, and math) are up to college standards and that they avoid the social pitfalls of campus life.

Curiosity is the rocket fuel of the academy. If you arrive with the tank fully topped up, you will likely find the experience exciting, demanding, and eye-opening. You will be one of the students who ask spontaneous questions in class, come to a professor's office with questions before the assignment is due (and not just to ask for an extension, heaven forbid), attend extracurricular lectures, and have trouble picking courses because there are too many interesting things to study. We love having you in class. You make colleges dynamic and exciting places to be.

We know that many of you will have looked at the test questions and wondered why they are relevant. They actually tell us almost everything we need to know about you. If you answered them all in the negative but still have great high school grades, you can probably survive college, but it may seem like a four-year stint in the dentist's chair — unless someone lights an intellectual fire under you. You will be clever but disengaged, not a happy state to sustain in college.

If you answered negatively but have average grades, then you might be able to complete college — maybe — but your experience will be a tough slog. You will probably struggle with basic assignments and will have trouble figuring out all the fuss about the college experience. What is average? Well, the mean grade point average for female high school graduates was 3.10 in 2009, and for males it was 2.90; B− for females and just under that for males.[3] If you answered negatively and have poor grades (anything under the average), you probably should not go to college. The combination of limited interest in the world and poor basic skills puts you at risk from the beginning. Find something else to do, because your college time (likely to be limited to one or two painful years) will be boring, unsatisfying, and a waste of everyone's time.

If you are in the final group, by the way, don't feel bad. About one third of college students are in this category, and they typically leave without a degree. It doesn't mean that they are bad people, or that they are necessarily unintelligent. It just means that they, like you, are not interested in what college has to offer, and don't have the skills to compensate for this lack of interest. They enjoy other things, and they will be happier and probably more prosperous doing what they enjoy rather than what parents and society think they ought to do. They should do what they love and what they are good at, with a firm eye on finding something that will provide a decent income.

Think of it this way. A person who doesn't like music or is not interested in how it is composed and performed is not at all likely to attend music school. Someone who hates competitive athletics does not go to an expensive month-long sports camp with top-notch coaches. People who find politics boring and unimportant rarely volunteer for election campaigns. Sending an uncurious young person to college is cruel and wrong, for the student and for the institution. College professors try to inspire these students, and sometimes they do, but in most cases it's like casting seed on stony ground, and it will not produce much of a crop. Test yourself. If you cannot pass the curiosity test, college is probably not for you — or at least it won't be a pleasant experience.

SUCCESS: PERSONAL QUALITIES THAT MAKE A DIFFERENCE

There are many ways to succeed in life, depending on how you define success. A rich family or a large inheritance can help — and family income and social position still constitute the single most important determinant of financial well-being in the United States. So much for the mystique of the classless society. But this country still has considerable mobility, both upward and downward. No one is guaranteed success in life; nor are young people necessarily defined by family circumstances. So don't be discouraged if you don't come from a rich family. Some of this country's wealthiest and most powerful people came from families of modest means and worked their way up the social, financial, and career ladders. Anyway, your goal should not necessarily be wealth and power, just something more attainable: an interesting and worthwhile life, and a certain level of comfort and security. It's easier to get there if your parents are rich or at least upper middle class, but it's not impossible (though it is more difficult) to get there if they aren't.

What personal qualities, then, are most likely to produce the kind of future that young adults want? Unfortunately, luck has a lot to do with it. Being in the right place at the right time, getting a unique job opportunity, buying the right stock or piece of real estate, or making a random choice that works out well are probably as important as some of the more classic characteristics in determining life prospects. But smart people capitalize on luck and do not turn their backs on life chances. Thousands of people had the opportunity to purchase mountain valley property in Colorado in the 1970s, when a few thousand dollars would have been enough to get a lot with a nice view. Not many people leapt at the chance. Those who did were likely to see their purchases turn into half a million dollars in a couple of decades, finding themselves set for life by a fairly simple — and, in retrospect obvious — decision made thirty years earlier. The same is true of buying Apple or Microsoft stock in the early days.

Researchers have been trying for years to unlock the secret to human success, without a great deal of consensus on the matter. For decades, they focused on IQ (intelligence quotient), believing, reasonably it seemed, that smart people would do better in life than not-so-smart people. That turns out not to be entirely the case. People with high intelligence (Mensa membership is restricted to the top 2 percent in testable intelligence) generally do well in their lives and careers, but not uniformly so. There are a lot of very smart, high-IQ individuals, often with impressive academic records, who have led quite average lives in terms of income and career opportunities, and others who have made a complete mess of their lives. Philosophy professors are usually highly intelligent, but they don't make millions — though at least they can be philosophical about it. Analysts also consider a new quantitative measure, emotional intelligence (EQ), which determines people's ability to understand, control, and direct their emotions. In our child-obsessed world, the emphasis on IQ and EQ proved very attractive to parents, who directed their children toward expensive IQ- and EQ-enhancing experiences (Mozart music in the crib, and so on), believing that they could, in the process, produce better career and life outcomes for their boys and girls.

We will leave the debate on fundamental brain or intellectual characteristics that determine personal success to the next generation or two of psychologists and neuroscientists. This does not, however, mean that we do not have strong ideas about the personal qualities that separate those who will succeed in life from those who will struggle (absent great luck or a wealthy family) to get ahead. Paul Tough's insightful book *How Children Succeed* is important in understanding the conditions that produce young people likely to have solid skills and the abilities necessary to make the most of their circumstances. In the somber opening to his book, Tough documents how early-life trauma — in the form of violence, conflict, family crisis, or poverty — can stifle individual potential to the point where recovery is extremely difficult. If anyone ever needs motivation for early childhood interventions (birth to kindergarten), *How Children Succeed* provides it in spades. If you have made it to the point of high school graduation, there is a strong likelihood that you did not experience early childhood trauma or, if you did, you have one of the other qualities that underlie individual opportunity.

Paul Tough argues that there are three characteristics that determine the chances an individual has to succeed:

- **Grit:** The path through life is littered with trials, crises, and failures. There is nothing about life in the modern world that is easy, obvious, or automatic. Successful people possess real grit — the ability to push through obstacles, respond to challenges, and dust themselves off even after major failures. The drive to succeed is strong in such individuals. They typically take a major setback as a learning opportunity rather than as a sign of fundamental weakness or shortcoming. Hardship provides important learning opportunities. Demonstrating the ability to work through crises is one of the most important illustrations of a person's capacity for personal growth, adaptation, and simple drive.

- **Curiosity:** Successful people are curious about pretty much everything. They tend to read a great deal and are constantly learning. They love to explore, experiment, discover, and understand. Teachers know the difference between someone who truly wants to learn and one who studies for a good grade. The former are treasures; the latter tend to whine a lot. The will to learn and the desire to discover sit at the core of all truly successful people.

- **Character:** Much as schools and society at large would like to reduce the requirements for success to a series of teachable moments or easily transmitted characteristics, there is, according to Tough, a great deal more at play. Personal qualities (that is, character) matter a great deal — trumping IQ and many other characteristics in determining the likelihood of success. A person of strong character has easily observable and highly desirable qualities: the ability to respond to adversity; real and sustained persistence; life focus, reliability, and trustworthiness; and an overwhelming work ethic. People with good character do not blame others for their shortcomings; instead, they grasp opportunities to learn and develop, and do not let life's misfortunes deter them from their long-term goals.

It's important to note that self-esteem is missing from Tough's description and from our list of crucial personal qualities. For the past generation, public schools and parents have been preoccupied with ensuring that children feel good about themselves — even if this means moving away from competition (too much losing undermines their self-esteem), not holding children responsible for meeting standards (too much reliance on arbitrary educational goals stifles creativity and undermines individual learning styles), and not drawing attention to differences in performance and ability (too much differentiation creates divisions within social groups and doesn't allow everyone to be a winner). Self-esteem, it turns out, is not well-connected to academic performance or career outcomes. This is a hard one to escape from, because the promotion of self-esteem is hardwired into modern society. We do not buy it — and nor do most of the key analysts in the field. Self-esteem is little more than contemporary edu-speak and is not connected to the qualities that generate success.

A PERSONAL SWOT ANALYSIS (SWOT STANDS FOR STRENGTHS, WEAKNESSES, OPPORTUNITIES, THREATS)

Here, perhaps, is the hardest bit. You are graduating from high school with decent grades. Your grades probably average over 80 percent — in many systems, this makes you an A student! Alas, this is not nearly the achievement that it was two generations ago. If you are right at 80, you are just below the average among students considering going on to higher education. Does this make you college material? We have already given you a couple of tests that should give you a bit of a sense of how you might fit at university. Here's another one:

SWOT TEST

1. **What are your strengths?** As with the other questions in this test, compiling a list — in this case of your strengths — can be difficult. You have to be brutally honest. A personal strength might not simply be the courses in which you had the highest grades (you might have had an easy grader for a teacher) but rather a field that you enjoyed and had decent grades in.

2. **What are your weaknesses?** Thinking of weaknesses requires introspection. How hard do you work? Are you really prepared to make major sacrifices in order to get ahead? Do you have a strong work ethic? Are you really ready to test yourself against the best?

3. **What opportunities are available to support your success?** The real challenge rests with identifying opportunities and threats. When it comes to opportunities, most students rely on parents, teachers, government, and the general "buzz" about the economy and about career possibilities. This advice is notoriously unreliable, offered by people who will not be living

your life. There are opportunities in emerging fields, such as nanotechnology. And, of course, there will always be jobs in the service and retail sectors. But where do you fit in?

4. **What threats could thwart your plans for success?** There are threats from Chinese and South Asian manufacturers and competition from professionals in India. Jobs are currently to be had in the American western resource sector, but many fewer will be available if pipelines and transportation links to markets are not developed. How will government programs and budgets affect your choices and chances? The prospect of another war — Afghanistan is supposedly done but there is a real prospect of another conflict in Iraq, this time with ISIS — could reshape personal opportunities within a few months. What happens if your family's financial situation takes a sharp turn for the worse? Are you ready for such a catastrophe?

Given that professional economists, demographers, and others have serious difficulties anticipating market and social trends, don't be surprised if you find forecasting the next year, let alone the next decade, to be extremely hard. The baby boomers are putting off retirement and holding on to their jobs, no one knows for how long, sometimes because they are paying for their children's or grandchildren's education! Restructuring inside companies and governments has eliminated thousands of middle-class jobs, just as closing manufacturing plants has removed thousands more (and unions, eager to protect existing workers, have increasingly turned to two-tier contracts to protect benefits for the older employees at the cost of new workers). Underemployment — getting a job that requires far fewer skills and less education than an individual has — has become widespread. In the United States, 25 percent of all retail workers have college degrees, as do 15 percent of all taxi drivers[4] and 15 percent of all firefighters.[5] Current estimates suggest that 50 percent — half! — of all college graduates in the United States are unemployed or underemployed after graduating. Colleges and universities, drawing on data from earlier decades, argue that the graduates will get their opportunities in due course, although the evidence for this statement is not very convincing.

Why? First, so many applicants have higher-education credentials that college graduates are getting jobs that used to go to high school graduates. Second, there are so many more people with undergraduate degrees than there are jobs that require degrees that many have to take work that does not require a degree — notably in the retail and service sectors.[6] Many college graduates are working alongside young adults who did not go to college at all, have four more years of work experience and earnings, and, in many cases, are receiving higher pay. And they find themselves several steps behind these young adults on the promotion ladder.

> **FOLLOWING YOUR DREAM ...**
>
> A friend's daughter had tons of academic and professional skills — but she really loved to cook. She cooked when she was a preteen, when she babysat, and all through high school. It finally dawned on her that she really, really wanted to cook. So she went to cooking school, got a diploma, and now, in high demand as a pastry chef, makes a decent living doing precisely what she loves to do. The most important part of this story is that her parents let her follow her passion and did not, as so many parents do these days, insist on her pursuing a more standard academic path. But, to prove the point that life is not fair, she came down with a serious back problem a year after landing a prime job in her field. She is now going back to community college and is trying to identify her second-best choice.

This situation should all be part of your SWOT analysis. Determining where you will fit in a rapidly evolving society and economy is no mean feat. We will come back to this over and over again: there is no substitute for real achievement — the top opportunities typically go to the very best — and hard work and good character will carry you much further than a basic credential any day. The top students in every field — including fields that seem devoid of career opportunities — will find meaningful and interesting work, although not without some difficulty.

BEYOND SWOT: KNOWING WHERE YOU STAND

The SWOT test leads to another series of questions that you have to ask about yourself as you make your plans for the next and crucial stage in your life:

- **How good are you at academics?** Forget your grades. Do a realistic assessment of your classmates. Are you the top student in the school? In the top ten? Here is your first wake-up call. There are hundreds of high schools in Texas. Even little Rhode Island has dozens of them. Each of these has a graduating class. Assume you are one of the top ten students in your school. This means that there are thousands of students graduating from the country's high schools who are of the same caliber and general ability as you. Are you ready and able to compete with the very best?

- **How hard do you work?** This is not a question just about academics. It relates to how you do your homework, to be sure, but also how you do with household chores, volunteer activities, and your part-time job. Do you tackle assignments — regardless of the nature of the work — with enthusiasm and efficiency? Or do you take your time or complain about what you have been asked to do? Which of these two types of person, by the way, would you hire if you were doing the hiring?

- **What do you do really well?** Think about your real interests in life. Make a list of the areas where you excel. These can be academic, physical, musical, artistic, or practical. Note if you are great at physics or English, but also if you are top-notch at carpentry or art. Give a lot of thought to this list, for it is going to be extremely important in defining your post–high school options. If, for example, you are not good at mathematics and you got your grades up to a competitive level only by taking the same course three times, you probably should not pursue a math-based college program — even if your parents really want you to take engineering or accounting. If, on the other hand, you are naturally gifted at mechanical or technical work to the exclusion of other more traditional academic skills, surely this should factor into your decision making.

- **What do you do badly?** Make a second list — and be really honest with yourself here — about the kind of things that you do badly. For the purposes of this exercise, consider "badly" to refer to those things in which you are in the bottom half of your peer group. If half of your high school classmates do something significantly better than you, whether it is writing, understanding world affairs, working with computers, grasping science, or fixing a bicycle or car, then you need to put this down. In some instances, these areas of weakness can be overcome. If you really want to pursue work in a field related to computers and you have minimal skills, challenge yourself. Take extra courses, outside of high school if necessary, to upgrade. A weakness need not be permanent, but a key weakness unaddressed can cause real difficulties down the road.

- **What do you really love doing?** This is where the difficulty starts, particularly if your parents have different ambitions for you. Many parents have dreams of their child becoming a doctor, lawyer, accountant, or engineer. Very few, it seems, fantasize about their child working at a day care center, working in a hydro-electric plant, getting a clerk's job in a state government office, or becoming a carpenter's apprentice. Dealing with your parents' hopes for your future can be a real problem — and it often starts with asking yourself these questions. You need to make a clear list about the things you really and truly love to do. What gets you excited in terms of study, work, and recreation? What kinds of activities make a real difference to your life and bring you simple and unadulterated joy?

- **How much does money matter to you?** You need to be completely honest with yourself and with your parents about this one. There are great jobs out there — social worker, musician, youth counselor, minister, preschool teacher, gardener — that offer full and fulfilling lives. But the pay is low, and working conditions can often be difficult. If money is a prime motivating factor in your life, then you had best take this into account. Many jobs simply will not provide the hundred-thousand-dollar-a-year salary, suburban house, holidays in the Caribbean, and two cars in the garage to which many of you aspire. If you want to earn a lot of money, there are ways of doing so: entrepreneurship (high risk, high potential return), medicine, accounting, some parts of the law, or real estate speculation. There are even a few places — Alaska still has some pretty neat opportunities — where it is possible to combine high wages and low skills. See what heavy-duty mechanics earn in the oil patch in Montana and North Dakota — you will be impressed — and they generally have not gone to college or, if they have, they don't use their training on the job. If money is the object, you had better have a prodigious work ethic, have a specialized skill, or be willing to follow the cash across the country and internationally.

- **How much do you know about the world of work?** You are facing one of the most important decisions in your life — preparing yourself for the workforce — when you know, typically, very little about career options. We know that high schools offer courses in career planning, but — based on the experiences of our children and thousands of university students — we sense that most teenagers don't take them very seriously. This is a serious question. There are thousands of careers available, from cat skinner (not what you think) to archivist. You could be a genetics counselor or a nanotechnologist. There is a large need for power engineers and millwrights, occupational therapists, glaziers, epidemiologists, diagnostic medical sonographers, speech pathologists, cost estimators, audit clerks, and a great many more.

- **Are you willing to relocate for work?** In your grandparents' days, there was little question — people would move to wherever a job was available. Mobility was the essence of an immigrant society. People used to move a great deal, following their dreams and job opportunities across the country and even around the world. This is still true for Americans, which is why there are so many Minnesotans in California these days, and Californians in Texas. It turns out, however, that many of you are not very mobile. People from Los Angeles, New York, and Chicago have trouble imagining life in small-town Iowa, coastal Alaska, or in the Appalachians. Young adults from Seattle and Portland (aka paradise) are notorious for refusing to leave. Highly motivated young people in the poorer states in the American South have historically been willing, even eager, to relocate to other parts of the country, but others have trouble leaving New Orleans, Detroit, Cleveland, or Merced, California. Ask yourself this question: Would you, a Bostonian, once you finish your schooling, happily relocate to Billings, Montana, a fast-changing city at the heart of the western oil boom? Would you consider a job on an isolated Indian reservation, where there is often an urgent need for professionals? Would you consider Oklahoma — yes, it is far from Hollywood, but any place that is home to the Sooners is pretty neat — where the economy is rebounding? How about Colorado Springs, Anchorage, or Honolulu, three of the most fascinating communities in the country? Mobility has always been the great equalizer in America, creating career and life opportunities for individuals. Look deep inside yourself. Will you move in pursuit of opportunity or do you expect opportunity to find you? (Subtle hint here: Mobility is one of the greatest keys to full career development. Staying put can lock you in a career and income box for life, even if it makes your mother happy.) Spread your wings: you might like the places you land, and you don't have to stay in one place forever.

- **Are you willing to create your own job?** We will come back to this point later, but entrepreneurship and self-employment are critical components of the modern economy. We have many self-employed people — taxi drivers, franchise operators, convenience store owners, tax specialists, and the like — but far too few entrepreneurs — the people who create companies, products, services, and jobs. Do you really want to work for someone else, or are you willing to set out on your own? Self-employment is growing rapidly — along with all of its freedoms and risks. Where do you fit in the spectrum from risk-taking to excessive caution?

PEER PRESSURE: RESISTING THE SWARM

One of the greatest challenges facing young adults is breaking away from the group. Much as everyone likes to believe that he or she is an original, a true individual, the reality is that we are shaped and defined by our genetics, environment, and social relations. Students from schools in wealthy areas are more likely to go to college than are those from poor districts. If you hang around with the swarm, your chances of doing well in high school decline and your postsecondary prospects get dimmer. We are conditioned by popular culture, peer attitudes, and a desire to fit in. This is simply the truth.

Ironically, one of the most significant outcomes of contemporary peer pressure has been the routine migration from high school to college. Everyone — from parents to friends — talks incessantly about it. In the best public schools, "Where are you applying?" and "Where are you going to college?" are standard questions. At elite American private secondary schools — which often advertise the success of their graduates in terms of numbers being accepted with scholarships into the best colleges — the pressure to write the SAT (formerly the Scholastic Aptitude Test, required for admission to many colleges) and prepare dynamite application letters is intense.

There is a certain lemming-like character to this movement toward college, for it is simply assumed that all right-minded young people will move from high school to campus, joining the mass competition to get a cubicle job (read *Dilbert* if you don't already do so: it's a fascinating and hilarious window on the world you have been trained for) and an entry ticket to the middle class. Politicians have picked up on this, of course, which is why they talk about college so much — and why President Obama has said that every young person should have the chance to go, or should actually go (he has been vague about which it should be) to college. The idea that there will be jobs for everyone with a degree or, equally problematic, that all of these would-be students are likely to succeed at college, is perhaps the worst conceit of the modern era, representing a serious misreading of the national and international job market and the capabilities of the younger generation.

Overcoming peer pressure is not easy. We appreciate that. College recruiters learned many years ago that one of the best ways of increasing applications from a specific high school was to convince a handful of popular kids to attend their institution. Once they had locked in these leaders — the captain of the basketball team and the head cheerleader were, stereotypically, the targets — others followed more or less automatically. There will be a very strong desire to follow your friends, both in the decision to attend college and then in the collective choice of campus, typically the one closest to your high school. Everything is familiar then, isn't it? You can take your social circle with you, stay in familiar territory, possibly live at home. All very comfy — but not a very adventurous leap into adulthood.

BE YOURSELF

Our advice, avuncular as always, is simple: be yourself; and, if you don't know who you are, find out. When the swarm forms up, make your own judgments about whether or not you want to join. Stand aside, look far afield, re-evaluate your SWOT analysis, and contemplate your future — for yourself and by yourself. Live your own life — not the one that your friends have outlined for you and for themselves. It's easier to give this advice than to follow it, but the results will justify the effort.

3

THE COLLEGE OPTION

TAKE THE TIME TO DO IT RIGHT

Many of you who are giving serious attention to your future will opt for college. Some of you will have made the right decision — for you, college is a great choice, and you are perhaps wondering why we are fussing about it so much. Your path is clear and, barring some unexpected misfortune, your academic success is assured — though not necessarily your career success.

For others, though, the decision is wrong. You will be disappointed with college and, in a year or so, you may wish that you had listened to our warnings. Going to college without thinking about what you are doing — treating it as an extension of high school, living at home, and following the high school swarm to the local campus, or picking a distant campus because you like the look of its web page — is not planning. This too-common approach is one of the reasons so many students struggle and fail in their first year. You can make the choice that's best for you and, if you decide on college, there are things you can do to prepare yourself for it. Take the time to do it right. This chapter is directed at those who have decided on college, and here we assume that you've made the right choice. Later chapters discuss other choices.

ADVANCED PLACEMENT

Perhaps you have taken advanced placement courses in high school (if you are in junior high, look into them). These are college courses offered in high schools in a variety of subjects, from art history to various branches of physics, to music theory, politics, and world history. Colleges often give course credit for them, and they are quite popular as a means of testing the waters and earning some credits. In 2013, 470,000 students took the English Language and Composition course. Taking advanced placement courses sounds like a great idea, but be warned: if you take a course and fail the exam, you may not be college material. A lot of students don't do very well in them: in 2014 the mean score for the exam in the World History course, which you'd think would be one of the easier ones, was only 2.66 out of 5. Even many students who pass these courses turn out not to be ready for actual college-level work, so take nothing for granted.

INVEST TIME IN YOUR PLANNING

Going to college is a very big decision — one that can cost you and your family sixty thousand dollars a year or much more, a total of at least a quarter of a million dollars, depending on how long it takes you to finish your degree, whether you get financial aid or not, and what costs you factor in (more later on costs). Some of your parents have money socked away for you, thanks to the tax system with its rewards for upper-middle-class people sending their children to college. However, many of you will have to rely on some combination of savings from work, loans (private or government), family support, grants, and scholarships. It's a long and quite expensive haul. Doing it right is important. Take the time to figure out which institution and program is best for you, realizing that there is a good chance you will get both wrong.

Consider the agonies of high school graduates across the United States. These students, and their anxious parents, are desperate to get into the prestigious college of their choice. The ones who consider themselves to be top-drawer, as the WASP elite used to say, apply to Harvard, Stanford, Yale, Princeton, and the other prestige institutions, which turn down more than 90 percent of applicants. And here is a college dirty secret. Because rankings of U.S. institutions are based, in part, on how "selective" they are in admitting students, some of the top schools deliberately encourage applications from students who have no chance of being selected. More applications = more rejections = higher ratings. And you, hopeful Harvard applicant, can easily become the fodder for this ratings war. But don't panic. There are close to five thousand U.S. colleges, not counting the for-profit institutions that are springing up almost daily. Only a handful of them reject anywhere near 90 percent of applicants. Some, in fact, accept everyone who applies. Even many so-called selective institutions make offers to over 70 percent of the people who apply. Relax — you will always get in somewhere. And if your grades are above the 80 percent level, you will be pleasantly surprised at how many fine, high-quality institutions want you — and your parents' money. The question is whether you really want to go, and whether you should.

Here is the basic math of the U.S. application process, using as an example a fine and creative institution, Colorado College, which is one of our favorites. Colorado College admits only 500 students per year and gets more than 3,500 applicants. "Oh, no," you wail, "I have only a one in seven chance of getting in." Not so. It turns out that many students apply to considerably more than one institution. So the college has to hedge its bets. Colorado College actually has to offer places to over 2,400 students in order to end up with 500 registered students at the start of classes. So, your chances of getting in are 70 percent, not one in seven. And Colorado College markets itself as a "highly selective" institution. Offer the same average to baseball batters and they would be ecstatic. Not bad odds, either, for a college applicant. Of course, it's different at Harvard, where in March 2013, 2,029 letters of acceptance went out to a pool of 35,023 applicants, a success rate of 5.8 percent.

Completely contrary to what you have been told, getting into a very good college in the United States is not overly difficult. Harvard? Yes. Swarthmore? Yes. But for a large majority of the best small, medium-sized, and large colleges and universities in the country, getting in is fairly easy. There is an entire industry of recruitment agents, postsecondary advisors, and college administrators who have a vested interest in exaggerating the mystique of American academic admissions. Well over half of the colleges in the United States — probably several dozen of which would be a great match for a college-destined student — are willing to accept almost anyone with a decent high school grade point average, and many will take mediocre students as well. American academic standards, save for a handful of elite programs in elite colleges, are not very high. Almost everyone with a high school average over 75 percent and the right mix of courses will be able to find a place at one of the country's universities. And with some five thousand institutions, and many for-profit institutions joining the ranks, to say nothing of the hundreds of online courses that are now available, there is no shortage of choice. In fact, you could argue that Americans have too many choices. It is a much greater challenge to find the *right* institution than it is to find an institution that will accept you. Have you heard about Georgia Gwinnett College, Keene State College in Keene, New Hampshire, or Carroll College in Helena, Montana? They are all fine colleges, offering excellent services for students, and they are much easier to get into than the so-called elite colleges that may well not match these institutions in terms of the quality of educational experience and career outcome. Because the local campuses are also often accessible, both physically and academically, you, like many students, may simply opt for the college closest to you. But, on the other hand, of course you need to be aware that cheap and close does not necessarily mean that it is the right choice.

AMERICAN COLLEGE INNOVATION

One of the great things about American colleges is that there is no end of innovation in the field. Consider two very different approaches. Peter Thiel, billionaire co-founder of PayPal, set up a scholarship program (twenty grants of one hundred thousand dollars each) to pay high-achieving high school graduates *not* to go to college, but to focus on business start-ups instead. At the other extreme, a group of academic adventurers have just launched "Minerva," which promises to reinvent and reinvigorate the idea of college. Minerva does not replicate existing college models. Instead, it offers a unique blend of online learning, face-to-face instruction, small classes, and international study experiences, which will see students rotate through a series of overseas campuses. Thiel's fellowship program and Minerva share several characteristics: a belief that the current college system is failing students, a commitment to flexibility and innovation, and an emphasis on attracting the best and brightest in America.

The application process for American colleges is one of the most complicated, costly, and demanding in the world. The high school graduation standards are much less rigorous than in Japan, Taiwan, or China, but the system makes up for this laxity at the college level. Many, but not all, institutions demand the SAT, an examination that tests writing, mathematical, and reasoning skills, and knowledge of current events. The best colleges require a full resumé — and it had better cover a lot more than academic activities if you want to get the attention of admissions officers at the top schools. There is also that special letter of application, now often ghost-written by professional (and expensive) admissions counselors. In these letters, you describe the connections among your experience, academic achievement, career aspirations, and extracurricular activities. If you end up applying to six or seven institutions — and many of them charge hundreds of dollars in application fees — you may have to write several separate letters, tailor your resumé accordingly, and explain how your unique characteristics make you the perfect candidate for success.

There are some shortcuts. Once you have filled out the forms for your top choice, you can usually get by with minor tweaks for the other institutions. One of our favorite ways to cut through the application red tape is through the Common Application Center. This service (www.common-app.org) allows students to assemble one application package that covers submissions to over five hundred colleges in forty-seven states. The members' list includes some of the big names (Stanford, Harvey Mudd, Whitman College, University of Notre Dame, and Yale) and some schools you may have never heard of (St. Olaf College, Pine Manor College, Keuka College, Salve Regina University, and Pitzer College) but that nonetheless warrant consideration. Of course, if your preferred institution(s) are not on the list, it is back to separate applications.

Popular culture provides some guidance, although you will find this unnerving, to say the least. In the TV series *The Middle*, a hilarious portrait of family life in Indiana, the oldest son, Axel, is athletically talented but an academic disaster. Of course, he gets a scholarship and heads off to school, where he runs headlong into an academic morass, floundering like a dinosaur in a tar pit. His ever-cheerful sister, Sue, fails at almost everything, but does well on a retake of her SATs and now can aspire to elite schools. Her middle-class family's reaction? To immediately seek out second and third jobs so that they can support her (unrealistic) aspirations. Interestingly, no consideration is given to the idea that Sue should work to save for her college education. The series *Modern Family* has comparable characters. Hayley, the eldest daughter of the Dunphy family, is a fashion plate and pop culture advocate, but a classic teenage airhead. She gets into a low-ranked and unnamed college, where she is promptly evicted for drunken behavior. Her hyper-academic sister obsesses about grades and college admissions to the point that she sends herself into psychological care. The family is preoccupied with college attendance, with nary a detailed conversation about the costs, real career possibilities, or anything remotely intellectual. You cannot escape the infatuation with college life in America even when you head to network television. Of course, if you want something intellectual, you can switch your PVR to *The Big Bang Theory*, nerd central if there ever was one, a classic portrayal of the intellectual aloofness and social awkwardness of the academically inclined (although Leonard's success with the physically attractive Penny gives hope for nerds everywhere).

By the time you get to eleventh grade, unless you are living in a cave you will have already had your fill of admissions advice from your parents, teachers, guidance counselors, and classmates. Almost every class is going to have a student — or ten — obsessed with getting into the "right" institution. In no other country in the world do students — including those of mediocre ability and questionable motivation — spend so much time thinking, planning, and debating postsecondary options. Going to university is a high priority in Japan, China, Hong Kong, Singapore, and South Korea, but families and students in these countries are much more realistic about prospects. Elite students focus on elite institutions; mediocre students set their sights on accessible institutions. In the United States, where most students are told repeatedly that they can "be anything they want to be" and that they are superbly talented, young adults devote a great deal of time and money to reaching too high. You know these students. They seem to devote hundreds of hours reviewing college guidebooks, drafting application letters, and, from early high school, building the perfect admissions resumé. Some have parents who made a huge effort to get their kids into the right preschool because that led to the right elementary school, which provided access to the right high school, which had a great record of getting their graduating students into Ivy League colleges. This effort, often completed at great cost, reinforces in the minds of all participants the importance of getting into college, a self-justification of the campaign to get the high school graduate launched properly.

It is at this initial step, unfortunately, that many college-bound students make a major mistake. Picking the right college is a difficult task that should be taken seriously. Focusing on the famous places, or the ones your parents attended, or the one closest to home, or the one with the best NCAA Division 1 football team is simply not good enough. Remember, there are more than five thousand colleges to consider. If you have the right skills and motivation, many will be ideally suited to you. But even if you are highly talented, some of the elite schools would be a disastrous pick. Consider one of our favorite small colleges, St. John's College, with campuses in Maryland and New Mexico. These are small institutions, with only four hundred students across all four years. Entrance standards are very high and the program is rigorous and demanding. Each year, students have to read a hundred of the best books of all time, and everyone studies mathematics. For the right students, there could be nothing more intense and enriching than spending four years with other young people who are eager to learn from the writings of the best minds in human history. For other students — the vast majority, in fact — this program would be an intellectual nightmare, with no competitive basketball team and no fraternities to offset the long reading lists.

There are many factors to take into account. Colleges pretend publicly that they are all the same, all great teaching and research institutions, but this isn't true, and students react differently to different colleges. Some students love the place where they earn their degree, while others forget about it and its faculty as soon as the degree is conferred. It's important to realize that not every college will suit you. This means that the most important part of your college journey begins while you are still in high school, likely in eleventh grade and continuing through your last year in school. Of course, you have to know yourself and be brutally honest about your strengths and weaknesses if you are going to make the right choices. If you permit yourself to be pushed in the wrong direction by parents, counselors, or friends, you could make a terrible decision. Similarly, you could make an equally disastrous choice on your own. There is a middle ground between following your preferences and instincts and going with the swarm. Finding that sweet spot will to a large extent determine the quality of your college experience.

We are unimpressed, by the way, with reports by institutions and ranking services about student satisfaction with their college choice. The rationale is much like that of approval ratings for car purchases. Individuals who opted to spend forty-five thousand dollars on a new car tend to validate their choice by later reporting their happiness with their selection — because to do otherwise suggests that they made a dumb decision. In college, this pattern is made even more meaningless by the fact that most students have no basis for comparison for their experience. Having considered a hundred colleges, the students choose one. They go there for four or more years and have an intense experience in the process. They are later asked if they made the right choice. How do they know? They did not go to other colleges for four years, so they have no basis for a legitimate comparison. To go back to the car purchase analogy, automobile buyers generally report positively on this selection (unless the car is junk) even though they have likely not driven in many vehicles other than their own. So, if a university reports that its students reported 94 percent satisfaction rates, file that information under M for meaningless. It tells you that people who had only one experience believe that, compared to the experiences that they did not have, they made a good choice. Hmmm ... not very convincing. Having said that, though, if you find a place where the "student satisfaction" rate, however measured, is particularly low, you will want to find out why before you commit yourself to the place.

Picking a campus is a delicate exercise, as you attempt to balance career plans, parental expectations, personal preferences, peer pressure, public recognition, and such intangibles as where your girlfriend or boyfriend has decided to go. We would urge you to do two things. First, give very careful consideration — as we have been urging you all along — to why you want to go to college and what you want out of it. If you have done that properly, the second stage — picking the right college — is going to be a lot easier. At this second stage, we beg you to get rid of preconceptions, particularly about the elite, expensive private institutions, the benefits of which, relative to lesser institutions, are exaggerated. Almost all of you have heard about Harvard, Yale, Princeton, Stanford, and UCLA. How many of you have heard of Hendrix College, a small school of 1,400 students that is one of three colleges located in Conway, Arkansas, a town of

50,000 that rarely makes the national news? But Hendrix is a high-quality liberal arts college, well recognized by its peers. It would be an excellent choice for a student keen about a small residential campus with a strong focus on social engagement, campus activities, and an old-style liberal arts education.

We will admit to a strong bias here. We are not enthusiastic about your going to the big-name research universities — like UCLA, Brown, the University of Florida, the University of Michigan — for an undergraduate degree. Smart, motivated students who go to these places will do fine, and the colleges do carry global brand recognition. It's certainly easier to sell a would-be employer in Japan or Singapore on the merits of UCLA than on those of Bates College, Evergreen State College, or Agnes Scott College — all fine institutions. Branding does matter, but not, in the long run, as much as the quality of the educational experience. There is a reason that Wall Street hires from the Ivy League Schools — although it actually has more to do with work motivation than the intrinsic superiority of their education. But if you are one of the prime college candidates — highly intelligent, curious, with a great work ethic and an openness to new ideas — we encourage you to consider smaller residential colleges. There are two areas where the United States truly leads the world in postsecondary education: the liberal arts colleges and the elite research universities, particularly at the graduate level. For the high school graduates looking to find themselves intellectually, there are several hundred of these small colleges (including well-recognized institutions like Swarthmore, William and Mary, and Lewis and Clark) that are absolute world-beaters. But again, do not be swayed by public recognition and the famous brands — you will often pay too much for the label and could easily find yourself in a school that is not well suited to your particular needs and interests.

If you want something really different, you might consider Deep Springs College, an "alternative" institution in the ranch country of California, forty-five miles from the nearest town of any size. It's a two-year institution with twenty-six students, all male (though this is under challenge). Founded in 1917, it is rooted in the three principles of academics, labor, and self-government. Students work twenty hours a week on a ranch the college owns, and they also control the curriculum, student admissions, and faculty hiring. Most go on to complete degrees at four-year universities, and over half eventually earn a Ph.D. The college's website[1] provides a good description of it. Clearly it's not for everyone, but for the right person the experience could be life-changing. (The recent documentary film, *Ivory Tower*, which is mostly about student debt,[2] has an interesting segment on Deep Springs.)

HISTORICALLY BLACK COLLEGES

Perhaps you are a student who will thrive at a "historically black college or university," defined as "an institution of higher education founded before 1964 with the intention of serving the black community." There are more than a hundred, the majority of them private institutions, the most famous probably being Fisk University in Nashville, founded in 1866. Quite a few of these colleges are well over a hundred years old, having been founded during the worst days of racial segregation: Florida A&M in Tallahassee, Claflin University in Orangeburg, South Carolina, and others, all of them fine institutions. We list the best ones in the Appendix.

These colleges were a response to formal racial segregation in America, which existed from the earliest days of college education until the mid-1960s. Some free blacks in the North did go to college before the Civil War, but for most African Americans, education of any kind was either difficult or actually illegal. After 1865, however, supporters of African American advancement promoted the development of colleges specifically for these students. At a time when almost all of the avenues to professional advancement were firmly blocked, the historically black colleges provided an essential opportunity for advancement. Generations of talented, ambitious, and highly motivated African American students bypassed the institutional barriers because farsighted promoters and supporters saw fit to underwrite the development of these exceptional institutions.

These are remarkable colleges, built as a rejection of assumptions about African American intellectual inferiority, and demonstrating to a long-ignorant national audience the enormous pool of talent and aspiration blocked from attending the country's colleges and universities. The names of the top private institutions — once icons for opportunity for African Americans — stand tall in the history of American postsecondary education. Spelman College, established in 1861, is based in Atlanta, Georgia, and is regarded as the best historically black college in the United States. Howard University, which opened in Washington, D.C., twenty years later, is one of the best known of the group, along with Morehouse College, another impressive institution. Booker T. Washington, one of the greatest African American minds in U.S. history, graduated from Hampton University in Virginia. Tuskegee University, located in Alabama, designated as a National Historic Site, was another of the post–Civil War academies that tried valiantly to open up opportunities for talented African American youth.

The historically black colleges, almost all small (between two thousand and seven thousand students), remain active and, in some instances, highly competitive and very selective. They are excellent schools, fired by a passion for African American advancement and a commitment to personal growth. They are more political than most colleges and universities, but nowhere near as much as outsiders expect. They are fine academic institutions with a superb historical pedigree, an honorable history of fighting against racism and injustice, and a deserved reputation for supportive student development.

As opportunities have expanded in public and private institutions, and as colleges and universities across the United States have tried to make themselves more open to African American students, the weaker historically black colleges have faced ever greater competition for students. It is no longer possible to argue that African American students are barred by race from entry to elite colleges and universities, though there's a stronger argument that many are barred by the economic disadvantages associated with race. Lower-ranked historically black colleges are struggling, having difficulty raising donations and dealing with declines in enrollment. If they disappear in the coming decades, or if they accept more non–African American students (a small number of the historically black colleges are already majority non-African American), a vital piece of the country's postsecondary system will have gone. At the same time, there is much to celebrate in the fact that African American students are no longer barred from entry into the nation's colleges and universities and that the once formidable barrier to black advancement has been dramatically breached.

FOR-PROFIT AND CORPORATE COLLEGES

The United States, which has the world's best network of private colleges and universities, also has a surprisingly diverse system of for-profit colleges and universities. This is a rapidly expanding group of institutions, some of a high quality and others, to put it charitably, of dubious character — or, to put it uncharitably, pretty fraudulent. The huge growth in post-secondary education of recent years, fueled by the belief that a degree or a diploma is the first requirement of a decent life, has created a seemingly insatiable demand for spaces in postsecondary institutions. And there is nothing that capitalism likes better than unmet demand, particularly in the middle and at the lower end of the consumer market. So, noting the thousands of students looking for credentials, parents and banks willing to fund advanced study, and significant criticism of the existing college and university system, companies jumped at the opportunity.

The for-profit institutions range widely in size and quality. The largest is the University of Phoenix, which is to postsecondary education what Denny's is to breakfast — inexpensive, formulaic, and predictable. It's simply enormous: different sources give different statistics, but in 2010 it claimed to have 470,000 registered students.[3] The University of Phoenix is not only online, either; it has face-to-face campuses in thirty-eight states and the District of Columbia. Twenty-nine percent of its students are African American. The university, which counts Shaquille O'Neal among its graduates and has Arizona Cardinals wideout Larry Fitzgerald sponsoring student scholarships, has run into trouble in recent years, with controversies over student loans and quality standards. One of the most complex for-profit institutions — Corinthian Colleges Inc. — grew by acquiring a variety of smaller institutions, creating a big online presence, and taking a very aggressive approach to student recruitment. Corinthian Colleges operates under the names of Everett College, Everest Institute, and WyoTech.

Corinthian and many of the other for-profit colleges capitalized on the flexible (critics would say preposterously loose) regulations of federal student aid and educational support programs. Some institutions receive 80 percent to 90 percent of their total budget from federal government loan programs, a unique twist on the concept of a free enterprise operation. In 2012 the *New York Times* reported that 96 percent of students at for-profits took out loans, as compared with 13 percent at community colleges and 48 percent at four-year public colleges. Many of the for-profit colleges, including several very sketchy law schools, encouraged weak and minimally qualified students to take out large loans to finance their college programs. Large numbers of these students failed to complete their studies but remained saddled with heavy student debt. Belatedly, the government became interested and started investigating a large number of the institutions for fraudulent behavior.

Corinthian, once a flagship for for-profit education, ran into serious financial and legal difficulties, despite receiving some $1.4 billion per year in federal funding. Accusations of misrepresentation of the costs of programs, employment opportunities, and likelihood of graduation swirled around the company. With several tens of thousands of students stuck partway through their programs and with no prospect of Corinthian rebounding, the U.S. government helped broker the sale of many of Corinthian's assets to Educational Credit Management Corporation (ECMC), a debt-serving company that, ironically, earns much of its money by fighting students trying to get out from under crushing student debt loads. ECMC, which took over many of Corinthian's campuses, has promised to turn the institutions into not-for-profit operations. Scandals have also erupted in for-profit law schools, several of which likewise played loose with academic standards and overproduced graduates for an already tight market.

The dramatic rise and controversial collapse of for-profit colleges is the greatest illustration of the irrational behavior of Americans during the college and university boom. While many private and public institutions raced to expand their student numbers, the pressure from the American public created even greater demand for college seats. The ever-opportunistic entrepreneurs jumped into the breach, responding to a seemingly inexhaustible demand for credentials. While there were good for-profit colleges — more than the news coverage suggests — the expansion brought out some of the worst excesses of American capitalism. Thousands of students, underqualified and ill-prepared, have been driven into bankruptcy, owing huge sums for government loans used to fund an incomplete or mediocre education.

A friend — newly separated, without a diploma or degree, and eager to get into a professional career — started searching for a psychology degree she could complete online. Inexperienced in the field, she identified a for-profit institution that would allow her to enroll directly in a Ph.D. program, offering full credit for her "life experience" and promising relatively quick progress to a Ph.D. in psychology, without the time-consuming steps of a bachelor's or master's degree. Suffice it to say that the degree, sure to be awarded if the fees were paid in full, would be worth little more than the paper it was printed on.

So, we have to end this section with a strong warning. Do your due diligence on for-profit colleges. Some of them are worthy, well connected to the workforce, and supportive of students. There's a list of them in the Appendix. The worst are little more than diploma mills. You might get your degree, but it will carry little or no weight with potential employers, and will provide few of the advanced skills that you assume you will get from your studies. Investigate them very carefully, be wary of sales jobs by commissions-based recruiters, anticipate sticker shock when you see the prices they charge, and double check with employers to see if the colleges have credibility in the workforce.

By the way, the for-profit colleges get much of their business from students who could not get into regular colleges and universities. If your grades and experience are insufficient to attract the attention of the public or not-for-profit institutions — we have already told you that it is easy to get into well over half of the colleges in the United States — then you probably should not pursue a postsecondary education. Many of the for-profit institutions prey on the unrealistic expectations of would-be students and their parents and try to convince them that they will succeed in their "student friendly" institutions. Resist! Going to college, for-profit or otherwise, when you are not properly prepared, is a bad decision. Do something else.

CORPORATE UNIVERSITIES

America is nothing if not educationally creative, and the emergence of corporate universities is one of the most fascinating parts of the country's educational transformation. In recent years, leading companies have established their own training and professional development institutes. There are now more than a thousand such institutions, ranging from small professional programs to large and complex operations like Hamburger University (run by McDonald's for some 7,500 students per year, mostly McDonald's managers) and Motorola University (which focuses extensively on Six Sigma management methods training). Some of the best known are Disney University, Charles Schwab University, Oracle University, University of Toyota, and Crotonville (run by General Motors). Few of them are available to recent high school graduates; they are designed for mid-career professionals and corporate executives.

Corporate universities are not degree-granting institutions in the traditional sense of the term, but they provide timely, relevant, and engaging educational opportunities. The work is often tough — attending a corporate university is no beach party — but most provide branded, high-quality professional educational experiences. These are not entry-level offerings and will not be of real interest until you are well advanced in your career. To a degree that few people recognize, corporate universities represent a long-term challenge to professional offerings and graduate programs, for they indicate that corporate America increasingly believes that it can better prepare graduates than standard postsecondary institutions can. Some believe that it is only a matter of time before such corporate-driven institutions start offering entry-level programs in the style of more traditional institutions.

FOR A GOOD LIBERAL EDUCATION

In our view, the ideal pathway for a talented, curious, and highly motivated young American student or international student who is looking for a general liberal education (as opposed to one interested in a more technical or scientific program) is to head to a liberal arts college for an undergraduate degree, followed by graduate studies or a professional degree at a top-flight research university or specialized professional school. Putting together those things America truly does best — the liberal arts college and the research and professional powerhouse — is still a very strong foundation for lifelong success. This is a positive way of saying something universities do not particularly want you to hear: that the undergraduate experience in even the top private research universities leaves a great deal to be desired, that heading to a low-quality public university can be very disappointing for top students, and that the undergraduate opportunities in the large public research universities can leave even the most ambitious students adrift and unfulfilled. Check out the sizes of the first-year classes at the University of Washington in Seattle, a top research school, and compare that to Middlebury College in Vermont. Decide for yourself if you are going to get personal attention in classes of 100 to 1,500 students or if you are better served in first-year classes of 15 to 20 students. Remember also that those very large classes are often split into lecture sections taught by young, untenured, underpaid, and sometimes unhappy adjunct professors. There are, of course, places that do both undergraduate and graduate studies particularly well, like the University of Chicago (a high-achieving favorite of ours, particularly as a center for intellectual rigor) and Princeton, but they are the exceptions.

Before you make your shortlist of your top schools, take a careful look at the Colleges of Distinction.[4] These small or medium-sized colleges focus on undergraduate education and on transforming the lives and opportunities of their students. They are teaching-intensive and highly supportive, and they do an excellent job of preparing their students for the top graduate schools, for professional study, or for the workforce. If you are launching yourself into a process that is going to shape your life and play a major role in determining your future prospects, you must start by moving past promotional brochures and the oppressive weight of popular culture. Let us be even more blunt. If you do not find it truly exciting to explore college opportunities, and if you cannot bring yourself to spend dozens of hours considering your options and looking for the best fit, then you are probably not going to get very much out of a college degree. Use this as a test of your determination and curiosity: if the exercise of exploring college options leaves you cold or uninterested, then perhaps you shouldn't go.

PLAN TO VISIT SEVERAL CAMPUSES

For most high school students, colleges can be imposing and even intimidating places. Since you may be spending four or more years at the place, there is a lot to gain from a campus visit, even if you avoid one of the promotional college tours and simply wander about with friends and family or on your own. A quick look at one of the huge classrooms — several of the biggest campuses have rooms that hold well over a thousand students — can be a real shock. The athletically minded should check out the sports facilities. Some campuses have superb gyms, pools, rinks, and fitness centers. Those institutions with NCAA Division 1 teams have some of the best athletic facilities anywhere, often hosting many Olympic-caliber athletes from around the world, though the average student may not have ready access to them.

You should take a good look at the residences too, particularly since we strongly urge you to stay in residence. They vary widely in quality: some are pretty spiffy; others are old and shabby. But then, how much are you willing to pay for spiffiness? You don't need a designer dorm room, though there are firms, one called Dormify, that for a fee will give you the dream dorm experience you clearly deserve. Pay close attention to student spaces — cafeterias, study rooms, lounges, and social rooms. Watch for special features — which aren't a vital part of the university experience but are designed to woo you — such as climbing walls, hot tubs, ski hills, and the like. You will be surprised by the difference between some public universities — many of which have been starved of building funds for years — and the more prosperous high-tuition private institutions. Heritage buildings add immensely to the ambiance of campus life. Many of the Ivy League institutions in the Northeast are remarkable places. We have a weakness for the "collegiate gothic" style of architecture, and Duke's beautiful campus seems to say "Ideas flourish here!" The same holds for many of the smaller nineteenth-century colleges, particularly in the East but including the best colleges in the Midwest and West — Lewis and Clark and Reed College are both beautiful places, as is the University of Oregon in Eugene. And Stanford, with money galore, manages to look both fun and wise. Some of the modern, urban universities, built when the utilitarian and ugly architectural style of the 1960s was in vogue, are awfully bland, but great things can still happen inside. Cal State Northridge is an easy-access institution north of Los Angeles; its California-bland architecture will win few hearts aesthetically, but it does well serving students requiring academic assistance.

Eating is a big part of the campus experience, and universities work hard to collect your food money. We are not fans of food courts, which typically feature chain restaurants, but there are great cafeteria facilities at many universities. When your parents aren't looking, check out the student pubs, especially for signs announcing music, comedy, and events other than just boozing. "All work and no play" and all that. But some places go overboard. Ignore the "best party school" lists (we include some in the Appendix). They are just weird. Arizona State University, which makes it high on the list of fun places, is actually one of the most diverse and academically creative institutions in the country. Go to ASU for the academics, not the basketball team or the parties. Dartmouth, a school with a wonderful academic pedigree and a reputation for student scholarship, has had a dreadful culture of drinking that has recently caused significant challenges to the campus community.

As physical places, colleges range widely, from barren suburban campuses to lovely pastoral settings. Urban colleges often sprawl over many city blocks, while the parklike campuses of the land-grant colleges occupy large areas. Their sheer size can be fairly intimidating. Some students love the intense urban feel of a place like Columbia University in New York City, while others find the downtown settings of the University of Southern California and the Washington University of St. Louis to be daunting and uncomfortable. Other students would find an isolated residential college — like Union College in upstate New York, Minot State University, or the University of Wisconsin Green Bay — to be intolerably distant from anywhere. Many of the country's universities — the Massachusetts Institute of Technology, University of Maryland, Ithaca College, and Drew University are good examples — are visually unimpressive, with blocklike hodgepodge buildings. MIT demonstrates that physical beauty and intellectual pre-eminence can be inversely correlated. The settings for a few campuses — College of the Atlantic (Maine), the University of Puget Sound in Washington State, Colorado College, Florida Southern, and Pepperdine University and Scripps College in California — are so stunning that some students undoubtedly decide to attend simply to enjoy what are some of the nicest college settings in the world. You are going to spend a lot of time on campus — make sure that the place feels good for you.

From the perspective of their physical space, all colleges accomplish their core functions in pretty much the same way. All the colleges have libraries (increasingly now more study halls than book repositories with the Internet providing access to so much information), lecture halls, faculty and administrative offices, sports facilities, and the like. Some look like large high schools; others like small cities. Some have invited commerce right onto campus (in the form of fast-food joints and stores); others are as sterile as a Stalinist government office. After the first blush of excitement — or dismay — whichever college you choose simply becomes your home. Note again our standard injunction about colleges. There is no right choice. What works for one person is precisely the wrong choice for someone else.

CHECK EVERYTHING OUT

Your campus visit, in person and online, should be much more comprehensive than a simple tour of the buildings and grounds. It is vital that you find the other services and supports that the college has to offer. Find out about the special programs for first-year students — you need to know what the institution does to help students adjust to the campus. Some smart campuses begin their outreach in the summer before classes start, giving incoming students a mental jump-start and getting them used to the rigors of academic life. Make sure you locate the writing, math, and study skills centers at the college. While you may think you won't need such support, the chances are better than even that you will. When you need help, you'll need it in a hurry. And, since your college career may depend on them, you need the services to be first-rate. At way too many universities, these fundamental services are seriously underfunded. It can often take weeks to get an appointment to even start the process of identifying the problems. There are other things worth checking out: counseling; career advising; cooperative education; health services; sex education; support for gay, lesbian, transsexual, and bisexual students; and the much-needed financial assistance. And don't forget the people in the registrar's office. They're the ones who handle all of your administrative work, process your grades, and otherwise monitor your progress through your years of study. Treat them with respect; they're not your servants, and they can be helpful in times of stress. It is here, by the way, that your parents' investment in your college education is most evident. The expensive private institutions typically have excellent student-support services.

They want you to succeed — and not just because a four-year student who graduates brings in a lot more money in his or her career than one who drops out after the first semester of the first year.

Some of the stuff you hear on a campus visit won't be of much importance to you. Guides will tell you about famous alumni, social life, guest lectures, major donations to enrich college life, and a great deal of other good news. You need to look more deeply. Even the weakest and poorest campus has a nice facility or two, and can often claim credit for a famous alumnus. Infamous ones too: Richard Nixon got his law degree from Duke, but they don't talk about that there.[5] In contrast, Kermit the Frog was granted an honorary degree Doctor of Amphibious Letters by Southampton College, New York, in 1996.

Try to get a sense of the people on campus. See if you can meet with some faculty members, departmental advisors (the people who guide you through your academic programs), and, in particular, the staff. It will surprise you to learn that support staff — departmental secretaries, janitors, cafeteria workers, residence advisors, reference librarians — can have a great influence on your enjoyment of campus life. Many graduates, reflecting back on their experience decades later, tell stories about the departmental secretary who guided them through times of trouble.

You need to find the campus that suits you, and you alone — not your friends, not your parents, and certainly not your high school teachers or advisors. Academic matters are, in the end, more important than the football stadium. Finding the right degree is

SAMPLE ACCEPTANCE RATES	
American Universities	
Institution	**Percentage of applicants accepted**
Stanford University	5.7
Harvard University	5.8
University of Chicago	8.8
College of the Ozarks	12.2
Rust College	13.9
University of Texas–El Paso	99.8
Bismarck State College	100
City University of Seattle	100
Daytona State College	100
Utah Valley University	100
International Universities	
Institution	**Percentage of applicants accepted**
Indian Institutes of Technology	2
The University of Hong Kong	9
The University of Tokyo	20
Oxford University	21
Cambridge University	22
Queen's University (Canada)	40

much more crucial than having a climbing wall in the gymnasium, a fancy buffeteria, or lap swimming in the college pool. But the people do matter a great deal. Look at the campus carefully — and find the college that fits best with your personality, aspirations, and academic needs.

DON'T BE TOO IMPRESSED THAT YOU GOT IN

Your mother's tears of joy when you open the letter of acceptance from (fill in the name of your college) are a tad over the top. It's not hard to get into a college in America, including some of the best in the country. The United States has hundreds of thousands of college spaces that it needs to fill every year and a limited number of truly qualified students. Save for a tiny number of schools that, as a matter of high principle, focus on academically challenged students, the colleges are seeking the very best students they can find. Most would, like Harvard, accept only students of supreme accomplishment, if only they could. Every institution would love to fill up with straight-A students who carry 95 percent averages, high-level athletic and musical ability, and tons of community service, but the reality is that they need to pay the bills. So, each year, each college reviews its cutoff point (the lowest grade average for entry), typically on a faculty-by-faculty basis. If there are a lot of applications, the cutoff rate goes up. If the application pool dries up — as happens quite regularly in areas like the Midwest, where there is a shortage of high school graduates — the institution will lower the cutoff point. There are many reasons why it's harder to get into the University of North Carolina (27.6 percent acceptance) than Northern Arizona University (92 percent acceptance), but even the most accessible institutions go out of their way to make it sound like a big deal that you were accepted. In such cases, it is not!

Americans are funny about college admission, clearly wanting everyone to go but perpetuating the myth that it is hard to get into a good college. Even Reed College, one of the very best in the United States, accepts a full third of those who apply. But "elite," in the context of colleges, means simply that the students on average are smart, or able, or intelligent, whichever word you like. In the United States, "elite" also often means that the college is unusually expensive. The fact is that really smart students do better at college and have much higher success rates. The less smart

GETTING INTO A TOP SCHOOL

Colorado College is one of our favorites. Its block program (students take one course at a time) is ideal for the truly curious and hardworking students, and a nightmare for the disengaged and uninterested. It is tied for the position of twenty-seventh top liberal arts college in the United States — but remember what we said about the unreliability of rankings. Fully 87 percent of students graduate on time. The campus has no classes over fifty students. Compare that to the megaversities in the big cities. Two thirds of the students are in the top 10 percent of their high school classes (which means that one third are not). The campus accepted 22 percent of applicants in 2013, which qualifies the school as the nineteenth most selective in its category. So, realistically, if you have a decent high school average, are in the top 15 percent of the students in your graduating class, and are inspired by the block program model, then Colorado College is well within your grasp. And this is one of the hardest institutions in the United States to get into.

ones have a high dropout rate. The easier it is to get in — the lower the standards, to put it bluntly — the smaller the percentage of students who graduate and, often, the less engaging the classes will be.

So, let's play devil's advocate for a second. The obsession with getting into the top schools is so pervasive that hundreds of thousands of young Americans spend a good part of their high school years positioning themselves for a run at an elite institution. While such a motivation is fine, it can be obsessive, particularly if a Tiger mom is pushing from behind. A talented student, say with an 84 percent high school average and a 1200+ SAT, can get into all but the top one hundred or so elite colleges — and even some of those are possibilities if the resumé is full (and true). But if students used their high school years to develop other skills — in community organizing, in athletics, in music or theater — they would be much better set up for life than if they devoted themselves wholeheartedly to the pursuit of a couple of extra grade points on their average. Indeed, we have seen many such students, pushed to the limit through high school, who crash and burn in college because they extended themselves fully in eleventh and twelfth grade and had nothing left in the tank for college. Personally, we much prefer the Reed College approach (they search hard for the "smart B," the well-rounded student of comprehensive potential rather than focusing largely on grades). If students and parents look beyond the branding of the best-known schools and consider the lesser-known but otherwise exemplary colleges across the country, they could make much more effective use of their high school years than they do at present.

Getting into a top American college and a high-demand academic program is an impressive accomplishment. But acceptance by an institution that accepts almost everyone is like being able to get into a new movie at the local theater. Show up at the right time, pay the entrance fee, and you are in. Not a major achievement. So, celebrate if you got into the college of your choice, but realize that this is not always a major accomplishment. And in neither case, we hasten to add, is it a guarantee of academic or career success. Remember (and keep in mind that television is mostly pretend but sometimes only too real) that Axel from *The Middle* managed to get into college when his high school performance was, shall we say politely, less than exemplary and that Haley, from *Modern Family*, also got into college when, as her sister pointed out cruelly almost every day, she left something to be desired on the academic front.

PICK THE CAMPUS, NOT THE CITY

Two of the strongest influences on college choice are contradictory: the desire to stay home with family and friends and the desire to take the fast track out of town. This is hardly surprising. Seventeen- and eighteen-year-olds respond to the challenges of growing up and their changing relationship with their parents in different ways. It's not unusual to have one sibling eager to flee the family home and another clinging to his bedroom. (The same holds true for parents. Some want the teenagers out of the house and away from town, while others, determined to postpone the empty-nest syndrome, dread the idea of their children moving away.) We hope that you will think carefully about your motivations for going to college — and for picking a campus that is either a longish bus ride away (you don't want Mom up every weekend) or all the way across the country.

There are many colleges and universities in towns of under 20,000 people — often called simply "college towns." Auburn, in Georgia, while best known for its football team (Go Tigers!) is actually an impressive university of 25,000 students, with a football stadium that holds 87,000+ fans, attached to a small town of less than 7,000. Almost every college town promotes the football team and, less prominently, the college.

Grinnell College, a classic liberal arts institution with 1,600 students and a superb campus atmosphere, is in a picture-perfect college town of fewer than 9,500 people. For students from New York City or Los Angeles, the adaptation to a small and isolated college town can be as daunting as an Oklahoma farm kid heading off to Dallas or Miami.

Many students, particularly from smaller towns and rural areas, are attracted by the allure of the big city, coupled with the chance to get away from home. But size is not the only determinant. While large, sophisticated New York is a student favorite, Boston is also a major attraction (and has the highest concentration of colleges and universities in the world), much more so than larger cities such as Chicago or Los Angeles. Duluth, Minnesota; Bradford, a branch campus of the University of Pennsylvania; Green Bay, Wisconsin; and other blue-collar towns are not drawing cards for their universities. While we understand the appeal of both small towns and big cities, we urge you to emphasize the campus rather than the surrounding community. Pick University of California Berkeley for its campus, not Oakland or San Francisco for their urban attractions. Don't be deterred by the size of Middlebury, Vermont (which is a lovely town anyway), but rather focus on the appeal of Middlebury College, one of the country's most impressive institutions. For the right student, the University of Texas at El Paso is an ideal fit, while for others Texas A&M is the perfect place. You study on the campus, not in the town or city. Don't make the location a major criterion for your college choice.

THINK SMALL

Except for the top-flight liberal arts and science institutions, the international reputation of a college is set by its faculty members and graduate programs. As an entering student, you need not be overly impressed by sky-high research rankings and the sterling reputations of leading faculty members. In fact, star academics only rarely teach undergraduate courses, so don't be too excited about being on the same campus as a Nobel Prize winner. Focus instead on the quality of the undergraduate experience. In one of the best books written on American colleges, *Colleges That Change Lives*, author Loren Pope argued that the best educational opportunities in the United States were to be found in small, specialized colleges, not in the big-name universities.

The biggest universities — particularly the large state institutions like the University of Florida, Florida State, University of Washington, or the University of California, Los Angeles typically cram first-year students into large lecture classes, often taught by graduate students and part-time instructors. You won't have much contact with your prof in one of these places; you'll just be a number. You don't want that, do you? While great things can happen on large campuses, even for first-year students, many will find the experience lonely and alienating.

We want all students to think very carefully about small-campus alternatives. Open-access institutions, places that take all applicants, like City University of Seattle and University of Maryland at Adelphi, can offer excellent student support and are good starting points for those who are anxious about the transition to academic work or who have weak high school records. Smaller colleges such as Bates, Middlebury, and others we have already mentioned have perhaps the best campus life in the country and great student-oriented facilities. There are dozens — hundreds actually — of small colleges, typically located in small towns, that offer superb undergraduate opportunities. They get far too little attention from high school students and parents, who are usually fixated on a dozen or so big-name institutions. What small institutions lack in star appeal and magnificent buildings, they often make up for in accessibility, friendliness, and support for students. Students at small colleges usually speak warmly about the experience, making friends and developing a strong bond with the institution. Talk to an alumnus of Franklin College (a thousand students, south of Indianapolis) or Pacific University (a thousand undergraduate students, in Forest Grove, west of Portland) and see what they say about their schools.

Americans love lists of winners, and colleges lend themselves to list-making, so here is one on this topic. A number of magazines — *Forbes*, for instance — identify the best "small colleges" in the United States, largely because these lists sell magazines. *U.S. News & World Report* might have gone out of business years ago were it not for the completely misleading annual ratings issue that sells in the hundreds of thousands and that, in our opinion, sends thousands of young Americans off to the wrong institutions each year.

On the subject of lists, you may find this one interesting: "50 Colleges and Universities with the Happiest Freshmen," published by the website collegechoice.net.[6] The site also publishes other listings: national rankings of liberal arts colleges, research universities, Southern regional universities, and so on. There's no lack of material for you to consider.

LOOK FOR SPECIAL FIRST-YEAR PROGRAMS

A number of American colleges offer dynamic first- and multi-year programs for elite students. These programs provide the best of the college experience: small classes, high-quality students, top-notch instructors, and an integrated, multi-disciplinary approach to learning. Students thoroughly enjoy these programs, which would appeal to any high school graduate with strong academic skills, a high level of intellectual curiosity, a willingness to test personal limits, and an impressive work ethic. These are not for the faint of heart. The workloads can be ferocious — but the personal, intellectual, and professional outcomes are superb. If you yearn to work with the best, want to be driven to be the best, and believe you have what it takes to sit with the elite students at top universities, then look at these programs. Here are some examples:

- Yale offers a program called Directed Studies, described as follows:

  "Directed Studies, a selective program for freshmen, is an inter-disciplinary study of Western civilization. One hundred twenty-five students are accepted each year. All students enrolled in Directed Studies take three year-long courses — literature, philosophy, and historical and political thought — in which they read the central texts of the Western tradition. The fall term introduces students to the principal works of classical antiquity and to the Judeo-Christian tradition. The fall term ends with the Middle Ages. The spring term begins with the Renaissance and ends with the twentieth century." That sounds fascinating to us. What do you think?

- There are a great many programs of this sort, far too many to list here, but you might be interested in the first-year Learning Communities program offered by Wagner College in Staten Island, New York.[7] The program involves "small groups [that] are placed in carefully selected field sites. This experiential learning component includes service learning, field trips, participatory learning and/or community research. Students typically spend three hours per week at the designated site observing the organization, its practices and its dynamics."

- Or the outdoorsy among you might consider the Adventures in Leadership program offered by Elon University in Elon, North Carolina. This involves "camping, hiking, climbing, rappelling and white-water rafting. The program will aid in your development of leadership skills, understanding of community and your ability to work in teams. Past participants say the most valuable outcome is the lasting friendships they have built. Accompanied by returning students, faculty and staff, participants will begin the adventure with group initiatives at the Elon Challenge course and conclude in the Appalachian Mountains of scenic West Virginia."

- How would you like to spend your first year in the Greek city of Thessaloniki, studying "the philosophical roots of our conception of justice — ideas of public justice versus private justice and the relationship between justice and power — examining the writings and theories of classic Greek philosophers." Look at the calendar of American University in Washington, D.C.[8]

- There are also single elite courses aimed at exceptional students. One of these (selected here at random) is offered by Curry College, a small liberal arts college in Milton, Massachusetts. Here you can take the First-Year Honors Program (FYHP), which "brings together a community of motivated, intellectually curious students from different majors who challenge and support each other while working closely with a faculty mentor. FYHP is a two-semester program consisting of a three-credit colloquium and regular co-curricular meetings where students, peer mentors, and faculty share a meal while listening to a guest speaker, viewing a film, engaging in discussion related to class, or participating in other activities." Lunch with a famous professor — you won't get that everywhere.

These are just few examples of elite programs. There are a great many others at a variety of colleges, far too many to list. At the end of this chapter we've included some web sources for you to search, if you are interested in this approach to college.[9] If you are a well-above-average student, an elite program or college might be perfect for you. American colleges offer some really excellent undergraduate programs, though your guidance counselors often do not know much about individual ones, if for no other reason than the fact there are so many of them. Such programs are hard to get into, often requiring evidence of a lot of extracurricular activity as well as top grades — which is one reason we recommend volunteering and gaining work experience in later chapters of this book. These programs, however, can be life-altering. They tend to offer smaller classes, intelligent classmates, top instructors, a strong focus on lifelong learning, excellent career potential, and true intellectual excitement. Imagine being in a class where everyone is smart: an exhilarating environment, and challenging too. If you are a good student, highly motivated, and have a strong desire to get the most out of your undergraduate degree, give these elite programs careful attention. Here, as elsewhere, Google is your friend.

Students who get into these programs rave about the educational opportunities and are impressed with the career possibilities that follow. You will also note a pattern here. The best programs are exclusive, creating opportunities for highly skilled and hardworking students. Average and below-average students, in contrast, have few such opportunities and are effectively blocked from the most interesting opportunities on campus.

SEARCH OUT FIRST-YEAR TRANSITION PROGRAMS

Unless you are a top-ten (as in the number 10, not 10 percent) student at your high school, the elite first-year programs are probably not going to be a possibility for you. If you are in the bottom 50 percent, and you still end up at college despite our warnings, there are transition programs for you. Most students turn to these programs after a semester or two of academic disaster. We urgently advise you to seek them out as early as possible, especially the pre-college classes, which offer a week or so of introduction to campus life. Take the study skills seminar, the time-management sessions, the exam preparation course, and the lectures on money management.

The best universities integrate the transition/introductory programs into their regular offerings. Colorado College is exemplary in this regard. The college believes that all students should be introduced to the world of volunteering. During the first two weeks of the first semester, all first-year students have to participate in volunteer activities organized by upper-division students. The opportunities range from serving at the Colorado Springs soup kitchen to doing environmental reclamation projects in the desert. With the entire institution committed to the enterprise, the campus buzzes with engagement and enthusiasm. Even better, fully 75 percent of the Colorado College students continue to volunteer throughout their undergraduate degree, with many establishing a life pattern of volunteering.

There are special programs for students who are non-native speakers of English (most of whom need every bit of help they can get — and many native English speakers need these programs too) as well as for international students, students with disabilities, Native American students, and even rural/smalltown students. Find the programs on offer before you settle on a specific college, and take them. Ironically, many of the students who sign up for these programs are the keeners, the ones who are already on a decent path for academic success. Students at risk, many of whom are not really sure why they are at college in the first place, often stay away until ordered to use them on threat of expulsion.

The people behind these transition and support programs really know their stuff. They have seen students at risk for many years. They know where students get tripped up, and none of your experiences will be very new to them. Dropping from A grades to D grades? Seen it many times. Struggling with your sexuality? Welcome to adulthood. Having trouble completing assignments? Join the crowd. Can't follow the lectures, and your notes don't make sense? Nothing new here. Social life on campus overwhelming your classroom work? A common experience. The academics and support people behind the transition programs are career savers. They are helpful, devoted to student success, and eager to get you on the right track. The best thing you can do, if you are at risk in any way, is to meet these folks early on and follow their advice to the letter.

Once classes start, any student who is struggling should go immediately to the academic support offices. (Make sure you find them before classes start. Searching for help when you're in academic free-fall is simply too late). If you start failing midterms, get bad grades (C or lower) on your assignments, or are not performing to your expectations (getting 75 percent when you are used to getting 90 percent is both normal in first year and extremely unnerving), seek out help. Do not wait until you have fallen behind or, worse, failed a course or, worse still, failed a whole semester. Most students at risk wait far too long. Students know if they are in trouble by the end of the first month, but most are too shy, too embarrassed, or too upset to seek help until the academic hammer descends on them, usually at the end of the semester. That is much too late.

What's at stake is not just whether or not you will be able to stay in college. It's also a matter of doing well on campus, enjoying the experience, and developing the skills you need. Cruising through to a mediocre degree is no great accomplishment. A transcript littered with failures and withdrawals is not an impressive start to your adult life. If you get into trouble, you must be sure to visit the academic support centers as soon as you get on campus. Sign up for the transition programs and learning skills classes. Attend faithfully. Pay attention! If you really apply yourself — and it's sad to think how few students take this advice and seek help only when they have already encountered serious failure — you can make up for the limitations of your high school career. Wait too long and you could well be back stocking shelves in the local supermarket before Christmas of your first year.

PICK THE RIGHT DEGREE

All of the work that has gone into picking a college can be undone by the hasty selection of the wrong academic program. This is actually the hardest part of the college selection process to get right. You have ideas about what you might like to study. Your parents are, most likely, fixated on a professional program — they love engineering, accounting, nursing, and anything that promises to be pre-med or pre-law. You could call it the "my son the doctor" syndrome, though women are now the majority in North American medical schools. Or you could call it the "big income" syndrome.

If you look at a college calendar, the range of offerings will baffle you. Is there life after college for someone with a B.A. in German? What are the benefits of environmental studies? Is there more to a kinesiology degree than being a high school gym teacher? What is biotechnology? Which one of ten majors in business makes the most sense? Should you go into a direct-entry program — one you enter straight out of high school, like engineering — or a more generic bachelor of arts or bachelor of science program that delays the choice of major (your main field of study) for a year or two or that lays a foundation for graduate study or professional school?

Colleges offer a great deal of advising help for students struggling to decide what they want to study. Despite this, you are pretty much on your own with this one. Advisors, parents, and others can give you endless amounts of data about job opportunities, earning potential, and academic and professional requirements — find out what it really takes to become a clinical psychologist before you blithely head off down that fascinating but long and complex path — but they cannot really answer the three most important questions:

- What am I really good at?

- What do I like to study?

- How can I convert this into a career at the end of my degree?

No one can really get inside your head and figure out what you enjoy doing and, even less, what you want to do as a career. Remember that, in your first year, you probably know about only a few of the jobs that might be available for you after graduation. Making a firm decision at age seventeen or eighteen, when your view of your own potential is as uninformed as your understanding of the world of work, is absolutely *not* a good idea.

CONSIDER BIBLE COLLEGE

Bible colleges, a remarkably large part of the American postsecondary system (there are at least 1,200 of them), provide a wide range of options for faith-based education and learning. They range from fundamentalist institutions — Bob Jones University is one of the best known — to the rigorously Catholic Ave Maria University established by Tom Monahan, owner of Domino's Pizza; Quaker campuses like Friends University; America's first Muslim liberal arts institution, Zaytuna College, in California; and Brigham Young, the university founded by the Mormons. Most institutions affiliated with the mainstream Christian institutions (Episcopalian, Catholic, Methodist, etc.) maintain a church connection, but the religious aspect of campus life has receded. Harvard, for example, was founded with strong religious connections, as were Princeton, Yale, and William and Mary. A few of these — Notre Dame is as famous for its Catholicism as it is for its football team — have retained a religious orientation.

For obvious reasons, church-affiliated colleges are not for everyone. Most are based in a specific faith tradition (some being much more flexible than others in accepting people of other religious backgrounds) and expect their students to adhere to the conventions and rules of the denomination. Their programs are actually quite broad academically, but understandably have a deep connection to the study of specific religions and spiritual value systems. Some — most notably those like Bob Jones University that are affiliated with the Baptist tradition — have extensive moral and behavioral codes that students must sign before they can be admitted.

Look at Biola University, Houston Baptist University, Bryan College (in Dayton, Tennessee, familiar to those who have read about the Scopes Monkey Trial), or Grove City College, in Pennsylvania, which refuses to accept federal funding and teaches "Bible-based conservative economics." These are but a few of the religious colleges available to you. Some offer full degrees and, in most cases (check this before you register), some of the courses you take can transfer to other universities. The Bible colleges have some of the most supportive and engaged social environments in American postsecondary education. They offer a fine alternative to public institutions and are ideal for religiously active students who are not fixed on a specific academic goal; want to enrich their religious understanding;

are considering the ministry; or are looking for a comfortable, encouraging environment in which to ponder their future.

LOOK NORTH, WAY UP NORTH

America has a strange relationship with Canada: it includes one of the world's most important trading partnerships, a historical friendship, a largely undefended border, and an almost complete American indifference to the country to its north. Canada offers a remarkable educational alternative, one that only a tiny handful of Americans take seriously. McGill University in Montreal attracts a fair number of students from south of the border; it is called "Canada's Ivy" as a result. American athletes, particularly in basketball and football, who cannot get a place in a top U.S. school will consider the Canadian possibilities.

Here are the two surprises about the Canadian system. First — and parents, pay attention — Canadian universities are an inexpensive option. Canadians pay about six thousand dollars a year in discounted Canadian dollars for tuition at universities, which all charge more or less the same; international students will pay between fifteen and twenty thousand dollars, or less than half that of an elite American college. Ah, but you say, these are Canadian schools, in a country more famous for hockey brawls and Arctic storms than intellectual achievements. Wrong! Canada has a strong and highly effective university system, much more equal and egalitarian than the American system and far more accessible. The country's top universities — the University of Toronto, McGill University, the University of Montreal, the University of British Columbia, and the University of Alberta — are among the top one hundred universities in the world. The University of Toronto is ranked more highly than such stalwart American universities as the University of Michigan, Duke University, the University of California, Los Angeles, and the University of California, Berkeley and Northwestern University. What is better, it is much easier to get into a top Canadian university than a comparable American institution. The University of Toronto is a huge place, though, with 67,000 undergraduate and 16,000 graduate students at its campuses. Surprisingly, only 625 of them were from the United States as of the fall of 2013.

Why do so few American students come north to take advantage of a system that is as good or better than elite U.S. colleges, no more difficult to get into, and dramatically cheaper? One reason is that Canadian public high schools are generally better than their American counterparts. American students coming directly to first year in a Canadian university might well discover themselves a little out of their depth, something they are not used to experiencing. But only a handful of Americans even consider leaving the United States, a serious and self-imposed limitation on students' options. Overall, the United States is seriously misinformed about Canadian realities. How many Americans know that Canada routinely places more cities in the list of the world's most livable cities than does the United States, that the Greater Toronto Area is one of the top-ten biggest metropolitan economies in the world, that the country has one of the best tax regimes and highest levels of personal freedoms in the world, and that the presence of a universal medical care system does not means that Canada is a raving socialist hotbed? Add in some other characteristics: Montreal is one of the most culturally rich cities in North America — think San Francisco with a French accent. Toronto is among the most multiculturally diverse in the world — a super-polite New York City. Vancouver has the most beautiful urban environment anywhere — Denver with an ocean! Calgary and Edmonton are as commercially vibrant as Dallas and Houston. Even the one great liability — Canadian winters — is exaggerated in the minds of most Americans. The area south of the Great Lakes typically gets more snow than the region to the north (although Montreal admittedly has more snow than any large city in the world). Vancouver has a better climate that Seattle (less rain). Winnipeg and Saskatoon are really cold in the winter — but consider these places rather like Minnesota with better food. And as a bonus, one cliché is true: when you bump into Canadians, they really do say "sorry."

Do yourself a favor. Consider the American options carefully, as we outlined above. But sneak your gaze over the border and a give a little thought to the opportunities available at Canada's fine universities and colleges. Canadian degrees are recognized by employers and graduate schools worldwide. In a number of fields, an undergraduate degree from a top Canadian university is considered to be in the same league as a top-fifty American college. All this and a lot cheaper too. So, overcome the anti-Canadian bias that is rampant in the United States and check out your neighbor to the north.

Americans who attend Canadian campuses find them welcoming, academically challenging, and quite social democratic in political tone. They are hotbeds of multiculturalism, actively liberal in a way that would drive Rush Limbaugh crazy, and with a mild but persistent current of anti-Americanism that is, ironically, less aggressive than at many American colleges, which in some cases are actively critical of their own country.

CONSIDER MILITARY COLLEGE

For those interested in a military career, with a strong sense of American tradition or a prodigious work ethic and a desire to test personal limits, U.S. military academies are a good alternative. The Citadel has attracted a lot of attention in recent years for hazing and the mistreatment of cadets, but many graduates swear by the demanding, even punishing, mix of scholarship, physical effort, and military preparedness. The military academies, topped (at least in its own eyes) by West Point, have done much more than train many generations of American military leaders. Many graduates have had fine careers in business and government (G.W. Goethals, who built the Panama Canal, and Duke's famous coach, Mike Krzyzewski, were West Point graduates, while two Nobel Prize winners — Albert Michaelson, who measured the speed of light, and President Jimmy Carter — were graduates of Annapolis Naval Academy), and even in professional sports (with David Robinson of the NBA champion San Antonio Spurs being the iconic example). The military academies fell on hard times in the 1970s, due to the combination of widespread anger at the war in Vietnam, anti-militarism across the country, the academies' resistance to admitting women, and increased public scrutiny about the hormonally charged residential and service environments. They have revived in recent years, due to the improved stature of the American military and the realization by some students and their parents that discipline, hard work, loyalty, and patriotism are missing in broader American society.

We probably don't need to sell you on the military life, because most people who choose it already know about its advantages (seeing the world, serving your country, gaining a totally secure career) and its disadvantages (periodic separation from family; the possibility of dangerous service in battles with Afghanistan, Syria, and ISIS). It's not a soft option. You have to be physically fit, and ten-mile runs and a boot camp atmosphere are features of all of the academies. You won't get much sleep, particularly in your first year. Before deciding, it would be wise to talk to someone who's been through the process. And you'd be smart to do some serious working out before going.

Although there is a tuition charge, it's usually waived, and officer cadets are paid a monthly salary. The military academies have high admission standards, both academically and in terms of character, and are not easy to get into. Support from a political representative — the higher up the political chain the better — is essential for admission to West Point. Summer work is not only guaranteed but compulsory, and you have a guaranteed career in the military after graduation (you have to serve for a number of years, and then you can leave if you want to). You get a first-class education in arts, science, or engineering, and your future is secure. America's military officers are quite well paid too: majors (eventually almost all officers will rise at least to this rank) top out at around $85,000 a year. Perhaps you will get to be a full general, at the top of the heap. At that rank the salary is $19,762.70 a month, and everyone salutes him (or her) — but of course no one joins the military to get rich. Given the strength of connections between the military and industry — it was President Dwight Eisenhower who described the "military-industrial complex" — there are also lucrative post-military opportunities in private security or industry.

If you don't want to go to college but you still find a military career attractive, you can go right into the services after high school. Here too, the pay can be attractive: you start off at a low level, but if you have a good career you can do quite well. And, with the almost inevitable American military adventurism, it is a fascinating — but often dangerous — way to see the world. Warrant officers' salaries top out at over a hundred thousand dollars. As with the officers' training schools, there's a boot camp to go through, and you have to be fit. If the life appeals to you, you should give the military option serious consideration.

AND DON'T FORGET THESE WORDS OF ADVICE

If you choose to attend college — and you will know if it's the right choice for you only if you do the research and are completely honest with yourself and those who care about you — then you can expect to be in for a challenging, rewarding, and life-changing experience. To make the most of this experience, we offer you this final advice (which will be applicable to the vast majority of college students):

- **Study what you love.** If you have a true passion for something, whether it is engineering or fine arts, you should seriously consider entering the field. If your parents want you to do something else, prepare yourself for difficult and lengthy talks. Arm yourself with details about work opportunities in your chosen area of study. Your naive assumption that your parents will be thrilled with your choice of Antarctic Studies will be quickly dashed, but their reaction can be offset when you demonstrate long-term and realistic thinking about the academic and career opportunities.

- **Love what you study.** While it is valuable, at the point of entering college, to focus on long-term employability, this works only if you actually graduate with a degree in a high-employment field. Studying something like accounting, which has high academic and professional standards, is worth the effort only if you end up enjoying the work and pass the courses. There is a simple test to help you here. When you visit college campuses, stop by the bookstore. Check the textbooks assigned for the courses you would be taking in your favorite subjects. If the textbooks interest you and if you find the material fascinating, you are likely heading if the right direction. If flipping through the pages gives you a headache or makes your eyes spin, you may be on the verge of making a bad choice.

- **Keep your options open.** While a few of the professional programs require first-year entry — where you make the selection right out of high school — others delay the final choice for a year or two. This is particularly the case in the arts and sciences, but also in most non-accredited business programs. (Accredited programs develop their curricula with advice from professional organizations and they are much more fixed and formal than most undergraduate fields.) Take advantage of the flexibility in these programs. Select your courses so that you keep your options open — this means that arts students should give serious thought to taking math and science classes in first year — and plan on spending a fair bit of time in first and second year reviewing options around the campus, and not just in the faculty or college that you entered first.

- **Prepare to work outside your field.** In most areas of study, your career options will be defined and shaped by the things you do outside class, including volunteer activities, extracurricular engagements, part-time work, and summer/co-op jobs. A degree in history or chemistry can be made much more powerful through the careful cultivation of your resumé and the accumulation of meaningful experiences. Do not fixate on your academic program as being the foundation for your career options. Many students who graduate with degrees in English, chemistry, environmental studies, or sociology end up with jobs outside their field of study.

- **Don't be afraid to change your major.** Students have a tendency to double down on bad program choices. Faced with overwhelming evidence that they either dislike a field of study or lack the basic aptitude for it, they will nonetheless persist, failing courses, falling behind, and, in many instances, dropping out of college. Switching programs is part of college life, and can often result in the complete transformation of your college experience. Before you jump from one degree program to another, spend some time checking out the other fields. Sit in on a few lectures in the other classes, speak to a professor or an advisor, and do some research on the subject and the career possibilities. In the end, however, you have to take the classes, complete the assignments, and sit through the examinations. Find something you like and are good at.

- **If college is not for you, leave.** We do not advise you to make quick and spontaneous decisions in this regard. Failing an assignment or a couple of midterms is not the end of the world. The transition to college is tough. Speak to an advisor or a favorite professor and talk to your parents before you jump. You might just be in the wrong program (see above). But if you find yourself skipping classes (the most worrying sign of intellectual disengagement), hating your assignments, panicking over examinations (pretty normal, actually), and getting terrible grades, there is a pretty good chance that you made the wrong choice when you came to college. You can wait a few months, until the college gives you a Dean's Vacation — a "go home for a semester or two" card — or you can make the choice for yourself. If the fit is really bad, and it is for close to one third of all of the American students who enroll in college, cut your costly losses early; explore other educational, training, or work options; and get on with life. And, remember this: colleges are eager for you to stay, since they need your money. Still, thousands leave early. College is not for everyone and, contrary to what you have been told, there are wonderful career options and high-income jobs available for people without college degrees.

We repeat: College is not for everyone, and you are not a bad person if you don't go to college, or if you decide to drop out if it isn't for you. The fact is, most things are not for everyone. Of your two avuncular authors, one is bored by classical music, and the other is bored by baseball — and we are both worthy people and fine citizens! Recently, a friend sent us a note about his daughter. Ponder this story (details have been changed or omitted to protect the identity of the student). She did well in high school, is smart and literate, and was pointed toward college by her extremely supportive parents, both of whom are professionals with two college degrees each. They thought they had launched her on the right career path. Then, a surprise: he told us that his daughter was in the process of switching from university (she was in Arts) to a technical school. She was unhappy at university although she hadn't said much and was prepared to soldier on until her parents brought the matter up. She now intends to get into gaming development — she wants to have a career in the digital gaming industry so she's looking for something more applied and less theoretical. She didn't enjoy many of the rhetoric/professional writing courses. Now that this decision has been made, she is a different person. Better still, the transition worked, and she is well on the way to a promising career in digital media. Smart young woman. Smart parents. Good decision. It's all about the match!

POSTSCRIPT: A WORD ABOUT COLLEGE AND RACE

You probably know this already, but it needs to be said: the college admission process does not operate on a level playing field — any more than the modern economy does. For the last thirty years, America's colleges have been battlegrounds for equality of opportunity, not equality of outcome. It has been argued, and the courts have agreed, that college admissions must take into account historical injustices, financial inequalities, gender issues, racial and ethnic differences, and other historic and sociological factors. There were good reasons for the adoption of formal and informal admission quotas, including decades of discrimination against women, African Americans, Hispanics, Jews, the disabled, gays, and others. Colleges had, for generations, been the preserve of white Anglo-Saxon males and had deeply entrenched systems for keeping others out. Harvard once had a quota on the number of Jews it would admit. The system had to change.

College admissions have now become race, gender, and class sensitive. Rather than selecting wholly on the basis of academic achievement (a system that itself had been curtailed in earlier years in the case of Jews, and more recently when Asian American applicants dominated the entering classes), colleges opted for a more flexible process. Special arrangements were made to admit more women, particularly in male-dominated areas like mathematics, engineering, and computer science. Colleges reached out to African Americans in particular, anxious to respond to generations of racial discrimination, weak inner-city high schools, and general socioeconomic challenges. They reasoned that an African American student from the inner city who got within a few points of standard entrance requirements had actually demonstrated greater achievement and potential than an upper-middle-class child of privilege, already blessed with many advantages. They also argued, again with good reason, that bringing the nation's cultural and ethnic diversity onto the campuses of America better prepared young people for the realities of national life.

In this regard, it's encouraging to hear that in 2012, 69 percent of Hispanic high school graduates were enrolled in a public postsecondary education, a percentage that was for the first time higher than that of whites. Hispanic enrollment at colleges and universities has increased 249 percent since 1996, and continues to grow,[10] though the high school dropout rate is still three times that of whites.

Institutions across the country started to aim for more representative student populations. Middlebury College's first-year classes are almost exactly 50/50 male and female — not a predictable outcome based on grades alone — and this first-rate school makes a sustained effort to attract students representing the ethnic and racial diversity of the country. Public institutions, particularly those of lesser quality and struggling to find enough students, exercise few such controls over enrollment; they follow an "everyone on board" approach. The results have been uneven, with many more women, significant increases in African American enrollment, restrictions on the number of qualified Asian Americans in some elite institutions, additional opportunities for Native Americans, and far greater sensitivity to issues of physical and learning disabilities. A young adult with Tourette's syndrome would have been hard pressed to find a spot in a top university thirty years ago. These institutions are now ready to both accept and support a much broader range of students.

The change did not go unchallenged. People barred from admission to top institutions or programs (particularly medicine or law) were incensed to discover that other people of lesser academic achievement — but appropriate minority status — had been accepted. They challenged the colleges and universities to abandon the preferential quotas and admission systems. As with so many other issues of this type, it was the courts that decided the matter, mostly notably in the Bakke case[11] of 1978, a landmark decision that upheld the use of race as a factor in affirmative action. More recently, the Supreme Court has weakened some of the affirmative action measures, making it harder for colleges to maintain quotas. The institutions were not deterred, in part because some had contradictory instructions from state authorities to do more to attract students from minority groups, but more because they were intellectually and politically committed to the idea of having a representative campus community. Other admission measures — such as giving priority to the top students from each school, which would include minority-dominated and inner-city schools, placing greater admissions priority on non-academic criteria — allowed the institutions to select more minority students without having formal quotas. Private colleges enjoyed greater freedom from such regulations, and some had greater success enrolling minority students. But even the elite schools, including Harvard, attracted public criticism and were forced to alter their admissions requirements.

Not everyone benefits from these initiatives. Several studies have shown that Asian Americans suffer from race- and ethnicity-centered preferences. Despite the fact that Asian Americans score consistently higher on SATs and other tests, Harvard University has seen a decline in the percentage of Asian Americans admitted. It appears as though Harvard's inclusion of more extracurricular activities as criteria played against — as would be expected — Asian American students, who are known for their single-minded pursuit of high grades. Caltech (California Institute of Technology), which retained its emphasis on academic achievement, saw no comparable decline in Asian American enrollment. The issue remains contentious and volatile. As *Asian Fortune* magazine reported,

> Today's landscape is, albeit not a rainbow-land just yet, not a far cry from it, either. The US Education Department predicts that this fall (2014) will mark the first school year where students of minority descent will constitute the majority of overall enrollment in the public education system, and the trend would continue thereafter. Which is to say, racial politics will no longer be the trials and tribulations for a small sector of the society, but an increasingly pressing concern shared by all Americans alike.

So long as access to elite programs and elite institutions is seen as the best pathway to achievement and prosperity, racial and ethnic politics, for better or worse, will be a defining characteristic of the American college and university system.

In short, ethnicity and minority status matter. Many institutions have special scholarships, bursaries, and work experience programs for minority students, disabled students, and other targeted groups. Many institutions look very closely at family and personal circumstances and give substantial credit for life experiences, even the unhappy ones. This may well be something you can benefit from. It is always a good idea to self-identify, not necessarily because you are looking for special favors, but because there may be support systems, financial assistance, special courses, or advisors and other benefits associated with your status. Do not decide for yourself that these arrangements are unjust or inappropriate; there is a long history of why colleges and universities provide such services and programs. They are simply part of the social and political reality of the modern postsecondary system and should be seen as one of the many resources available to individual students.

4

THE COMMUNITY COLLEGE OPTION

GO TO COMMUNITY COLLEGE: THE ROAD TO EMPLOYMENT

Community college is often the right choice for young people graduating from high school. But while many students, particularly those who are technically inclined, attend community college as a first choice, the reality is that a great many — too many — Americans are obsessed with going to a degree-granting college or university. College is a great choice for the right student, but it should not be an automatic first option. Pay close attention to the junior colleges/community colleges across the United States, a vital but underestimated part of the American postsecondary system.

One of us has a son, a fine, intelligent fellow who earned a B.A. with a major in philosophy from a university in the East. This led to a series of not very satisfying jobs, none of which, of course, had anything to do with philosophy — except perhaps that his degree helped him be philosophical about them. After a few years he decided that he was going nowhere at this, so he enrolled in a community college and earned a two-year certificate in civil engineering. The math courses weren't easy, and quite a few of his classmates dropped out, but he worked hard and earned his qualification. He then got a job as a project manager with a large construction firm overseas that did paving and similar contracts with the government. Five years later he is the district manager, earning six figures. University made him learned, perhaps, but community college made him employable.

University and college graduates take note: attending a community college or technical school may be a highly attractive and relevant option for you. An increasing number of college graduates are choosing to attend community college or technical school *after* receiving their bachelor's or master's degree. Many of them enjoyed college or university, learned a great deal, and absorbed the terrific educational experience that university boosters like to talk about. But their degree did not lead them into the kind of career they wanted, so they went to a community college to learn a practical skill.

As you contemplate your future, we want you to give careful attention to community colleges. For many students, the community college or junior college is an important bridge between high school and college/university. The junior college offerings consist of university-level courses, typically available for transfer credit (that is, you can use these course toward your college or university degree). Junior colleges provide excellent options for several groups of students:

- those who cannot afford high college fees and can continue their education only in the less expensive local college;

- those who, for personal or other reasons, need to stay at home in order to continue their studies;

- those who did not do well academically in high school but think that they have the potential for continued growth. (They may not, of course; many students are overconfident; the experience of students seeking to overcome poor academic performance through the college system is often not good.);

- those who require personal attention and would benefit from the smaller classes and greater care that is often available in the smaller institution;

- those who (along with their parents) are worried about the social transition from high school to a large metropolitan university and who would benefit from the more personable atmosphere of the junior college; and

- those who really do not know what they want to do academically and professionally and are looking for a respite from a career-making decision while continuing to make some progress toward an eventual diploma or degree.

In other words, there are a large number of high school graduates who would do well to consider the community college/junior college option, rather than immediately heading off to a big campus or elite institution. As a long-time fan of *The Middle*, we watched with horror as Sue Heck, the chronically optimistic and cheerful underachiever, headed off with her father on the college tour. If ever there was a person suited for junior college and a few more years under her parents' care, it is poor Sue!

But community colleges are much more than this. If you are interested in a practical career, and are looking for a program of study that produces career-ready graduates, then community colleges have a great deal to offer.

COMMUNITY COLLEGE, TECHNICAL INSTITUTES, COLLEGE AND UNIVERSITY: KNOW THE DIFFERENCE

There's a wide variety of community colleges. The junior colleges focus on the first two years of college study, although they often offer career and technical programs as well. The standard American community college provides a variety of academic and technical options, from college transfer courses to adult basic upgrading, professional and career development courses, technical diplomas, and many short and special purpose offerings.

Community colleges and technical schools don't have the status or prestige of colleges and universities. You can see it in their facilities. Top private colleges and even public universities have magnificent old-style buildings and fancy new ones, often adorned with the names of donors, that say "big-name architect designed me." Their laboratories are among the best in the world, their libraries impressive, and their recreational facilities top-notch. For state governments, universities are showpieces of prosperity and a commitment to excellence.

Community colleges and technical schools are more practical places. Not for these institutions the soaring foyers, public art, and spiffy architecture that characterize many university campuses. This is beginning to change: there are impressive new college and technical institute buildings, of which Santa Barbara City College, a campus that is as attractive and enticing as its wonderful host community, is a very good illustration. But the campuses of the Lake Area Technical Institute in Watertown, South Dakota, or the North Iowa Area Community College (even the names are unimaginative — we tried chanting "Go, North Iowa Area Community College," and it just didn't work) are more typical. The facilities at these schools are functional and very serviceable. In effect, they reflect the practical ethos of the institution and the "let's get to work" ambiance that dominates the place.

We urge you to look past the buildings, ignore the traditional North American attitudes about junior/community colleges and technical institutes, and see what training and skills opportunities they provide. For many Americans, turning away from the traditional college is a real challenge. We urge you to consider doing this. Your future might well depend on your review of these alternatives.

So, to start, let's define the difference between the institutions. The American Association of Community Colleges (AACC) lists more than 1,200 two-year institutions (with more than 13 million registered students), which define themselves as community colleges, institutes, and technical institutes. AACC is currently engaged in a comprehensive rethink of their role in light of shifting demographics and economic realities. Their key report, which highlights the degree to which they see the community colleges as being crucial to national success, has the ambitious title *Reclaiming the American Dream: Community Colleges and the Nation's Future*.[1] The association understands its central — but underappreciated — role:

> Community colleges are a vital part of the postsecondary education delivery system. They serve almost half of the undergraduate students in the United States, providing open access to postsecondary education, preparing students for transfer to four-year institutions, providing workforce development and skills training, and offering noncredit programs ranging from English as a second language to skills retraining to community enrichment programs or cultural activities.

Globalization is driving changes in the American economy, and the need for an educated workforce has never been greater. The majority of new jobs that will be created in the next few years will require some postsecondary education. In addition, the demographics of the workforce are changing. As a result, employers increasingly rely on the very students who currently are least likely to complete their education.

Without community colleges, millions of students and adult learners would not be able to get the education they need to be prepared for further education or the workplace. Community colleges often are the access point for education in a town and a real catalyst for economic development.

You will notice in this statement the mix of economic practicality and social mission. Community colleges do not obsess about the cult of excellence (as important as this can be) but rather celebrate access. Open access means that everyone above a particular age gets in, regardless of age or academic qualifications. Classes often include a mix of eighteen-year-old recent high school grads, forty-year-olds making mid-career transitions, thirty-year-old mothers returning to school after their kids have gone off to school, and ex-military making the shift to the regular workforce. There will be brilliant students who should have gone straight to a top college, educationally challenged individuals who will not last long, people who have great ability but are having difficulty readjusting to the classroom, and time-servers who are in community college simply for lack of alternatives. The sitcom *Community* captured the academic diversity of the community college crowd, but not so much the age and occupational range of the standard class.

Colleges and technical universities and technical institutes are often lumped together, but there is a difference. Colleges are non-degree-granting institutions that focus on shorter, less-technological programs, while technical universities and technical institutes offer diplomas and full degrees, emphasizing programs of study — in medical fields, animation, digital technologies, and the natural resource sector, among others — that require more intensive study. But while technical universities and technical institutes award degrees, they don't offer the basic research and broad education that you will find in a university. We deal with community colleges in the remainder of this chapter, and we discuss technical universities and technical institutes in Chapter 6.

It should be noted that a number of technical universities and technical institutes started out as community colleges, and expanded and upgraded what they had to offer. They continue to provide community college–type programs along with the more advanced technical institute programs. So don't be surprised if you find the kinds of programs described in this chapter at a technical institute as well as at a community college.

UNDERSTAND WHAT COMMUNITY COLLEGES HAVE TO OFFER

The community colleges offer a large range of programs, from adult basic education to university transfer courses, but they generally don't offer degrees (some offer "applied degrees"). Students can select from the trades (brick and stone mason, electrical technician, heavy equipment operator), paraprofessional programs (legal assistant, office manager, bookkeeper), and social service and health care studies (early childhood care worker, social work assistant, practical nurse), among others. Some colleges offer highly specialized career programs, such as the automotive collision technology program offered at the North Central Kansas Technical College, the theatre arts program at Snow College in Utah, or computer-aided design drafting at Southeast Community College in Lincoln, Nebraska (a school internationally renowned for excellence in producing precision production graduates).

The colleges, many of which operate a network of small campuses, emphasize accessibility and low cost, allowing people to study close to home, restart their education, and adjust their careers. Some colleges cover large areas or large populations: the Los Angeles Community College District (LACCD) system is the largest in the United States, including nine separate campuses:

- Los Angeles City College

- East Los Angeles College

- Los Angeles Harbor College

- Los Angeles Mission College

- Pierce College

- Los Angeles Southwest College

- Los Angeles Trade-Technical College

- Los Angeles Valley College

- West Los Angeles College

This massive system has over 135,000 students, over half of whom are Latino and another 15 percent African American. On the diversity score, LACCD has more Latino and African American students than all the campuses of the University of California system combined. Close to a quarter of its students do not have English as their first language. Forty percent of them are over twenty-five years of age. LACCD, like all American community colleges, is a unique combination of first-chance, second-chance, and last-chance institutions, particularly for students from underserved, minority, and economically distressed populations.

Michigan has twenty-eight community colleges — more if you include "tribal colleges" that operate in the state, and some more specialized institutions. The Michigan community colleges include

- Alpena Community College

- Bay College (Escanaba)

- Mott Community College (Flint)

- Delta College (University Center)

- Glen Oaks Community College (Centreville)

- Gogebic Community College (Ironwood)

- Grand Rapids Community College

- Henry Ford College (Dearborn)

- Jackson College

- Kalamazoo College

- Kellogg Community College (Battle Creek)

- Kirtland Community College (Roscommon)

- Lake Michigan College (Benton Harbor)

- Lansing Community College

- Macomb Community College (Warren)

- Mid-Michigan Community College (Harrison)

- Monroe County Community College

- Montcalm Community College (Sidney)

- Muskegon Community College

- North Central Michigan College (Petoskey)

- Northwestern Michigan College (Traverse City)

- Oakland Community College (Bloomfield Hills)

- St. Clair County Community College (Port Huron)

- Schoolcraft College (Livonia)

- Southwestern Michigan College (Dowagiac)

- Washtenaw Community College (Ann Arbor)

- West Shore Community College (Scottville)

- Ferris State University (Big Rapids)

- Bay Mills Community College (Brimley)

- Northern Michigan University (Marquette)

- Wayne County Community College (five campuses)

- Lake Superior State University (Sault Ste. Marie)

The commitment of Michigan's government to provide ready access, close to home, for as many citizens as possible, is clearly evident in the very wide geographic distribution of the campus network. The challenge in Michigan is different than in Los Angeles, because the collapse of Detroit, the challenges facing the automobile sector, and the general deindustrialization of the American industrial heartland has brought the connection between education and training and the workforce to the fore. Massive retraining programs are underway as Michigan tries to rebound from a huge economic meltdown. For individuals, the community college system is the front line of personal reinvention and preparation for the economic revitalization that they hope is coming to Michigan. For the State of Michigan, the community colleges play a central role in determining the future of the state economy and the reinvention of the Michigan economy in an age of rapid technological change.

The Michigan community college system faces, therefore, the challenge of offering traditional college programs plus new economy opportunities for companies responding to global and technological opportunities. Consider, for example, the program offerings, which include a large list of academic transfer offerings, at Henry Ford Community College, an institution serving Dearborn, a community hard hit by the decline in the auto sector. The program offerings are comprehensive and diverse, but not as cutting-edge as those provided at the technical colleges and technical universities. The strength of many urban community colleges lies in their comprehensiveness; one of their challenges rests with maintaining their broad variety of programs with funding that is always limited, and the difficulty of responding to the realities of the economy. The college offers a remarkable variety of programs (not all at every place) that range from Advanced Machine Tool Technology to World Languages, from Welding Technology to Baking and Pastry.[2] The college truly has a program for everyone.

5

TECHNICAL UNIVERSITIES
AND TECHNICAL INSTITUTES

UNDERSTAND THE TECHNICAL UNIVERSITIES' AND TECHNICAL INSTITUTES' UNIQUE MISSION

Of all the postsecondary options in the country, the most effective in preparing graduates for employment are the technical institutes and technical universities, perhaps the most underappreciated institutions in North America. Technical universities and technical institutes are also described as technical schools, advanced colleges, or, globally, polytechnics, a name that has not taken hold in the United States. Most Americans lump community colleges and technical institutes together, a perspective that ignores the unique mission and special status of the technical institutes. They are large, growing, well-connected to industry and business, obsessed with the career outcomes of their graduates, and of impressively high quality.

Let's start with the institutions that you probably know the best: technical universities. The United States has a series of technical universities, proudly declaring their commitment to practical and applied research and teaching. These most famous ones — Caltech (California Institute of Technology) and MIT (Massachusetts Institute of Technology) are among the most highly regarded and successful postsecondary and research centers of any type in the world — offer undergraduate and graduate degree programs and maintain first-rate research and training facilities. The Colorado School of Mines is arguably the best mining-focused research school in the world, with some fast-rising Chinese institutions nipping at their heels. Companies and governments love them, providing ample cash and funding superb facilities. So, as you search for possibilities, make sure you check out the places mentioned above as well as others, such as the Florida Institute of Technology, Michigan Technological University, the Polytechnic Institute of New York University, Texas Tech University, and Worcester Polytechnic Institute, among others.

The Rensselaer Polytechnic Institute is one of our favorite places, offering a unique blend of programs and courses. It is a private university in upstate New York, with some seven thousand students. It also illustrates the diversity of the American postsecondary system, the capacity of an almost two-hundred-year-old institution to keep up with the times, and the existence of universities that will define the next century. If you are looking for a school that is devoted to preparing graduates for the jobs of the future, not the positions of the past, then Rensselaer is worth a serious look. The institute offers programs in architecture, business, engineering, humanities, arts and social sciences, IT and web science, and science. In addition to practical and standard degree programs, their interdisciplinary offerings, shown here, are an enticing blend of the very best in twenty-first-century education and training:

- Applied Science

- Biochemistry and Biophysics

- Bioinformatics and Molecular Biology

- Design, Innovation, and Society

- Ecological Economics, Values, and Policy

- Electronic Media, Arts, and Communication

- Environmental Science

- Games and Simulation Arts and Sciences

- Information Technology and Web Science

- Interdisciplinary Science

- Minds and Machines

- Product Design and Innovation

- Sustainability Studies

- Systems Engineering and Technology Management

Georgia Tech, to use an example of an institution with a superb record for promoting entrepreneurship and engagement with the business community, offers a similarly broad range of programs and career opportunities. It is one of the top-rated public institutions in the country — including all colleges and universities — and has an excellent engineering program. The list of undergraduate programs includes some basic science and social science programs, but overall it is like a handy guide to the most career-relevant and high-demand employment fields of the coming decades. Check out these offerings:

- Bachelor of Science in Architecture

- Bachelor of Science in Industrial Design

- Bachelor of Science in Computational Media

- Bachelor of Science in Computer Science

- Bachelor of Science in Aerospace Engineering

- Bachelor of Science in Biomedical Engineering

- Bachelor of Science in Chemical and Biomolecular Engineering

- Bachelor of Science in Civil Engineering

- Bachelor of Science in Computer Engineering

- Bachelor of Science in Electrical Engineering

- Bachelor of Science in Environmental Engineering

- Bachelor of Science in Industrial Engineering

- Bachelor of Science in Material Science and Engineering

- Bachelor of Science in Mechanical Engineering

- Bachelor of Science in Nuclear and Radiological Engineering

- Bachelor of Science in Applied Mathematics

- Bachelor of Science in Applied Physics

- Bachelor of Science in Biochemistry

- Bachelor of Science in Biology

- Bachelor of Science in Chemistry

- Bachelor of Science in Earth and Atmospheric Sciences

- Bachelor of Science in Physics

- Bachelor of Science in Psychology

- Bachelor of Science in Business Administration

- Bachelor of Science in Applied Languages and Intercultural Studies

- Bachelor of Science in Computational Media

- Bachelor of Science in Economics

- Bachelor of Science in Economics and International Affairs

- Bachelor of Science in Global Economics and Modern Languages

- Bachelor of Science in History, Technology, and Society

- Bachelor of Science in International Affairs

- Bachelor of Science in International Affairs and Modern Language

- Bachelor of Science in Literature, Media, and Communication

- Bachelor of Science in Public Policy

The students who attend these technical universities are usually not looking for a good time or a general education. They come to the schools knowing precisely what they want out of an education and their degree, and bring a practical, work-focused perspective to their studies. There is a different kind of energy at these institutions, as they are not really about general education, personal growth, social engagement, fun, and recreation. The institutional passion is preparing young people for career opportunities, commercial innovation, technological discovery, and practicalities. It is easy to get excited meeting with the students and faculty of these institutions — they are hands-on kinds of people, eager to get practical and to make their own way in the world.

In no way are these technical universities inferior to regular colleges and universities. The best ones have sky-high admission standards; getting into Caltech, MIT, or Georgia Tech is equal to getting into the best institutions in the world. Their faculty members are among the best on the planet. They attract hundreds of millions of dollars in donations. Companies fund and support their research institutes and, most importantly for you, they line up to hire their graduates. The incubators based at these schools produce hundreds of start-up companies each year, contributing to America's still impressive reputation as one of the world's most innovative and entrepreneurial nations. We are great fans of technical universities and urge you to give them serious and detailed attention.

Sadly, too few American students devote enough effort to the study of math and science in high school to be eligible for attendance at these first-rate, career-focused institutions. As a result, they rely heavily on international students and the children of new Americans who, to the great credit of the facilities and the young adults, have managed to avoid being sucked into the anti-math vortex that pervades the modern American high school system.

While the technical universities have the highest profile in this category, there are many other technical institutions — two-year technology-focused colleges — available across the country. Technical institutes are career-focused, equipped to provide practical training developed in cooperation with employers, and strongly influenced by advanced applied research. Because of their high quality, they usually attract many more applications for popular programs than they can fill. As a result, the applied teaching and research profile of the technical institutes has begun to get increasing attention from the public sector and more money from governments. Like the colleges, these technical schools are often highly attractive options for people who already hold degrees. If you are one of these people, you should look very closely at the technical institutes. Technical institutes are career-oriented, high-technology and professionally focused, and deeply engaged with national and international businesses. They are not designed to be easy to get into — they are as committed to excellence as the top universities, and do not have the open-access policy of the community colleges. They offer the most practical education and training system available in the country.

DON'T GO TO A TECHNICAL UNIVERSITY OR INSTITUTE EXPECTING AN EASY RIDE

You know that we admire community colleges, colleges, and universities, and these institutions will continue to offer high school graduates fine options. But if you're looking for a postsecondary education that is designed to link you directly with the workforce, then the technical universities and institutes are the strongest choice for the twenty-first century. But you must have some focus, for these are not places for people who don't know what they want to do. They look for highly motivated, energetic students with the background and skills needed to succeed in what are often very technical or scientific fields. These places are not like high schools, where the priority appears to be making you feel good about yourself, or university, where the less hands-on standards of the lifetime academic are applied. Technical universities and institutes get students ready for business, both by providing the skills training and by introducing them to the pressures, conditions, expectations, and demands of the modern workplace.

If universities were on top of the employment realities of the 1970s and 1980s, the torch has now passed to the technical universities and technical institutes and, to a lesser degree, the community colleges. These institutions offer practical education for a practical age. They provide a range of certificate, diploma, and degree options, have strong ties with employers, and offer solid employment prospects for graduates. They are well-connected to contemporary technological realities and offer students excellent laboratories and training facilities. Their degree programs, in particular, are intensive and highly focused, with a strong emphasis on project and personal work. Some of the technical institutes now offer a range of four-year degree programs — some college people don't like this much — and many of these programs are gaining a real foothold in the marketplace, particularly in terms of prestige and status.

Studying at a technical university or technical institute is not an easy ride. Precisely because they are so well-connected to the workforce and employers, these institutions know that their graduates are expected to make a rapid transition from study to paid employment. The teachers and programs are demanding and very results-oriented. In many of the programs, the approach to learning copies a lot from the paid workforce, particularly in the attention given to deadlines, specifications, and client service. In short, you can't goof off there and hope to succeed. Technical universities and institutes are not for the swarm.

MAKE SURE YOU HAVE FOCUS AND COMMITMENT

We asked you before to do a full and honest assessment of yourself. If you are unsure of your commitment to a specific technical or professional field, you would be better off taking a more general practical education in a college or a more open-ended academic course of study at a university (or, even better, taking time away from advanced studies until you are ready to make a real decision). Colleges and universities are better suited for people uncertain of their career path and interested in exploring options. Technical universities and technical institutes demand, and get, more focus and more commitment. Give them careful attention if you are practical, want a well-paid job after you are finished your studies, are comfortable with technical work, and possess a strong work ethic.

We have told you, repeatedly, that the job market is tough and getting tougher. But there are actually many jobs out there — well-paid, dependable, and practical jobs. Many of the most lucrative positions are technology-based, requiring a combination of intelligence, creativity, and practical ability. Employers are constantly complaining about their inability to find the right workers for the most urgently needed positions. While they carry no guarantee of employment — no one knows what the next decade will bring — the technical institutes are the most promising route to those jobs.

Here is another fact — and potentially an unhappy one. Many of the top programs at the technical universities and institutes are hard to get into. Some, like those for dental technicians, can have years-long waiting lists. Unlike colleges and universities, which can always squeeze more students into a five-hundred-student classroom, most polytechnic programs can handle only a fixed number of students, with the limits set by the facilities, the work placements, and the need for instructors to provide individualized instruction. They work to align their programming with the marketplace and thus take care not to flood the workforce with too many graduates.

Getting admitted to Rensselaer Polytechnic's superb electronic media program — to select only one example of dozens — is harder than getting into most of the colleges and universities in the country. Many of the medical technology, digital design, and career-ready programs have hundreds of students trying to get in. In fact, many university graduates are among those competing for entry-level spots in the polytechnic programs. While the technical universities and technical institutes remain among the best-kept educational secrets in the country, a growing number of young people have figured them out.

LOOK FOR THE BEST POSSIBLE MATCH

Technical universities and technical institutes work for another reason. They are closely attuned to the changes in the North American economy, right down to the level of individual programs. While universities have no compunction about producing thousands of surplus psychology graduates ("Let the students decide") and while community colleges graduate a steady stream of heavy-equipment operators, hairdressers, and other skilled workers ("Career preparation is our specialty"), the technical institutions work more closely with the business community and government to determine actual workplace demand. While they do not always get it right — some technical graduates do have trouble finding work in their chosen field — they try a lot harder than community colleges and universities do.

The technical universities and technical institutes talk routinely with business — benefiting by getting access to the best pieces of technology so that graduates are ready to make a smooth jump from their studies into the world of work — and adjust their program intakes on the basis of declared industry need. Trying to maintain a match between the production of graduates and workforce requirements is a hallmark of technical school planning. We hope that they resist the pressure from students and governments to focus — as community colleges and universities do — on meeting student demand rather than workforce needs. They will be sorry if they go down that path, the one that has severely undercut the utility of general arts and sciences programs.

It is time for parents, in particular, to understand the enormous potential and opportunities that rest in the technical universities and technical institutes. The question is not "Which institutions are the best?" but rather "Which institution and what program is best for this particular student?" At this point, Americans focus on the first question and largely ignore the second. Parents, guidance counselors, and institutional recruiters need to help you, as a high school graduate, to shift your focus and search for the best possible match, rather than following the swarm to the supposedly most prestigious institution. Your career depends on it.

EXPECT A HANDS-ON EXPERIENCE

The technical universities and technical institutes specialize in moving students into work-type settings quickly. While there is classroom work in even the most technical programs, students generally spend a lot of time in laboratories, machine rooms, or other simulated workplace environments. Technical schools typically require students to do a lot of project and teamwork, to complete personal projects, and to connect classroom tasks with workplace experience.

Importantly, this applies to the technical schools' research activity as well. A growing number of faculty members at the technical universities and institutes manage research projects, most of them co-sponsored by business and industry. The basic, curiosity-based research that dominates universities is not much in evidence here. Because these schools (save for the top-end technical universities) do not always have graduate students, undergraduate students end up working on many of these projects. The opportunity to participate in major company- or industry-focused research projects is a huge advantage to a technical diploma or degree program. It is an oversimplification to say that technical school and community college students learn by doing while college and university students only read and talk about their subjects: many university programs, from digital arts to engineer and nursing, in fact have a lot of practical elements. However, in the technical world, practical, hands-on experience is fundamental to the programs and, therefore, to student preparation.

One of the implicit commitments the technical universities and technical institutes have with employers is that the graduates of their practical and applied programs will be career-ready when they leave the institutions. Many college and university leaders argue the opposite: that businesses have to take a much more active role in preparing university graduates for jobs. In the current environment, where companies feel under enormous pressure to hire people who can move quickly and effortlessly into the workforce, the defensive college and university arguments simply reinforce the general notion that universities are not connected to workplace realities. We have never heard the president of a technical university or technical institute make such a claim. Indeed, the opposite is true, with the technical schools routinely asking the business community how the schools can best adapt their curriculum and practical training to better prepare the students for jobs.

PREPARE CAREFULLY BEFORE APPROACHING A TECHNICAL UNIVERSITY OR INSTITUTE

So, how do you approach a technical school? There is no simple answer to this question. The country's preoccupation with colleges and universities is so strong that parents, students, and counselors are used to standard structures (faculties and colleges) and programs (arts, science, business, medicine). MIT, Caltech, and Georgia Tech, along with a few other institutions will be familiar: admission to these schools is on par with the very best colleges in the country. But most technical schools do not have the same cachet as these, and it requires more intensive investigation and planning to benefit from attending one. When you check out colleges, you will typically find that the first year is devoted to general studies — in the arts, science, or business — with the final decision about the primary field of study postponed until second or even third year. This is a strength of colleges, for it works on the assumption that students need a fair bit of time on campus to understand both program and career options, to experiment with familiar and brand-new areas of study, and to discover their passion. Students who come to university to study in the arts might take courses in such diverse areas as history, biology, German, economics, and psychology in the first semester alone and could easily end up shifting their planned major 180 degrees from where they started.

In contrast, while technical schools allow shifting and refocusing, they assume that students have prepared carefully for their advanced study and have a good idea of what they want to learn. But here is the trick: technical programs are different, the range of opportunities is much greater, and they are best suited for young adults with a real sense of purpose that focuses on a practical career. Like colleges, they are not for everyone. In fact, one of the things we worry about is that the greater career success enjoyed by technical university and technical institute graduates will lead the swarm to shift their focus from colleges to universities to technical schools, reproducing the overcrowding and overproduction of graduates that has become the hallmark of the university system. So, do yourself a favor. Don't rush off to a technical school simply because it is more attuned to the realities of the twenty-first-century economy. Check it out carefully — and, as we constantly urge you to do, test what you see against your abilities, your passions, and your interests in life.

LOOK TO POLYTECHS FOR A REGIONAL OR SPECIALIZED FOCUS

A number of polytechnical schools have a strong regional and/or industry focus, something that is not often true of the regular kind of college. An example is the Colorado School of Mines, in Golden, which focuses on engineering and applied sciences, particularly in connection with the earth's resources, and ranks well among the nation's postsecondary institutions. The Florida Institute of Technology, in Melbourne, has a campus at Jensen Beach specializing in oceanography, underwater technology, and marine biology. The New Mexico Institute of Technology, in Socorro, is one of the best small science and engineering schools in the country. If you are interested in any of these things, a bit of web searching will give you many possibilities to consider.

EXPECT PRACTICAL TRAINING, NOT BEAUTIFUL CAMPUSES

Because technical universities and institutes are different from universities — both in terms of their general applied focus and their emphasis on specialized programs — they should be approached very differently. College recruitment highlights campus life, residence opportunities, institutional status, and heritage. Contrast the magnificent buildings at the College of William and Mary, a three-hundred-year-old institution that virtually screams "smart people study here," with the bland practicalities of MIT, a monument to serviceability and function with barely a tip of the hat to aesthetics. The social side of the technical school experience is not the equivalent of that at a college. The campuses are practical, dominated by laboratories and workrooms more than leafy walkways, huge libraries, and big residence complexes. They do not highlight intercollegiate sports (though some of the bigger technical universities, like Texas Tech, play football with the best of them), even though they have many generous donors, and, except for the elite institutions, they generally lack the prestige usually associated with universities. What they do provide is great preparation for the workplace, practical facilities that are often among the best in the country, a sustained commitment to cutting-edge learning opportunities, and an overwhelmingly practical approach to education and training. Do you want to cheer on a college football team or train for a good, practical career? Your choice.

Technical universities and institutes, like community colleges, spend less time and effort trying to recruit students, and are thus better suited to students who search them out than to those who have been drawn in by an effective video pitch, recruiting speech, or promotional campaign. The reason is simple. Unlike colleges and public universities, which are largely undifferentiated, technical schools are highly specialized: they know what they are and what they offer and they make much less of an effort to attract students to their institution. Universities want you to pick them out of a crowded field. Technical universities and institutes know that they are unique and they count on students to seek them out.

They certainly know that employers direct students their way and, on a regional basis, each of the technical schools has a strong reputation for responding to the needs of the workforce. Consider it a key part of your self-evaluation process. If you are sufficiently motivated and organized to discover the technical school that has what you want, the school is likely to be keener about your application. If you need to be wooed, then you are probably not well-suited to the technical university or technical institute environment.

If you are practically inclined, and if preparing yourself for a specific career (often with high and steady income potential) is your top priority, you should do a detailed investigation of all relevant technical schools. For the technically oriented, look at the applied science and technology programs. Students with a business or social service orientation will find a full range of offerings that rely much less on a high school science and mathematics background.

VISIT A TECHNICAL UNIVERSITY OR INSTITUTE

Catalogue listings tell only a small part of the story. The technical schools require more detailed investigation if you are to find the right match. You have to go well beyond perusing a school's website and reading its promotional material. Make sure you attend an on-campus technical university or technical institute orientation night (going to the career fair is a poor second choice, as you will be speaking to recruiters and not to the professionals and specialists in the field). Look at the laboratories, drop in to the bookstore and look at the course texts in the programs you are considering, and see if you can sit in on a class. Remember that American institutions see you more and more as a customer than as a student, and they are much better than in the past about accommodating special requests.

If you have narrowed down your field of study, see if you can examine a work site or company specializing in a particular area. Technical careers are unique and highly specialized, in the main, and your enthusiasm for a program is likely to be closely tied to your understanding of the career possibilities associated with it. Technical schools are best suited to students with a clear focus and an understanding of what they want out of their education and career. Unlike universities, which appropriately emphasize breadth of knowledge and the opportunity to shift direction, technical universities and technical institutes are very career-obsessed. If you are too, then they could easily be the perfect match.

6

USING VOLUNTEERING
AS A LAUNCH PAD

BE PART OF THE ENGAGED MINORITY

What a contradictory lot you young people are these days! You millennials — Generation X, Y, Z, or whatever it is now — are a strong breed, but you are also the most studied and the least understood group of young adults in generations. Reporters, always keen to know what you're thinking, say that you have a strong interest in helping the poor, engaging with the world, and working for social justice. The truth is, however, that many young people are far more interested in social media, video games, and earning (and spending) money. This discrepancy is only natural — asked to tick off your interests, you of course will choose "saving the environment" over "hoisting some brews," even as you head off to the pub.

But you aren't all like this. For a minority of young people, engagement with community is a crucial part of their lives. They have already been actively working to better the world, through their faith communities, Boy or Girl Scouts, 4-H, U.S. Army Cadet Corps (or other branches of the armed forces), environmental groups, and other agencies. You may be one of the 3.2 million members of Dosomething.org, a web-based volunteer initiative designed to mobilize youth to address the most pressing challenges of their time. These young people — and the adults who inspire them — are the backbone of society, and critical to the pursuit of social justice in our time. It is to them, and to people who might like to be like them, that this chapter is addressed.

Volunteerism, though certainly praiseworthy on its own, is not often seen as a strong element in career-building. It is viewed as a separate activity that reflects the spiritual or social justice part of a person's makeup, rather than as an integral part of personal or professional development. We wouldn't want to downplay the humanitarian zeal and the concern for others that drives the volunteer impulse. Bless you for sharing your time and talents with those who really need them. At the same time, there's no denying that such activities also have a practical side, and here we will also emphasize how they can be extremely valuable to your career and your adult life.

VOLUNTEER AS A WAY TO GIVE SOMETHING BACK

Let's deal first with the cynical aspect to volunteerism as a means of puffing up your resumé. In the United States, where competition to get into the elite universities and colleges is intense, having impressive volunteer activities on your record can push your application closer to the top of the pile. Employers, too, love to see signs that there is a heart and soul behind the job experience and credentials. Even more crudely, many want to know how you used your out-of-school hours. What answer do you think looks better to a prospective employer? "I worked at the food bank!" "I have memorized the life history of the Kardashians" "I chilled with my bros!" or "I am in the top ten thousand worldwide in Call of Duty: Elite!"

Naturally, the free-enterprise system being what it is, a few enterprising individuals have seized the opportunity to make money from the altruism of others. There are actually companies that charge a fee to match students' interests with volunteer opportunities. They realize that their clients want to be seen helping the disadvantaged, but without getting their hands dirty or dealing with really poor or sick people. These firms match clients with highly visible "volunteer" opportunities — those that are good for Facebook pages and resumés but that actually accomplish very little. At their worst, these involve staying at a high-end hotel and making brief visits to a developing world orphanage or an AIDS hospice so that the client can be photographed "helping" the disadvantaged. Pretty slimy, to be sure, and so transparent that it is unlikely to fool people for long — though there seems to be money to be made in it. If you hire one of these outfits for the sole purpose of making yourself look good, shame on you too.

You need to always remember that by both historical and global standards, people in the United States are among the richest in the world. Remember that there are more than a billion people who exist on less than a dollar a day — less than the cost of a regular chocolate bar, or a third the cost of a Starbucks Caffè Mocha. It's hard to put a firm number on the relative wealth of Americans, but let's give it a go. Wealth is defined in many ways, most typically by individual and family income. By these standards, the United States has long ranked comfortably in the top ten countries in the world. But money in the pocket is only one measure of wealth. A wealthy person or wealthy society should be able to count on many non-monetary benefits. After all, what value is it to have stacks of money but live in constant fear of being robbed or killed, as is the case in many countries around the world? So, a proper measure of "wealth" should include other factors — such as life expectancy, access to health care (we will not enter the "ObamaCare" debate, but you need to know that the rest of the world is aghast at America's expensive and far from universal health care system), educational opportunities, the status of women and children in society, safety within the home and the community, freedom from war and domestic strife, fresh water, unpolluted air, freedom from hunger, and decent shelter and clothing. By these standards, the average American is probably in the top 2 percent of all of the people who have ever walked the face of the earth.

As a country, the United States is more violent than other industrialized countries, and imprisons people at an astonishing rate, often for minor drug convictions. We don't want to get into the gun culture debate, but suffice it to say that the United States has issues. And America is now the world's leading peacemaker and police officer, meaning that young Americans have a much greater chance than the Japanese, Swedes, or Thais of dying in a foreign war. Yet even with these qualifications and dangers, the United States is a comparatively wealthy, peaceful, safe, and open society, which is why so many people long to immigrate to the country.

If you have any kind of social conscience, you will have to agree that your wealth carries at least some national and global obligations. (If you don't, feel free to say "whatever" and skip ahead to the next chapter, but remember that you will be missing some real rewards). People have, argu-ably, an obligation to give back — through their effort or their money — to the less advantaged. Many Americans feel that the federal, state, and municipal governments handle these responsibilities at the local, regional, and national level — funded, of course, from tax revenue paid by the taxpayers — and that Washington discharges our global responsibil-ities through foreign aid contributions.

The uncomfortable fact is that, in terms of proportion of gross domestic product devoted to foreign aid, the United States is well down the list of donor countries, at 0.19 percent; the most generous countries, Sweden, Norway, and Denmark, each give more than 0.8 percent of their GDP. The American commitment to foreign aid has never reached the internationally recommended target of 0.7 percent of GDP, and his-torically much of the aid has been tied to sales of U.S. foodstuffs and machinery — which of course is good for the national economy. Even the Canadians, who are far from generous in international terms, devote 0.32 percent of their GDP to international aid. (Some of you will — with some justification — point to massive U.S. military expenditures, much of it used to protect foreign nationals or to challenge or hold back vicious regimes.)

It falls on individual donors and volunteers to take up the slack. Americans do respond generously, as they did following the 2004 tsunami in Southeast Asia, the devastating 2010 earthquake in Haiti, and the 2013 typhoon in the Philippines. Americans are equally generous to the cam-paigns run by the Red Cross, Oxfam International, Heifer International, World Vision, and hundreds of other charities. Local charities, including the United Way, Catholic Charities USA, Feeding America, and Salvation Army, raise hundreds of millions of dollars and provide services across thousands of communities. Americans volunteer at food banks, attend fund-raising auctions and concerts, sponsor children in the developing world, and worry about the misuse of donated funds by crooked foreign governments. Americans are reasonably generous people, although the largest share of tax-deductible donations goes to faith communities (over 30 percent of the total), which pass some of it along in the form of foreign or domestic aid.

VOLUNTEER AS A WAY TO DISCOVER YOURSELF

We see volunteerism as an opportunity for you to connect with people, communities, and countries much less advantaged than you may be. Volunteering carries a number of personal benefits. You will, through volunteering, develop a much greater understanding of and empathy for people who are poor, physically or mentally disabled, living with a personal or natural disaster, or otherwise struggling to make it through life. You may — particularly if you work directly with people in need (as opposed to through third-party organizations) — develop real compassion, acquired through thinking about the differences between your own life and the lives of other people who suffer through no direct fault of their own. Your appreciation for the complexities of the human condition will grow immensely if you make connections with people from other communities, countries, societies, and cultures.

By volunteering, you will test yourself in many difficult and complex ways. Dealing directly with hungry people is never easy, and it is much more challenging when you know that you will not face real privation in your life at home. The first exposure to real poverty is, for most people, a real eye-opener, upsetting their understanding of humanity and sparking a concern for social justice. Encountering widespread and deliberate environmental destruction, the brutal mistreatment of women, religious or cultural discrimination, massive slums, inadequate water supplies, and the like will have a profound impact on your world view. Some of you will be unaffected and simply see your wealth and comfort as something you have earned or deserve by natural right. A significant number, though, are changed forever, and set forth on a life marked by concern for others.

Volunteering will probably not transform you into a humanitarian like Mother Teresa (who worked for decades with the poor and ill in India) or a social activist like Suita Guota (Jobs With Justice), Ai-Jen Poo (Domestic Workers United), or George Goehl (National People's Action). Not that it would be a bad thing if you became saint-like, of course — it's just unlikely. At root, the fundamental benefit of volunteering for you is that it will make you confront yourself and draw attention to your assumptions about both your place in the world and the challenges facing the poor, the dispossessed, and the uncared for. As a bonus, it will set you apart from the swarm.

Volunteerism provides enormous opportunities for intense and rewarding local or global exploration. You can work on a Habitat for Humanity International project in your community, building homes for people who need basic shelter, or you can join a group working in Mozambique to build houses for women and children affected by HIV. Save the Children permits you to raise funds locally to support educational and health programs in the developing world. Youth-oriented charities, including Kaboom! (playgrounds), Share Our Strength (food for the poor), and Newborns in Need (clothing for infants) provide opportunities to help young people. Right to Play takes the joy of exercise, games, and competition around the world — and it needs hundreds of volunteers! There are thousands of charities doing great work at the local, national, and international levels.

We want you to consider spending a few months or even a year or more volunteering before you go on to postsecondary education or into the workforce. Young people often feel real pressure to get on with life, only to head off into a field of endeavor for which they are ill-suited. You are likely seventeen or eighteen years old. You are a young adult, probably with at least six decades of life ahead of you. Taking a year or two to help others is only a short detour from whatever path you choose. Volunteering can provide you with a life-changing perspective on the world, a way of placing your options and opportunities in a broader global context. People have been doing this for generations, heading off to help in Christian mission fields at home or overseas (the Church of Jesus Christ of Latter Day Saints has this down to a global art form), joining international aid organizations to provide crisis assistance in times of natural or human disaster.

The Peace Corps is probably the best-known example of the volunteer spirit among young Americans. Founded by executive order of President Kennedy in the spring of 1961, it was designed to promoted world peace and friendship through the overseas service of trained young people. Up to 2013, over 215,000 Americans had served in it, and it continues to attract about 10,000 applicants a year, some with specific skills, and others simply willing to go and help where needed, working in about 70 countries. This is an organization with a long and honorable history, and it may well be something you would like to participate in. Volunteers are usually college graduates, though relevant experience can be substituted for this, so for most readers of this book, it would be an experience for later. It would be a tremendous post-undergraduate opportunity for students planning to continue to graduate school. Information is available at www.peacecorps.gov.

Of course, you can always help out in your home community or region. There is never a shortage of opportunities at seniors' homes, elementary- and pre-schools, drop-in centers, agencies working with people living with mental and physical challenges, environmental organizations, and many, many others. You could easily put together a full slate of commitments without going more than a few miles from home, discovering opportunities to engage with local citizens and the community at large. To a degree that very few people appreciate, the country runs substantially on volunteer labor, and you can do much worse than join the huge volunteer army that keeps America moving.

MAKE SURE THE COMMITMENT YOU CHOOSE IS RIGHT FOR YOU

You have to be careful in selecting your volunteer opportunity. Some people find it hard to witness extreme poverty. Others find serious diseases upsetting. Many Americans, raised with the uncrowded spaces and large expanses of this massive country, have trouble dealing with the huge, overcrowded, and chaotic slums that surround major cities in the developing world.

You have to be honest about your comfort level with different cultures and communities. North American women, raised in open and generally welcoming conditions, can chafe at the restrictions governing their actions in fundamentalist regions and under oppressive regimes. There are many dangerous parts of the world — all of them desperately in need of volunteers and assistance — that would frighten even the bravest people. Be sensible about these things. Just imagine how your parents would react to hearing that you had decided to spend a year in Afghanistan, Somalia, or Yemen. You can volunteer without making a martyr of yourself or putting yourself at unnecessary risk.

VOLUNTEER OPPORTUNITIES FOR YOU TO CONSIDER

- Help out in a hospital, orphanage, or center for children with disabilities.
- Assist community-based political organizations.
- Support training initiatives for dispossessed workers.
- Work on agricultural projects, including local food security activities targeted at the urban poor.
- Support children and families suffering from HIV/AIDS.
- Teach English as a second language or assist in understaffed schools.
- Volunteer with public health programs.
- Help preserve and interpret historic sites.
- Get involved in business development and micro-business activities.
- Assist with youth sports and community cultural activities.
- Help with environmental reclamation and conservation initiatives.
- Participate in important local or international research projects.
- Perform with and assist community arts organizations.
- Help Habitat for Humanity complete building projects.
- Support journalists and social activists with public awareness activities.

Multiply the number of items on this list by the scores of countries urgently requiring assistance, many with hundreds of communities or rural areas. The world is not short of opportunities to help.

REMEMBER THAT VOLUNTEERING CAN HELP YOUR CAREER

It's not all self-sacrifice. There's a practical benefit to volunteering. The first priority should always be the opportunity to help others. From start to finish, benefits to yourself should be secondary. But it's a happy fact that properly selected volunteer activities can make a major contribution to your career possibilities. Admissions officers love to discover that a top student has a solid social conscience. Employers are more impressed with young people who have made a commitment to helping others than with those who spent their summers serving at McDonald's or Bubba Gump Shrimp Company, or their gap year working as a retail clerk in the downtown mall — or even backpacking around Asia, though that can be a positive experience too (see Chapter 8). At a simple level, therefore, volunteering looks good on future job applications.

The career-boosting benefits of volunteering go well beyond building your resumé, important as this can be. If you have selected your volunteer activities properly — working with the poor in Guatemala looks a great deal better than helping out at the high school graduation ceremonies for an elite, expensive private school — you will have told people evaluating your file a great deal about yourself. Your volunteer activities should have several of these characteristics: take place over the longer term (four months to a year), include work that is clearly humanitarian or related to environmental or social justice issues, take place in a different cultural setting, present personal challenges (physical, psychological, emotional, or cultural), and provide practical experience.

That last point is crucial. Eventually, when you get back to America, you will want a job, either right away or after some kind of postsecondary education or training. Picture an employer reviewing two resumés, both from young people with the same level of education: university, college, apprenticeship, or just high school. One stayed at home, had several part-time, low-skill jobs, and now wants a real job. The other spent a year volunteering in South America, developed Spanish language skills, and began as a teacher in an elementary school but ended up as the manager for the local food cooperative. Remember that, as an employer, you are looking for standard employability skills in your prospective workforce. Compare a volunteer and a non-volunteer in these categories: breadth of experience, organizational skills and experience, humanitarian qualities, confidence in speaking, evidence of work ethic, commitment to personal development, professionalism, international awareness, growth potential, openness, and creativity. Which one comes out on top?

This is not to say that local or national volunteer activity is without real merit. Indeed, a full-time local volunteer will likely stand out above the crowd of young people who have had stay-at-home, low-skill jobs. But from a career-building perspective, an international engagement grabs greater attention. Everyone from family members to admissions officers and future employers is impressed that you joined the Peace Corps, spent half a year in the favelas in Brazil, taught in an elementary school in Ghana, built flood-control systems in Sri Lanka, or supported a major conservation effort in Nicaragua. Supporting the local food bank, volunteering with a youth sports initiative, or visiting the elderly in a hospice are all valuable activities that reflect very well on you. They simply do not generate as much spontaneous interest as a long-term international engagement.

The most crucial element of volunteering is that it opens your eyes to your own strengths and weaknesses as well as to the opportunities and challenges of the modern world. Whether you volunteer in your home community, elsewhere in the United States, or in another country, you are going to expand your horizons, learn a great deal more about the world, and enhance your future employability.

7

TRAVEL: DISCOVER THE WORLD

LEARN FROM THE KIWIS AND AUSSIES

We are firm believers in the importance of seeing the world. Rather than rushing off to university, college, the workplace, or some other activity, many of you would benefit from leaving the country and traveling. We are not talking about a week in Florida on a spring break–type party, a month overseas on familiar territory, or a visit to a luxury holiday resort. We are thinking about a carefully planned, well-researched, life-enhancing encounter with other countries. Done properly, an extended period of travel can have a positive impact on your life. It can change both your view of the world and the trajectory of your career. Knowing the world and understanding the limits of your ability to adapt to the complexities of humanity can be pivotal to your future.

For many young adults and their parents, the idea of spending a year abroad is a positive way to bridge the gap between school and adulthood and the life of work. Young Australians and New Zealanders often build the "gap year" into their transition to adulthood. European youth travel extensively within the continent, aided by low prices for air and rail travel; the Germans love to head for wilderness areas. Well-to-do Asian youth — particularly from Japan, Hong Kong, and the wealthy enclaves in China — show up on youth trips, camps, and other adventure activities in countries around the world.

By contrast, the custom of postponing the leap into postsecondary education or work — of going outside the country to discover more about the world — is not well-established among young Americans. With some exceptions, you tend to stay close to home, and, when you wander, you usually head for safe, English-speaking places. You have usually traveled only on standard, risk-free trips to Disney World, Hawaii, England, or Niagara Falls. Young Americans do not typically visit much of their own country, let alone travel to Zambia, Indonesia, or Bangladesh. You often go into your adult years having visited very few places and knowing very little about the world beyond what you learned in school — which, for many of you, is not very much.

For a large number of young people, there is no great need to move forward with their studies, to sprint into the world of work — although, of course, there are those who are forced by family and financial circumstances to get on with adult life as quickly as possible. If you can manage it, you should consider spending a significant period of time — four months to a year — traveling inside or preferably outside the United States (even Canada is worth a look!!).

Put aside your travel paranoia, shift out of your comfort zone, and give careful thought to how you might explore a world that you perhaps don't know very well. There is a complex and exciting world to discover. The so-called "gap year" is a simple concept: you save up the funds to travel, buy an inexpensive ticket, decide where you are going to go (often with friends), and head off on a grand adventure. You will, if you plan your extended travel properly, learn a great deal about yourself and your place within the world as a whole.

Aussies and Kiwis, living in countries that still have some nostalgia for British traditions, have colonial memories that lead them to travel to the "mother country," restoring family and cultural connections to the British Isles. Americans, with so many different nations of origin, have no such common destination — although a sizeable number of anglophiles do make the trans-Atlantic crossing. Travel farther afield. A visit to India will demonstrate the power of one of the world's most dynamic and complex societies. Traveling across Europe will fill you with a sense of historical and cultural wonder. Walking through the streets of the intense and rich city state of Singapore will alert you to the potential of Asia. Traveling from the attractive and sophisticated city of Montreal through the plains of Saskatchewan to the oil-patch hustle of Calgary and the spectacular beauty of Vancouver will remind you of the power and possibilities of Canada, the quiet and ever-so-safe giant to the north. Driving from

Cape Town to Johannesburg will reveal the wealth and grinding poverty of South Africa. A few days in Moscow and St. Petersburg will demonstrate the combination of imperial majesty, Stalinist oppression, capitalist excess, and post-Communist decay that makes Russia so fascinating. Travel the world. Know the world. Discover yourself.

PAY FOR YOUR YEAR OF DISCOVERY YOURSELF

Maybe it is because we have nine children between us, making us cheap in the extreme, but we are not fans of free rides. If you are thinking of a year of traveling — and we sincerely hope that you will give this very serious thought — then start saving as early as possible. Many travelers work from the end of school into the early or late fall, then leave for eight months or so, giving them the option of starting school the following September. If you are frugal and really want to travel, you can save a fair bit of money during this period of time. There are many ways to add to your savings: high school graduation gifts from parents and grandparents, saved Christmas cash, money set aside from part-time work during high school. Parental support is always a possibility for well-to-do families, but we would not recommend that even wealthy parents pay all or a large part of the cost.

It's not as cheap as it was fifty years ago, when one of us traveled across *Europe on Five Dollars a Day*, to cite the title of the popular guidebook — but it still can be done at reasonable cost. Young adults who plan for their travels, pay all or a substantial portion of the costs involved, and spend frugally while on the road will get far more out of their experience than those who are simply given the whole thing as a present. There are many benefits to this approach, including the early experience with financial planning, the careful budgeting during the last stages of high school, attention to detail (such as who pays for the inoculations, which are generally not covered by health insurance), forward-looking preparation, and the delayed gratification that this entails — the satisfaction associated with taking responsibility for a big undertaking, the freedom that comes from paying for a major initiative oneself (making it harder for parents to direct the travel schedule), learning about foreign currencies and currency fluctuations, and the money management necessary to stretch the funds for the whole trip.

It's also a good idea to build work into your travel plans. By working along the route, a young traveler can easily double or triple his or her amount of time on the road, and pick up some experience along the way. There are useful working visa programs for young workers in Australia, New Zealand, and the United Kingdom. These visas are easy to get, flexible, and let you prolong your stay by working, generally in an unskilled job. There are many opportunities for English-speaking au pairs and nannies across Europe and Asia — many young women (and not just young women) capitalize on such opportunities and use a few months' work to extend their travel time.

Work and save before you go, and then find occasional work during your travels. Convert a month-long visit to Europe into a year-long adventure around the world. As much as you possibly can, pay for the trip yourself. Convert your first major experience after high school into a declaration of independence. Traveling the world on someone else's dime is an extension of adolescence — fun but without the maturity, responsibility, and freedom to make your own choices. You are a high school graduate. You are about to make huge life choices that will frame your adulthood. You can start by taking full responsibility for financing what could and should be both a grand adventure and the launch of adulthood.

BE ADVENTUROUS, BUT BE CAREFUL

The worst thing that you can do with your travel time is to gather together with some high school friends, settle on an itinerary by consensus, and then head out together in a prolonged extension of a high school field trip. You may have one good friend who shares your interests and wants to explore, but making the journey into a group exercise is not the best way to go.

There is no fixed plan or direction for your travels. Some will head to the United Kingdom and Europe — expensive, familiar, easy to get around, and rich with history and culture. Many, fleeing Northern Tier–state winters, will target Australia and New Zealand — two great countries that have the advantage of being cheaper than Europe (but not much), with better work opportunities, great weather, and some of the most diverse and beautiful scenery in the world. We are all for these, but, as we have already indicated, we favor a journey that takes you off the familiar and easy path.

Avoid the danger zones. One important sign of maturity — and one way of stopping your parents from having a fit — is to deliberately avoid conflict regions. If you want a test of this, go to the library and take out a copy of Robert Young Pelton's *The World's Most Dangerous Places*. Leave it sitting on the living room table. Watch your mother age before your eyes. Expect to be taken for a serious walk by your father. There are so many wonderful and fascinating places to visit that you do not need to put yourself at risk. If you want to go to the Middle East, pick Turkey, Qatar, and the United Arab Emirates, not Saudi Arabia, Iraq, or Iran. Stay away from Kashmir on the India–Pakistan border, but do seek out the major cities in India.

Think about the world's greatest cities — London, Paris, Stockholm, Istanbul, Copenhagen, Sydney, Auckland, Hong Kong, Singapore, New York, and, yes, Montreal, Toronto, and Vancouver, three of the most interesting and diverse urban places on the planet. Don't avoid the poorer cities: there are some — São Paulo, Rio de Janeiro, and Buenos Aires are good examples — that are impressive, modern cities with huge slums.

Take in some of the world's greatest human-made wonders, like the Great Wall of China, the Hermitage in St. Petersburg, the Eiffel Tower, the pyramids of Egypt. Ride the Japanese *Shinkansen* (bullet train), and visit the Acropolis in Athens, the Coliseum in Rome, Stonehenge in England, and the Old City of Jerusalem. But these are the easy and obvious ones. Find a hundred places you have never heard of and never anticipated, for in these unexpected discoveries lie the real mysteries of humanity. Head for Tromso, Norway, one of the world's great cities. Visit Nara, Japan, only a short distance from the business centers of Osaka and Kyoto. Go to Angkor Wat in Cambodia. Try a couple of the remarkable Great Walks in New Zealand. Skip Sydney, Australia, and spend a few days in Melbourne, but then head to Perth and Darwin, which are far more interesting places. Check out the remarkable city of Curitiba, Brazil, one of the most innovative in the world, and stop in Vanuatu in the South Pacific. Don't get hung up on Moscow, but try to get through to Yakutia in the middle of Siberia. Check out the largely abandoned villages in rural Portugal or the techno-impressive cities of

Umea, Sweden, and Oulu, Finland. Visit Qatar, and see what billions in petro-dollars can buy.

DO A REALITY CHECK

Here is one of those periodic tests that we inflict on you. If the lists above do not make you curious, if you did not grab an atlas or travel book or go online to check some of them out, you have just revealed a great deal about yourself. The places above — and thousands more — are wonderful. Visiting them should make your heart soar (or plunge, depending on your reaction to some of the hardships). If you were unmoved, if the prospect of exploring the world simply left you cold, you are not a bad or terrible person, but you are likely to remain place-bound for much of your life, and your world will be limited accordingly.

But you have just learned an important lesson: you like the familiar, you like being comfortable, you are not adventurous (at least not yet), and the idea of traveling does not inspire you. Incidentally, and this is a crucial point, you may not be ready for university either — if you cannot be inspired by the prospect of exploring the world in a physical way, it is unlikely that exploring it mentally through literature, history, geography, sociology, politics, or any other field will appeal much to you.

CONNECT WITH ASIA

As you plan your trip, make sure that you include Asia in your travels. For a growing number of young Americans, the continent is at least some-what familiar because it's part of their family's history. The large numbers of young Indo-Americans, Chinese Americans, Pakistani Americans, Vietnamese Americans, and other Asian Americans have obvious reasons for connecting with Asia.

For Americans whose cultural and ethnic origins are in Europe, North America, South America, or Africa, Asia is often remote and mysterious, if not threatening. Asia is the land of the Chinese economic juggernaut, the broiling Indian cities, South Korean technology, Japan's anime, Pakistan's political instability, Vietnam's wartime legacy, and thousands of other things. It is hot, except where it is cold, densely crowded except where there are large stretches of almost open land, industrially competitive save for regions where hundreds of millions subsist on hardscrabble farming, democratic where it is not run by dictators and one-party states. Asia is a land of a million contradictions, the source of much of the world's economic anxiety and its hope for future prosperity.

As you prepare for a twenty-first-century life, you have to come to terms with Asia. The West has viewed the emergence of the region as an economic powerhouse, with two of the three largest economies in the world, as a threatening development. But in fact, Asia's economic power is a return to form. Before the onset of industrialization in the late eighteenth century, China was the world's largest economy and Asia was globally prominent. Colonialism, wars, Communism, and American expansionism allowed the West to overtake Asia and even to subjugate much of it. No longer. The ascendency of Asia will be perhaps the most important phenomenon of the twenty-first century.

While parts of Asia are no-go zones — stay away from Burma, many parts of Pakistan, and any part of the continent experiencing civil unrest or insurrection — most of it is safe for you. The U.S. State Department's website provides excellent advice for anyone thinking of traveling in the region — read it carefully and take the advice. Common sense prevails. Get caught with drugs in Singapore or Thailand and you won't be home any time soon, if ever. Engage in anti-government protests in China and don't be surprised if the authorities are seriously unimpressed. For a young North American woman, wandering into the bar culture in parts of Japan can bring serious problems.

A well-planned trip should include a substantial amount of time in Japan (the safest and most accessible country in Asia), China (and don't stay in the big cities the whole time, for the rural areas reflect the mistakes of the past and the greatest challenge for the future), Hong Kong, Singapore, and South Korea. Vietnam is well worth a visit as it is a potential economic powerhouse, still recovering from both the long war with the United States and the decades-long boycott that followed. Laos and Cambodia are interesting, but travel is more difficult. Indonesia has some very accessible places — Bali is a major tourist destination and Jakarta is a modern city — but many of the hundreds of islands that make up the country are difficult to reach and somewhat uncomfortable for travelers.

Thailand is a diverse country and is well worth the trip — but the parts that attract young people are best known for wild partying. Real dangers lurk there. Be careful. Follow the cultural circuits in the country and the rewards are significant.

Many travelers have difficulty with South Asia — Bangladesh, India, Sri Lanka, and Pakistan — but the region is more accommodating than most expect. There are serious extremes of wealth and poverty, and the misery in some of the major urban slums and poor rural areas can be very upsetting to well-off Americans. Still, this region is experiencing an interesting combination of rapid population increase and economic growth, political instability and democratization, religious tension and multicultural collaboration, technological innovation and ancient class systems. We would describe Asia this way: you have to see it to believe it. Besides, many of the patterns of your life, economic and otherwise, are going to be set in Asia. Get used to it and get to know it.

HAVE FUN WITH YOUR PLANNING

If you are keen, do not just follow our lead. Explore — online and in books — and discover the parts of the world that interest you. You'll love some of the places you go and dislike others. In the process, you'll create a personal mental map of your world, and figure out your own place within it.

With these warnings in mind, have fun with your planning. The preparations can be enjoyable and even exciting. Here are some things to look for:

- **Multi-stop around-the-world tickets!** One of the best travel deals in the world. For about $3,500, you can go all the way around the world, provided you keep going in one direction.

- **International Hostelling Association memberships.** Another of the best travel deals in the world. Youth hostels are typically well-situated, inexpensive, safe, and well-managed. Staying at an accredited center carries many benefits in terms of accessibility, reservations, local knowledge, Internet facilities, and the like.

- **Tour companies specializing in trips for young adults.** There are many of these around, the New Zealand experience being one of the best for young people — light on the luxury, heavy on the camaraderie and fun. These are typically inexpensive, enjoyable, and well-organized tours that combine the best of sightseeing with opportunities targeted at young adults.

- **Ways to connect traveling and volunteer activities.** Habitat for Humanity, for example, arranges tours in association with many of their building projects.

- **Vaccinations.** Go to the local travel medicine center, give them a list of all of the countries you will be visiting, and roll up your sleeve (or lower your drawers)! Get all of the vaccinations you require, especially those for diseases like dengue fever, hepatitis, malaria, and yellow fever. Trust the specialists. They know what you need and they are more cautious than you are. If anything, get more vaccinations than you might need, not fewer. We can assure you of this. You do not want to get sick with a tropical or strange illness in a country without a proper health care system. If you are one of the people who think that vaccination is a Big Pharma plot, stay home, unless you have a death wish.

- **Good travel insurance.** The best agencies offer excellent local support in most countries and move quickly to get you into top-quality hospitals (which are very different from those provided to the local population). Do not skimp on the insurance arrangements and make sure you have full coverage.

- **Local cellphone service.** Coverage is excellent in many countries. Rural Vietnam is typically better and cheaper than many places in rural America, for example. The problem comes with the roaming charges for your North American telephone service. In most countries, it is much — as in a huge amount — cheaper to buy local pay-as-you-go service than to pay your domestic wireless service provider. Most international airports have cheap and reliable wireless sales counters.

- **Travel guides and books.** You can get quite a bit out of a decent travel book — Lonely Planet and Rough Guide publish excellent ones — and more people learn about the history, culture, and politics of foreign lands from these guides than from traditional sources. We strongly urge you to read serious books of history, politics, society, or current affairs before you head into a new country or while you are there. You will get much more out of your travels than if you try to pick up background and information on the fly. And with Nook, Kindle, or iPad readers, you can pack a hundred books with less weight than a single hardcover book.

BE PREPARED FOR A LIFE-CHANGING EXPERIENCE

Will traveling make you a better student or employee? It's hard to say for sure. Travel — and we are talking here about four to twelve months, not a quick trip to the Dominican Republic to lie on the beach — will certainly make you a more interesting person. It will broaden your horizons, make you more self-reliant, build your confidence and independence, introduce you to the importance of cross-cultural understanding, and expose you to both the richness and the poverty of the world. The maturity level of young people who have ventured far from home, making their way with care and attention to detail across many countries, is often profoundly different from that of an average high school graduate.

When you are on the road, you will confront a hundred significant choices a day. Lie on the beach or visit a world-famous museum? Share pizza with friends from the hostel or spend a very risky evening with rowdier folks you met at the bar? Jump on a bus heading into remote mountain villages or stay in the safety of a familiar major city? Change your schedule so you can help stomp the grapes in a winery in Spain or stick to the plan that you set out six months earlier when you had no sense of the possibilities. You will make judgments about new friends and travel companions. You will negotiate with your partner or group about issues large and small. You will adjust to new foods, accommodate different social and religious conventions, and learn to operate in a wide variety of political, legal, and economic environments. You will cope with crises, some of them potentially serious, and learn to negotiate, navigate, and otherwise fend for yourself in very complex settings.

We do not want to oversell the economic and career value of a year of travel. Very few employers are going to hire you as a vice-president on the basis of the two months you spent climbing and hiking in Nepal or working at a winery in New Zealand. The right kind of travel — have we warned you about avoiding the debauchery zones in Thailand or the pot cafés in Amsterdam? — will draw the attention of admissions officers and human resource recruiters, if only because it makes you more interesting than your competitors who have not wandered very far from Rhode Island, Austin, or Modesto. As well, you will likely be much more interested in the world and could develop a lifelong fascination with the people, economies, and politics of the places that you visited.

What are you searching for? The answer is simple: yourself and your future. To find either of these, you will do well to embrace the challenge of travel, move away from where you are comfortable, and see just how far you can push yourself. There is great pleasure to be found in discovering yourself and learning about far-off places. Do this with joy, careful planning, strict money management, and a desire to become a true citizen of the world.

8

ENTREPRENEURSHIP: WHY WAIT TO BE YOUR OWN BOSS?

LOOK INTO ENTREPRENEURSHIP AS A CAREER

There is a great deal of talk in the United States these days about the "skills gap," the "knowledge economy," and the value of a postsecondary education. The country has a more serious deficit, however — and here is perhaps the greatest opportunity for young people — in the field of entrepreneurship. Entrepreneurs are the people who start and run businesses, not those who apply to work for them. And they are a breed apart. There aren't enough in this country, but perhaps you are one of them.

When people try to explain why the United States still has (for the moment at least) the world's largest economy, they usually think first of the country's remarkable risk-taking environment (unless they're on the political left, in which case they give other reasons: the legacy of slavery, capitalist exploitation, and the like). Gambling is in America's blood, right down to bankruptcy laws that enable people to write a bad debt experience off their books, to bounce back from financial crisis, and to plunge boldly back into the world of business creation. The country is crazy about its financial high-rollers. How else can the attention paid to a high-stakes gambler and loudmouth self-promoter like Donald Trump be explained, when serious and far more important people like Yo-Yo Ma, Noam Chomsky, Daniel Boorstin, and David Frum are little known outside select circles? There are other countries with a finely tuned entrepreneurial drive — Israel is a world leader, and places like Japan, South Korea, Taiwan, and Singapore have well-developed business development cultures that drive their economies. But no one really does business quite like Americans.

America is a major player on the entrepreneurial front. From the days of John Jacob Astor and Andrew Carnegie, to Thomas Edison and Henry Ford, and through to Bill Gates and Steve Jobs, America has always put its leading entrepreneurs on a pedestal. No country does celebrity entrepreneurship quite like the United States. Check out your local bookstore and you will be amazed by the number of books by and about American entrepreneurs. Jack Welch is a national business guru. Warren Buffett and George Soros get instant attention, and so do Mark Zuckerberg, Jeff Bezos, Larry Page, and Travis Kalanick. Female entrepreneurs attract attention, with the performance of such business people as Judy Faulkner, Oprah Winfrey, Tory Burch, and Arianna Huffington standing out from a growing crowd. Have you heard of Evan Spiegel (Snapchat), Howard Schultz (Starbucks), or Jack Dorsey (Twitter, Square)? The vast majority of American entrepreneurs never make the front pages of the newspapers, rarely write books about themselves, and generally garner very little attention. But at the local and regional level, these entrepreneurs are highly influential.

> **STOP RIGHT HERE …**
>
> Do you recognize all or any of these names? Are you curious about them? Remember the curiosity test; you can look them all up. As well as the ones mentioned on this page, how about Tim Ferriss, Godfrey Sullivan, or Bre Pettis (all of whom are on *Forbes*'s Top Entrepreneurs of 2013 list), or Ray Kroc, Sam Walton, J.P. Morgan, Charles Schwab, or Alfred Sloan from an earlier generation? You may have noted that all these names are male, but that trend doesn't have to go on forever.

America treats entrepreneurship much as it does professional athletics, developing talent young and pushing it through the system. You'd have to be a hermit not to know a fair bit about the career and life opportunities in entrepreneurship. There are even a number of organizations directed at young entrepreneurs. Here are a few:

- Kauffman Youth Entrepreneurship

- Junior Achievement

- Growing Up CEO

- Girls Going Places

- Students for Independent Free Enterprise

While much of these organizations' emphasis is on traditional for-profit enterprise, the United States hosts support programs for would-be youth entrepreneurs, including Youth Venture (associated with Ashoka), Echoing Green, and Young Women Social Entrepreneurs. The Yoshiyama Program, operated by the Hitachi Foundation, focuses on entrepreneurial solutions to local poverty. Young people who are intrigued by the prospects and opportunities associated with running a business should check out these and other organizations. You can focus on developing entrepreneurial talents or devote a comparable amount of time and energy to figuring how you can prepare yourself to work for someone else.

EXAMINE YOURSELF: ARE YOU A BORN ENTREPRENEUR?

University professors have intense debates about whether or not entrepreneurship can be taught. It does seem odd that these people, secure in their tuition-supported positions, would be teaching young people how to take risks, make business-threatening decisions, and deal with commercial reality. The consensus, however, appears to be that people can be taught to understand entrepreneurship. And — if they have the basic skills and

---

DOES COLLEGE DESTROY ENTREPRENEURSHIP?

One of us signed up for one of those amazing self-help, self-promotional seminars for which America is understandably "famous." Robert Kiyosaki, author, investor, and promoter extraordinaire, was promoting his latest book, with the provocative title *Why "A" Students Work for "C" Students and "B" Students Work for Government*. The message was simple — school systems drain the entrepreneurial spirit from young people and do not prepare them for independence and creativity — and the lecture was interspersed with lengthy group discussions among attendees. It was an awkward experience. The facilitators, well-dressed young men and women, walked around the room, alert to the slightest sign of declining interest or disappointment, working hard to keep everyone's head in the game. Since this was not a book-promotion event, there was an alternative motive. Kiyosaki and his colleagues were touting an investment plan — yet another real estate promotion play promising maximum return for minimal effort. What made this event unique was Kiyosaki's seductive argument that academic achievement was antithetical to entrepreneurship and risk-taking. The idea that going to college destroys risk-taking and innovation and initiative is not one we'd necessarily endorse, though Bill Gates and Steve Jobs might have agreed with Kiyosaki at the beginning of their careers. Certainly, though, you don't need a college education to be an innovator.

mindset — they also can be taught how to capitalize on their abilities and convert motivation, commercial ideas, and energy into a successful business. Put a different way, a lack of guidance and preparation can make the path to successful entrepreneurship even tougher than it already is.

But maybe you are one of those who have natural entrepreneurial skills in their DNA. You are the one who is always looking for an opportunity to make money, who organized the spring break skiing trip and made a nice profit from it, who rebuilds cars and sells them for a 40 percent return on the initial investment, who took the sleepy little concession stand run by the student council and turned it into a big money-spinner, who started tweaking some computer programs in high school and ended up creating three apps that are now hosted on the Apple website. A born entrepreneur is not just the smooth-talking used-car salesperson type, although some of you out there are like that as well.

The really transformative entrepreneurs do not just sell, speculate, or develop (all fine things); they also create. And they create not only new businesses but also new products and even entire commercial sectors. Steve Jobs, Bill Gates, Jeff Bezos of Amazon.com, and Martha Stewart are great examples. Another example is Mark Zuckerberg, founder of Facebook, who took some basic computer code and converted it into a hundred-billion-dollar enterprise.

Young millionaires flourished during the dot-com boom in the late 1990s — and some of them, the true entrepreneurs, survived the bust. They took their digital earnings and invested them in new companies and new ventures. They built on their initial technological innovation, used the money to invest in other businesses, and continued on in a life of commercial creativity. They now form the foundation of the high-technology industry in the United States, although they are no longer the geeks and hackers of earlier days. Most importantly, these high-tech businesspeople made entrepreneurship acceptable and even exciting, in a way that business development, auto parts manufacturing, and construction never did.

It turned out that the most successful ones — Gates and Jobs being the best examples — were far more than techies who got lucky on the digital bubble; instead, they were

> **READ THE RECENT BIOGRAPHY OF STEVE JOBS**
> Are you anything like him?

savvy, high-risk entrepreneurs sniffing out profit and opportunity by staying just ahead of the global technological curve.

CONSIDER SOME BASIC QUESTIONS

Some people are meant to be entrepreneurs, but most are not. True entrepreneurial spirit — by which we mean the ability and drive to create, not simply the capacity to turn a profit — is extremely rare. When the two elements merge — entrepreneurial spirit and core business ability — the results can be spectacular, as successful entrepreneurs and investors demonstrate.

At this stage in your life, you can consider some basic questions:

- Do I like making money?

- Do I enjoy taking risks?

- Am I really, seriously, over-the-top dedicated and hardworking?

- Am I willing to "eat what I kill," or live off of what I earn from business?

- Do I learn quickly, from both life experience and organized education, so that I can get the core skills I need to succeed?

- Do I insist on being my own boss?

If you can answer these questions with a resounding yes, then you should seriously consider starting your own business, during or after high school, or after university or college.

Now consider a second set of questions:

- Do I like to invent or create things?

- Do I like figuring out how things work — or do not work?

- Do I find myself a little out of sync with my classmates, seeing the world somewhat differently than others?

- Do I think I am right most of the time — and am I willing to work hard to prove it?

If you answer the second set with a strong affirmative, then you are a creative thinker, a "do-er" with real imagination and the capacity to anticipate change. This might make you an artist, a writer, a politician, or the leader of a social movement.

Now, if you answered yes to both sets of questions — the first about your drive to make a profit and the second about your imaginative side — you might be on the path to being a true twenty-first-century entrepreneur. If you think that this defines you, don't neglect this aspect of your personality. The true twenty-first-century entrepreneurs are the innovators who sustain and improve prosperity, who make their families, communities, and country better. It is a real gift to be truly business-minded. It is wonderful to be intelligent and creative. It is extremely rare to be all those things. For these true twenty-first-century entrepreneurs, the future can be a bonanza. And our world could use a lot more people like them.

LEARN FROM LIFE, NOT SCHOOL

High school does not create entrepreneurs — nor, with some exceptions, does university or college. Most teachers, civil-servant-like and unionized, don't have the skills to teach entrepreneurship. If they did, they wouldn't be teachers. They might be friendly to the local businesspeople, and might even create some policy space for them in the school. But they are not going to do very much to turn students into entrepreneurs. Classes on business focus on the basics of law, policy, and bookkeeping — not on the blood and guts of starting, building, losing, and selling a start-up business.

Universities and colleges have stepped into the game, offering all manner of courses, programs, targeted residences for young entrepreneurs, extracurricular activities, awards, clubs, and other related initiatives. Boot camps, like any one of the hundreds of college- and university-based programs for young entrepreneurs that work outside the conventional classroom to help young creative people convert ideas into businesses, are all the rage.

At this point in your life, you are pretty much on your own. Unless you have a favorite high school teacher with an entrepreneurial bent (there are a few), a family friend who serves as your mentor, or entrepreneurship running deep in the family, there will not be a lot of help for you. Entrepreneurs stick out from the crowd — there will not be many classmates who understand what motivates you or who share your passion for business or creativity. You should seek out people who think as you do. Real entrepreneurs in the community — the Big Men and Women about Town — are probably your best bet as mentors. These successful people are often among the very best supporters of young entrepreneurs and can be a huge help in the future. They are often surprisingly accessible. They know what it took to launch their careers, and are often on the lookout for bright, talented young entrepreneurs.

START SMALL – AND YOUNG

While there are many examples of successful entrepreneurs who came to private business later in life, most entrepreneurs seem to have a lifetime fascination with the field. The central characteristic of young business leaders is that they are willing to work hard to get rich. These days we have almost lost one of the most important points of entry for such people. Not so long ago, when almost every house in town had the paper delivered, preteen boys and girls by the thousands walked American streets each morning, delivering the daily paper. The job of a paper carrier involved running a mini-business: selling subscriptions, delivering the paper (subcontracting when away on holiday), collecting money, keeping the books, dealing with deadbeat subscribers, and, eventually, pocketing the profits. This is almost gone now. Adults deliver most newspapers — kids deliver the free flyers, which is not at all business-like — and there are so few subscribers that many of those delivering papers drive from one to the next. The really difficult and character-building parts — which involved collecting money, recording income, and paying bills — have all been replaced by online billing and payment systems. There were other options: shoveling snow, mowing lawns, running a juice stand in the summer, and so on, and some of these are still around.

The main point is simple. Even preteens could get a start in business. You are probably all puzzled by this, because most of these junior entrepreneurial opportunities have evaporated over the last twenty years. This does not mean that there are no jobs for young people — thousands of people work in family businesses or local stores, restaurants, and service outlets. And there are still babies to be sat — the current rate where we live is upwards of five dollars an hour. But that's not entrepreneurial; it's more like getting paid for doing chores.

We have seen a slow and steady decline in tiny owner-operated businesses, the kind that taught hard lessons about commerce — getting even well-to-do adults to pay their newspaper subscriptions on time was often challenging. Think of the shifts that have occurred. Recent immigrants, mostly adults, have taken many of the jobs formerly done by young people. Online billing and payment systems have eliminated the need to collect payments personally. Parents are much easier on their children and often provide them with an allowance that covers more than they could earn through operating a small business. Few young people go door to door to solicit snow-shoveling or lawn-mowing business — and the ones who do are often college-aged or new immigrants, and only rarely teenagers.

So getting experience in entrepreneurship is a little harder than in the past, but is far from impossible. Starting young is essential, in business as in athletics, music, writing, or any other worthwhile endeavor. Malcolm Gladwell's observation that achieving excellence and pre-eminence requires some ten thousand hours of practice holds for business as for anything else. If you want to hone the skills of a high-achieving businessperson, you have to practice, learn, practice, and, when you are feel you are almost there, start practicing again and again.

This is easy to understand in the context of hockey, music, or painting. Very few people become quarterbacks on the Green Bay Packers without countless hours of practice. The first violinist in the Philadelphia Orchestra might have been a child prodigy, but that skill was then developed, sharpened, and improved through years of practice. We don't think about marketing, human resource management, investing, bookkeeping, product development, supply chain operations and logistics, innovation, and risk-taking in the same terms, but becoming a successful businessperson or commercial leader is no different. You have to work at it.

You can follow the standard pattern in North America — coast through high school and then head to college or university for a diploma or degree in business. Then, armed with a college or university credential, you will do what most young Americans do, which is search for a job with a decent employer. Postponing your plans to become an entrepreneur makes sense in one regard. In today's business environment, you will likely need advanced technical or professional skills. Including some advanced education in your development is a wise idea. But you need to develop the basic habits and mindset early. If you wait till your mid-twenties to begin, your dream of starting your own company, launching a new project, or becoming a true entrepreneur will almost certainly never be realized.

Start now. Hit it hard. Find a business opportunity. Do your research. Plan carefully and thoughtfully, and then move on it. You might start very small: mowing lawns for the neighbors, washing cars, or providing some other basic service. Be good at it. Deliver a top-quality service or product, and do it with full attention to your customers and your business. Hire someone to help you. Set up proper books. Figure out the licenses and regulations. Take the idea of launching a business very seriously; give it the same amount of attention you might later spend launching a college, polytech, or university career.

The learning benefit of a year or two spent running a small business is immense. You will be laying the groundwork for later ventures into commerce, and you will also discover whether you thrive — or shrivel — under the pressures of

DON'T JUMP WITHOUT PREPARATION

It takes real guts to take the first step, to launch into business. If you cannot bring yourself to jump, or at least to take a significant step, you will have learned a great lesson about yourself.

But, if you are going to jump, do your homework first. Plan carefully, with close attention to the details:

- Is the idea sound?
- Do you have the money?
- Who is going to do the work?
- What is the market and audience?
- Do you need a business license or any other approvals?

Review everything with a mentor, preferably a businessperson who has been down this path before. And with the work down and the planning well in hand, do it.

Remember: Nothing ventured, nothing gained.

running a proper business. Some young entrepreneurs take a big leap, buying into a more sizeable business and running the company while continuing their studies. (If you can stomach an old Tom Cruise movie — and this one is actually pretty good — watch *Risky Business*. The business model is lucrative but hard to sell to your parents — he turns the family home into a brothel when his folks are away. But, as he soon discovers, there is form and structure to every successful business.) Our point is simple. Entrepreneurship is both a skill and a passion. You have to develop the skill and feed the passion. You can and should start young and start small.

BE PREPARED TO TAKE RISKS – AND TO GO BACK TO SCHOOL

Business is about risk above all else. It involves taking a calculated gamble about commerce and personal choices. You are putting it all on the line — your money, your time, and your reputation. Once you hang out your shingle (put out a sign to announce the start of a new business, typically in law or medicine — another reference that means nothing these days), your name and your business idea are open to the public. What you thought was a terrific idea — delivering cakes and cookies to children's birthday parties — could easily go down in flames. These days, the Internet makes it easier to hide your commercial experiment. Your attempt to make money by being the 694th iPhone application offering fart sounds could collapse in digital humiliation, but the odds are very good that few people will learn of your embarrassing experience. Remember, too, that most successful businesspeople started and failed several times before they found their niche.

The position of being a young entrepreneur holds a great deal of promise. You will find out whether you like the field and whether you have the nerve, work ethic, and determination to succeed — and the brains to know when to shift gears, close down shop, move to another business idea, or adapt to changing circumstances. The chances are quite small that you will, as a teenager, find the business that will propel you through life. What you will find is whether entrepreneurship is for you, if not immediately then when you have prepared yourself better for the real challenges.

So, to encourage you, here are the top five lessons that we think you will gain from running a small business when you are young:

- **You will figure out if entrepreneurship is for you.** Most people will never be entrepreneurs. You need to find out whether you have what it takes, and whether you have the ideas and the creativity to look at the work around you and find a way to make money.

- **You will discover the strong connection between work ethic and personal outcomes.** If you work harder, you will likely make more money. Slack off as a small business owner and your income plummets. This is one of the most important life lessons.

- **You will find out if you have good business sense.** While there are many technical aspects to running a successful business, the key attributes are less formal. You will find out whether you have the *instincts* to identify opportunity, the *strength* to bargain hard, and the *integrity* to build a proper business.

- **You will discover your openness to risk.** Business is about taking calculated gambles on a daily basis. If the thought of life in a risk-filled environment is stressful and unnerving, you'd better plan on a different career.

- **You will quickly learn that ideas and work ethic are not enough on their own.** You will need technical and professional skills — keeping the books and paying taxes is essential. Being a smooth-talking, hardworking, amiable salesperson is not sufficient on its own.

Teenage businesses can bring in hundreds of dollars a month, enough for a lot of iTunes downloads and regular visits to the movieplex. Really successful ones — and there are hundreds of such young businesspeople out there — can make thousands of dollars a year. With a little family financing, hard work, and some good luck, you could have a solid business in operation.

But you may find out that this is not enough. One of the big discoveries for many budding businesspeople is that they need additional skills — technical, professional, or commercial. Having money is much better than the alternative, but is often not sufficient on its own. For people wanting to make the most of their careers — and to push their business abilities to the maximum — commercial success often leads to college or university for the specialized training that is required for real success.

Don't be surprised, therefore, if you find out that your success as an entrepreneur leads you to an accelerated program of self-improvement and further discovery. Indeed, now that you've experienced that remarkable combination of risk, effort, intelligence, and commerce, you might well find that you are much more motivated to do well academically than those around you. After all, you've learned all about opportunity costs and are making significant sacrifices to be back in school — and you have your eye on a much bigger prize, specifically the wealth and freedom associated with being an independent businessperson.

YOU'RE ALSO HELPING YOUR COUNTRY

Remember that it's not entirely about you. While entrepreneurship can lead you to an exciting and rewarding career, there are also vital nation-building elements to this kind of activity. We live in a globalized and highly competitive world. Americans compete for business — and therefore for jobs, wealth, and stability — with entrepreneurs and innovators in countries around the world. Those places that win at the entrepreneurial game — and again we draw your attention to places like Israel, Taiwan, and Singapore that are doing particularly well right now in this regard — stand to prosper in the coming years. Canadians, in contrast, have fallen back on their natural resource wealth to sustain their very high standard of living. America remains the gold standard for entrepreneurship, but it is fair to say that the competition is gaining ground.

People love to talk about the well-established innovation clusters, like Silicon Valley in California, the medical technology center in Boston, and the impressive concentrations that have emerged in Austin, Texas, and San Diego, California. There are some new groups developing across the country, in places as diverse as Aspen, Colorado; Portland, Oregon; and the Raleigh-Durham Triangle in North Carolina. In between, there are vast expanses where twenty-first-century innovation is thin on the ground, where the business community relies on traditional fields (resources, agriculture, tourism, and government services) rather than emerging technologies. There are government and banking programs by the dozens, as federal and state governments and financial institutions seek to promote business development. But the country needs more. In particular, the United States requires that even more young people consider entrepreneurship as a career. For some, this means nothing more than gut-wrenching risk-taking — a flyer on local real estate that might turn into a lucrative land development business. For others, years of advanced study in engineering, applied science (love that biotechnology, nanotechnology, and quantum computing stuff), and business are required to make a move into their highly technical sector. For all of these future business leaders and entrepreneurs, it requires a particular cast of mind — one that is freed from the need to follow the well-trodden path to the human resources office or the employment center, that finds risk energizing, that builds off of a formidable work commitment, and that has real staying power.

If the United States is to flourish in the twenty-first century, it urgently needs builders, thinkers, risk-takers, creators, and innovators. It needs young people with the verve and enthusiasm to tackle the challenges and complexities of the global economy. These people — and perhaps you are one of them — have the ideas or business drive to create new companies and produce the thousands of jobs that the country requires to sustain its enviable standard of living. We do not do particularly well in this regard at present, in part because we spend so much time and effort preparing young people to work for others. The United States has historically been a nation of risk-takers and entrepreneurs, of investors and company builders. There is no guarantee that this pattern will continue into the future. Without a steady infusion of new entrepreneurs, America will quickly fall back to the pack.

You will know if you have what it takes in terms of drive, energy, and determination. If you don't, that's okay too — we don't either, and we've had happy and productive lives. Business is not for the faint-hearted, and entrepreneurship is not for the weak. Nor, interestingly, is it restricted to the smartest or those with the best grades. (In a variation of the Kiyosaki book we mentioned earlier, one of the standing jokes about universities is that they are where A students teach B students so that they can work for C students.) Entrepreneurship is more about mindset and work ethic than it is about intellectual capacity and high school grades. If you have it, or if you think you have, immerse yourself in the sector. Hang out with those motivated by business. Figure out where opportunities and your interests collide. Explore and try it out. The country's future might well rest on your success. And if you do really well, you can make a point of hiring some of the brainiacs from high school to work for you.

9

GIVE WORK A CHANCE

GET A JOB

Not so long ago, work was a standard part of growing up. Young people worked on the family farm or in the family business. They looked forward to getting a first job at a restaurant or local store. With little cash in the average kid's pocket, even a minimum-wage job was a confidence and income builder. The pattern is changing, meaning that more young people are heading to college without a great deal of work experience or even a first taste of paid employment. Odd, isn't it, that you should head off for more education, primarily to prepare you for the world of work, when you have little or no experience actually working for someone. The once vaunted Protestant work ethic that supposedly drove the Industrial Revolution in Europe and the United States appears to be eroding, much to the detriment of the younger generation.

The reason for this shift seems to be that young Americans have busy lives these days, but these lives do not always involve working for money. School takes up a considerable amount of time. Many of the best students are heavily involved in extracurricular activities — competitive sports, student government, volunteer groups, music, or drama. Add to this the inevitable summer camp, family travel and socializing, video games, and what have you, and there may be little time left for employment.

Others of you are, in fact, working. You sell tickets at the movie theater, hand out the fries and donuts at the fast-food restaurants, work the counter at the local store, and otherwise serve in the army of part-time, low-wage workers that keep the service economy going. Fewer of you have *good* summer jobs, in part because desperate university students and recent graduates are grabbing most of the decent positions. And even the old entry-level posts in the retail stores and restaurants are going to adults (many of them new immigrants) and your new competition — senior citizens looking to supplement their incomes. For those of you in low-income families, these jobs are absolutely crucial. They allow you to save for college or university or (especially for immigrants) supplement the family income.

Here's the point: you don't work because you love the smell of stale french-fry oil or because staying up past midnight to vacuum spilled popcorn off a theater floor feeds your love of the arts. You work because you want to and have to — and in doing so are developing attitudes toward life and responsibility that will serve you well in the years to come.

If you aren't poor, you work because you want the extras. Your parents won't cough up for the latest Samsung Galaxy, they balk at paying for your girlfriend's ticket to the movies, they make you cover the cost of insurance and gas for your car, or they refuse to buy the beer (or substance *du jour*) for your weekend parties. (You won't be surprised to learn that we're on your parents' side, most of the time.)

But there's a benefit to work that goes beyond getting money for fun. First, you learn the discipline of the workplace — showing up on time, being responsible, doing your job well, responding to criticism, taking direction, and the like. Second, you learn the direct relationship between work effort and the stuff money buys. Want the new cellphone that costs $750? Even the most math-challenged can figure out that at a job that pays $10 an hour (minus taxes, some benefits, the costs of getting to and from work, and related expenses), it will take close to a hundred hours of work to pay for it. That's a lot of fries served. And what good is the phone without a monthly data plan? Welcome to the world of McJobs.

Despite the various good reasons for working, it is parents who, in a growing number of middle-income and wealthy families, provide a first line of defense against the horrors of paid work. After all, if one of Mom and Dad's goals is to protect you from a blue-collar, working-class life, they're hardly going to applaud your decision to clean toilets at the local hotel, cut grass for the city, do telephone solicitation, or deliver pizzas.

So here you are, a few weeks or months away from graduation. You still don't know what you want to do. Your parents, teachers, and guidance counselors keep yammering away about preparing yourself for the world of work, picking a career, studying for a profession, or otherwise finding a way to pay your way through life. But at a basic level, you have only a theoretical idea of what they are talking about. What is this work stuff? What's it like to work from nine to five, or two weeks on/two off on the night shift, or as a casual employee? And what are offices like? Factories? Construction sites? Retail warehouses? Telemarketing operations? You have to make a choice, but on what basis? A few days of job shadowing? Presentations at Career Day? A little online research? Get real. None of this is worth a bucket of warm spit, to quote an American politician of an earlier day (except he didn't say "spit"). Here's a radical thought: get a job!

BUY SOME TIME

There's no rush to get to college, a polytechnic, or community college. If you aren't yet convinced that postsecondary education is right for you — at least not at this moment — then don't go. We've argued earlier that there are other choices — travel or volunteering, for example — that you should consider very seriously. But why not consider the world of work? In many parts of the country, there are reasonably good short-term jobs available for bright, hardworking young people. We are not talking here about great careers necessarily, but rather about experience-enhancing opportunities to test yourself and to try out the working life.

Consider it an exercise in buying yourself some time. Get a job and set a financial goal or purpose (save money for a trip, postsecondary education, a car, a place of your own, whatever). Don't just wander aimlessly into the workforce. Those who do will often pop their heads up twenty years on and discover that they're in the same place. Plan your entry into the job market with the same kind of energy and thought you might otherwise give to going to college or university. Done properly, spending a year or two in the workforce could well prove to be precisely the right thing for you to do. And even if you wander aimlessly into a low-end job, it will be a learning experience, as long as you don't get stuck in it.

For young people who have never held a regular, long-term job, employment is as foreign a territory as the favelas of São Paulo. There are wonderful and difficult people in almost equal measure. There are great jobs and terrible jobs. Try inseminating cows (with a gizmo, not — um

— you know what we mean) if you want a rough introduction to the realities of life. If that is not your style, get a job in a slaughterhouse or swab toilets in a nightclub. You could also work with mentally challenged adults (one of life's most surprisingly rewarding opportunities), assist with the production of live theater, work backstage at a concert hall or for a minor league baseball team. Work can be — and almost always is — challenging, fun, awful, hard, disappointing, and fulfilling, sometimes all at the same time.

The message here is simple: try out work right out of high school. You will almost certainly discover that the kind of job you get is hard, doesn't bring in much money, and doesn't seem to have much of a future. It can also be a great incentive to go back to school.

APPROACH YOUR FIRST JOB AS A LEARNING EXPERIENCE

Of course, not everyone who leaves high school for the workforce ends up in a low-income, dead-end job, destined for a life with few prospects for happiness or a high income. Stephen is one of these exceptions. He is a super-bright lad, truly gifted with computers. Early on, while still in high school, he presented himself to one of the leading technology entrepreneurs in the country and said he wanted a job. He had nothing to sell. So he did some voluntary work, and then convinced the company to take him on. With nothing more than a high school diploma, he became a valuable member of the company. Several years later, he was earning a big salary — and attending university part-time at the insistence of his employer, reinforcing his self-taught skills with some brain-enhancing learning. Stephen shows that great things can result from leaping feet first into the workforce. But there are only a handful of Stephens out there.

If you are one of them, you might find your niche in life as fast in the world of work as in university, or faster. Do what he did. Talk yourself into an entry-level job. Watch closely. Give careful thought to where you can contribute. Speak respectfully and politely to your superiors — being a smart-ass may be cool in school but it doesn't work well in real life — and show you are really interested in the job. Ask questions by the hundreds. Do research in the evenings. Ask more questions. Show them you are interested in business, and in their business in particular. Remember, by the way, that not asking questions and not showing any interest tells your employer a great deal about you. Regardless of the business, taking a sincere interest goes a long way. You will be amazed by what you can learn about companies, agencies, human relations, business operations, and management styles simply by being alert and attentive.

If you approach your first job as a learning experience, as well as a way to make some money, you will benefit enormously. You'll find out much more about what you like and dislike — sales or human resources, warehouse operations or being a waiter — and you'll discover where you have special skills and aptitudes. This is a trial-and-error approach that carries very little risk and considerable potential benefit. Imagine going to college or university and then discovering that you dislike your chosen field (this happens a lot to teachers and lawyers, if they can find work at all these days). Give work a chance and grow along with it.

DON'T FORGET WHAT IT'S ABOUT: MAKING MONEY

Work is, in the end, about making money. You will hear a lot of self-actualization stuff about finding a job you truly love or doing something that develops your full potential. Lovely, if you can get it. Most people go to work to pay the bills. They may not get much satisfaction in collecting garbage, filing legal papers, stocking grocery store shelves, or handling government forms, but they need to make a living and they try to find the best job that they can. Our guess is that around 10 percent of all working people have jobs that they really enjoy or that bring out the best in them. Most others just earn a living. You need to as well. So if you decide to take this approach after high school and go looking for a job, tackle the experience as an exercise in money management.

The brutal truth about minimum wage is that it's a life of poverty, or semi-poverty. The federal minimum wage in the United States is $7.25 an hour, with some variation among the states. Forty hours of work per week brings in $300, which, assuming fifty-two weeks a year with a couple of weeks off, amounts to $15,000 before income taxes. Suppose you end up with $12,000. Can you live on that, outside your parents' basement? Our bottom line here is that it's fine to take a minimum-wage part-time job while you're in high school because it's a good way to learn about the world of work, and if you can't think of anything to do after high school, it's probably better to take this kind of job than lie around the house playing computer games. But it's a lousy plan for the long term.

FIND A JOB WITH IMPACT

Getting a job right out of high school need not mean taking any minimum-wage opportunity that comes along, but you have to be realistic. Not many places, outside a few high-wage, high-cost communities in the Montana and Wyoming oil patch, are going to pay twenty dollars an hour for unskilled work. There are great opportunities in the retail and service industries — admittedly the kinds of jobs most parents and guidance counselors sneer at a little — and jobs that could really expand your horizons and give you deeper insights into the world around you. Do things you haven't done before. This is an experiment, after all, and it's designed to help you learn about yourself.

Consider some of these possibilities:

- **Work with animals.** Apply to a veterinary clinic, a zoo, a ranch, or the local animal pound.

- **Work with seniors.** The number of homes and activity centers for seniors is growing by the week. Seniors have amazing stories to tell, and being with them can deliver a much-needed jolt of humility.

- **Work with new Americans.** There are hundreds of not-for-profit centers offering settlement services for recent immigrants to the United States. These folks really need friendly, kind, and knowledgeable people to help them. A fair bit of the work involves looking after children, through language lessons and babysitting.

- **Work with children.** While most of the jobs in the field are now filled by people with college diplomas and university degrees, private daycares, private schools, and the like can offer the chance to work with children.

- **Find a basic job in a professional office.** Every law firm, architecture office (our favorite), and accounting company has basic jobs that have to be done, from filing and delivering mail to completing forms. These are remarkable places to experience. The people are smart and engaging, and often like to mentor young folks. (In major American firms, by the way, these jobs are going to university graduates — and many of them are unpaid internships!)

- **Get an entry-level job with a not-for-profit organization.** Each community has many charities and other not-for-profit agencies. These low-budget operations often need help with basic tasks. They can provide you with an excellent window onto a complex world that most people never see.

- **Work in construction.** While the well-paid jobs require a formal trade or certificate, most construction sites need someone to clean up, load and unload supplies, and otherwise support construction activity. You may find that there is benefit in physical labor and real pleasure being part of the construction of something new. Start your search with small contractors or renovators.

- **Find a job with a moving company.** If you have a strong back and like large-scale puzzles, a job with a moving firm can be attractive. The work is demanding, but the challenge of getting goods in and out of trucks and homes can be quite intriguing.

You get the point. There are jobs available for unskilled, entry-level workers. You have to work hard to find a job — college and university graduates are shouldering their way into the positions that used to be left over for people coming out of high school — but there are possibilities out there. Find something that stretches you or that tests something you are considering for a career. Walking down the street to the fast-food store shows a desire to earn and to work, but does not show much initiative or creativity.

By the way, many employees with these organizations start as volunteers. So, if you are hoping for a full-time job of this kind after high school, consider volunteering with an organization in eleventh or twelfth grade.

PROVE YOURSELF THROUGH WORK

Contrary to what you have been told repeatedly by parents, teachers, and others, you have a lot to learn and are largely unproven. Graduating from high school, even with an 80 percent average, is no great shakes. That makes you only a little impressive. You are not likely going to set the world on fire, find the job of your dreams, or soar with the eagles. Life just isn't like that, and all of the self-esteem-building exercises you have been through have done you a grave disservice.

Here are the top five things that most young people of this generation have to prove. You don't necessarily have to prove all of them, but you do have to prove some:

- **that you can tackle real and sustained challenges** — academic, technical, or otherwise;

- **that you can succeed on your own**, without parental intervention or special conditions;

- **that you are capable of hard work** on a regular basis;

- **that you have realistic expectations** about your abilities and responsibilities; and

- **that you can handle hard physical labor.**

Half a century ago, only a minority of people finished high school and only a few went to college. Now, young people are almost forced to graduate from high school and are pushed strongly toward postsecondary education. Regardless of which route you take, consider this your declaration of independence. To this point, most of you have relied very heavily on parents, teachers, and other adult mentors to make your decisions and to shape your lives. Now the safety net is gone and you are on your own. Many of you will delay this process, either by staying at home or by going to college or university, as selected and paid for by your parents. Indeed, young North Americans have got into the habit of prolonging their dependence on their parents into their late twenties and sometimes beyond.

Resist this, if for no other reason than that employers and others evaluating your file like to see signs of early independence. Once again, think about an employer choosing between two comparable candidates. One struck out on her own after high school, found work, moved out of the family house, and then presented herself for a job opportunity. The other stayed at home, still relies heavily on parental financial support, eats for free, and uses the family laundry and other facilities. Which of these people would you think an employer would see as more responsible, self-reliant, and mature? We know which one we would select.

As you see, we have strong views on this topic. Many young Americans, in our experience, have a deeply flawed work ethic. Jobs are hard, even the ones that are not physically or emotionally demanding. It's not easy to take orders from others, especially if you think they're idiots, as they may well be. Showing up at work — on time, in a good mood, ready to work even if you aren't — isn't easy either. But life is no walk in the park and it's vital that you understand this as soon as you possibly can.

WHAT WE DID

We took different approaches to work when we were young. Bill spent high school summers in the army reserves, starting at age fifteen (he lied about his age to get in, though of course we don't endorse lying), then worked driving an ice-cream truck the summer after his first year of university, saving enough to spend the next summer in Europe. He then got his ideal summer job, as a member of the Fort Henry Guard in Kingston, Ontario. This work involved foot and rifle drill, firing the large guns, and giving tours, and culminated in a trip to the Royal Tournament in London and then to Expo 67, the World's Fair held in Montreal in 1967.

Ken always worked — delivering papers, mowing lawns, shoveling driveways, and learning that the extra things he wanted from life, mostly outdoor gear and baseball gloves, were better if earned through hard work. His first real job, as a librarian's assistant, combined the formalities of a job with his deep love of reading. But then, between years of university, he worked on highway crews and in fishing camps.

Both of us worked while we went to university — Ken at gym kiosks and Bill as a residence don in graduate school. And we like to think that we developed and/or possessed a strong work ethic that has served us well into adulthood.

DON'T UNDERESTIMATE WHERE WORK CAN TAKE YOU

Some of you have had very privileged lives, others much less so. The United States is one of those countries where all of you have an opportunity to progress to the highest levels in the workforce, the professions, and public life. But the honest truth is that this country does not exhibit perfect equality. Those who are born rich will likely die rich. Many rich people of your generation have done nothing to earn their wealth. Teenagers from middle- and upper-middle-class backgrounds have huge advantages over those from the working poor or welfare families. For most of you, the path forward has been sketched out, if not fully defined, by the time you leave high school.

But work can be the great equalizer. A well-to-do, highly educated person who does not work well with others is likely to crash and burn (unless his parents own the business, in which case life really is not fair). A young adult from a disadvantaged background who possesses a strong work ethic and has the ability to apply her skills will generally do well in life. The reality is that work is where expectations, abilities, and effort collide — producing winners and losers in the great economic race that is modern life.

Here are two closing bits of advice. First, if you already have a university degree, and are holding down a McJob, get out of it as soon as you can. There's nothing wrong with your job, but unless want to make a career of it, leave it ASAP. This book gives all sorts of advice that is applicable to your situation, and you should look especially hard at the college and technical school options, though a bit of volunteering wouldn't hurt either. But don't stay where you are, unless your heart is set on the food or retail service sector. Those jobs are fine, but if you wanted service as a career, you wouldn't have gone to university in the first place, would you?

And finally, *don't take your mother to a job interview.* Believe it or not, many young people do this — and parents have been known to follow up after the interview, often to complain about their child not being hired. Make your job hunt your own, and handle the interview processes yourself. Consider this Test One of whether you're really ready to step away from the nest. If you're not, then we're officially worried about you!

10

APPRENTICESHIPS
AND THE SKILLED TRADES

FIND OUT ABOUT APPRENTICESHIPS

In some countries — Germany, for example — apprenticeships in the trades and technical fields are central to the education system, the economy, and middle-class prosperity. In the United States, unfortunately, apprenticeships are a seriously neglected option for young adults. However, in the last few years the federal government, increasingly preoccupied with correcting the "skills imbalance," has begun to offset the general disfavor in which apprenticeships and the skilled trades are held. Basically, the government wants more young Americans — that's you — trained for the skilled trades so that the country can lessen its dependence on imported labor. President Obama's support for apprenticeship training is usually drowned out, however, by his relentless promotion of college and university education. Let's hope the government's effort succeeds despite the country's preoccupation with white-collar education, for the skilled trades offer strong career possibilities, good incomes, and interesting and demanding work.

An apprenticeship is essentially a matchmaking arrangement that brings together someone who wants to develop a specific skill with an employer who is looking for a worker and is willing to provide training. The government plays a crucial role in the apprenticeship programs, providing funding for students and/or employers and establishing national standards that ensure the validity and transferability of the credentials. Most of the work — 90 percent in most cases — takes place on the job, with the rest being done before, during, or after at a training institution. The U.S. government strongly endorses the idea of registered apprenticeship programs:

> Registered Apprenticeship programs are operated by both the private and public sectors. Sponsors include employers, employer associations and joint labor/management organizations. Program sponsors pay most of the training costs while simultaneously increasing the wages of the apprentices as their skill levels increase. Registered Apprenticeship training can be competency based or time based with training generally ranging from one to six years depending on the needs of the program sponsor. For the apprentice, this translates into an educational benefit worth $40,000 to $150,000. Because the training content is driven by industry needs, the end result of apprenticeship programs is extremely well trained workers whose skills are in high demand.[1]

The apprenticeship system is, as a consequence, surprisingly robust, with over 440,000 trainees and more than 250,000 participating employers, industry associations, and other partners. The U.S. government recognizes that support for apprenticeships is widespread, indicating that employers in many sectors (see the list below) are active participants in the program. The Department of Labor has a long list of possible apprenticeships, in a large variety of occupations, from able seaman to accordion maker, from x-ray equipment tester to arc welder.[2] It's a long list, covering a wide field of activities, and it's well worth checking out. The government's apprenticeship hub makes a strong case for the value and attractiveness of this training system, identifying the benefits that apply to all participants.

For employers, the benefits of these programs include

- skilled workers trained to industry/employer specifications to produce quality results;

- reduced turnover;

- a pipeline for new skilled workers; and

- reduced worker compensation costs due to an emphasis on safety training.

For apprentices and journeyworkers, benefits include

- jobs that usually pay higher wages;

- higher quality of life and skills versatility;

- portable credentials recognized nationally and often globally; and

- an opportunity for college credit and future degrees.

For the nation, benefits include

- a highly skilled workforce;

- an increased competitive edge in the global economy;

- a system to contribute to and sustain economic growth; and

- a reduced need to import skilled workers.[3]

There are hundreds of apprenticeship programs in the country, covering a wide variety of trades: welder, childhood development practitioner, baker, alarm and security technician, composite material laminator, florist, hairstylist, and many more. Each apprenticeship has entrance requirements (hint: keep up the high school math), but the focus is on the development of specialized skills through direct participation and careful oversight by an experienced tradesperson. Expect to be surprised by the variety of fields offering apprenticeships. The U.S. Department of Labor lists a few of our favorites:[4]

- Able Seaman

- Acoustical Carpenter

- Aircraft Mechanic, Armament

- Animal Trainer

- Artificial Glass Eye Maker (or Artificial Plastic Eye Maker)

- Bank-Note Designer

- Ben-Day Artist (we bet you don't know what that is!)

- Brilliandeer-Lopper (a gem and diamond worker)

- Candy Maker — they pay people for jobs like this?

- Card Cutter, Jacquard (textile and fabrics, not Las Vegas gaming)

- Cartoonist, Motion Picture

- Crime Science Technician (be the next CSI star!)

- Marine Engine Machinist

- Master Homeland Security Specialist

You will learn more about the complexity and diversity of the modern workforce in half an hour on the apprenticeship website than you likely would in four years at college. It takes a lot of skilled, talented, and motivated people to keep the modern economy and society operating at full speed. A surprising number of the jobs and opportunities go to registered apprentices, and not to college and university graduates.

Note, by the way, the government's emphasis on "registered" apprenticeship programs. There are thousands of opportunities for American workers to learn skills on the job, typically by accepting lower-wage work for the opportunity to learn practical skills. These arrangements work reasonably well, but with one huge qualification: you will lack a credential. A registered apprenticeship program leads to an official credential, one that is recognized across the United States and, often, internationally. Unless you stay within one company, work for yourself, or find flexible employers, having the skill but not the credential can be a real liability. The registered programs are more formal, have substantial technical and in-class components, and require extensive recording of hours of work and the nature of supervision provided. In return, they provide a certificate of completion — what the U.S. Department of Labor calls the Journeyworker ticket, which is highly transferable and readily accepted and recognized. The registered apprenticeship is more onerous and can take a fair bit longer, but typically brings more job opportunities and a higher salary.

The apprenticeship system works in the opposite direction from the standard college-polytechnic-university system. At a college, technical school, or university, students explore areas of interest, graduate, and then try to match themselves with an employer. With an apprenticeship, the initial matchmaking occurs at the beginning, before the work and training begin. It's not uncommon for high school students who are proficient in the skilled trades to start working on their apprenticeship while in high school and to proceed directly into a paid position after graduating. The wages typically improve as the apprentice takes on higher-value work, operates more independently, and starts to show the benefits of the hard work and training.

These apprenticeships, which can be completed over as few as one and as many as five years, typically involve paid employment (at a lower rate than for a fully credentialed skilled tradesperson). In some trades, you can start the apprenticeship in high school or do most of your classroom training before you start the work experience. At the end, apprentices receive their full qualification in the form of a journeyworker certificate

THE JOYS OF WORKING WITH YOUR HANDS

In the distant past, we used to celebrate the talents and work ethic of the small farmer, who was seen as the backbone of Western civilization. Most of these types of farms are now gone, replaced by industrial-sized mega-farms. We then passed through a time when the skilled tradesperson — factory worker, construction worker, equipment operator — was seen as the core of American prosperity. These jobs are still around, but our attentions have shifted to more sedentary, cleaner work of a clerical nature.

There are all kinds of jobs that are decent and have merit — whether it's filling out forms or repairing airplanes, writing computer code or building a new church, working in a bank or operating a gas plant. There is, however, something special about working with your hands, creating new things, repairing stuff, and keeping machinery humming. Tradespeople make vital contributions to our collective well-being — and they often enjoy and take great pride in their work. Look at construction workers at the final stages of a housing or office construction project, or oil rig operators when they strike oil, or electrical workers as they scramble to re-establish power lines after a storm. There is tremendous value in having the ability to work with tools and technology, to solve practical, real-world problems, and to build and maintain things.

or similar designation. The certificate is the marketable piece — the apprentice is not tied to the employer for life and can now move freely within the industry and across the country on the basis of possessing a well-understood set of skills and abilities.

Apprenticeship programs don't have automatic entry. Remember that employers are making a real — and expensive — commitment to the apprentice in terms of wages, oversight, and training. They hope and expect that the apprentice will stay on with them after getting the certification, which means that there is a high correlation between being taken on as an apprentice and having an ongoing job at a decent income.

Here's how the system works in the construction industry. You can find a sponsor for your apprenticeship by finding an employer yourself, going through a union, or approaching the apprenticeship and training committee in your state and in the sector of your choice. Most employers want you to have at least a high school diploma, not because it necessarily prepares you for anything but as proof that you can stick to and finish a task. Your work experience is monitored very closely and documented by the employer, particularly in those fields called "compulsory trades," where everyone working in a trade has to be in a certified apprenticeship program. You are responsible for the classroom part of your program, which is generally not paid for by the employer. Apprentices are paid between 30 and 50 percent of the regular wage of the certified journeyworker at the beginning, with increases possible as skill level rises. Most construction apprentices work about 80 percent of the year and take courses during the rest.

DON'T SHY AWAY FROM PHYSICAL WORK

Apprenticeships are attractive for a number of reasons:

- **They lead to good jobs**, with a decent starting wage (remember you are unskilled when you start).

- **They provide on-the-job training** with expert supervision and a lot of practice.

- **They include classroom instruction** to provide the technical background that you require. Don't underestimate the challenges of the classroom work. This is real-world stuff, with much less margin for error than in a first-year biology or sociology class. These courses are often very demanding, and rightly so.

You may be wondering why you weren't told about this. The answer is simple: far too many Americans shy away from working with their hands. This country was built on the backs of men and women who worked as cooks, welders, pipefitters, carpenters, electricians, and mechanics. Despite the current craze for "white-collar" careers, these jobs and many like them are as important now as they ever were, and they are often well paid. America has long depended on immigrants to take up the hard and unattractive work. It is important to remember that, in the mid-nineteenth century, the Irish were to the United States what migrants from Mexico and Latin America are at present. At the beginning of the twentieth century, the arrival of hundreds of thousands of immigrants from eastern and southern Europe (particularly Italy) provided the crucial industrial and trades workers.

To learn a trade was once a standard American option, particularly for people from working-class backgrounds and for immigrants. With the resource and industrial sectors booming in the decades after the Second World War, working with one's hands was a well-paid and attractive way of life (it still is for those not blinded by the lure of a college degree). For people newly arrived in this country, moving from rural areas to the cities, or coming of age in the booming economy, the opportunity to work in a skilled trade and find employment (often in a unionized shop) in the auto sector, forestry, general manufacturing, construction, health care, and many other fields was highly attractive. These jobs paid well, once the trade union movement gathered strength, and required hard and highly technical work. Skilled tradespeople were valued by employers and took great pride in their work, as they still do.

But the skilled trades seem to have lost their buzz in North America. While swarms of young people head to university, college, and technical programs for which they are often ill-suited, the country's companies scour the world for skilled tradespeople. In the resource sector, in particular, the United States is once again doing what it did in the 1950s and 1960s: importing thousands of highly skilled immigrants to take jobs that too few Americans are trained to fill.

Of course, all Americans want the "good life," however they define it. But in these uncertain times, they tend to swarm like Los Angeles commuters on the infamous freeway system, all heading in the same direction but increasingly jammed together. Right now, that direction is focused on office work. But if you think that's the ideal life, start reading *Dilbert* cartoons or watch *The Office* on TV. Forget Google and Apple. They're the fantasy employers, with their campus-like atmospheres, games rooms, and free cafeterias — but you won't likely get to play games with them. In the United States, not surprisingly, working for the federal government is pretty high on the list of jobs people want, even if government is far from popular in the country at large. It's what the Chinese call the "iron rice bowl" — safe, secure, well-paid jobs with excellent benefits — but there are lots of pointy-headed bosses there too. Not enough young people grow up aspiring to be electricians, machinists, or pipefitters, despite the demand for these trades and the good wages associated with them.

And not many parents push their children in these directions, even if such important work has deep roots within their families. For the majority of American parents, "rescuing" their children from a life of physical labor appears to be a high ambition. It's not that they dislike the skilled trades. Goodness knows they call on plumbers, electricians, and carpenters to fix things, and most know that the skilled tradespeople are crucial to the economy. It has more to do with core values and expectations.

Parents usually want better lives for their children than they had themselves — and not having to work with your hands is part of this dream. It's an odd way to look at the world. A plumber typically makes more money and has more interesting problem-solving work than a clerk in a government office. But in our day and age, white-collar work — with a cubicle and desk, or, if you are really good, an office of your own — is perceived as high-quality and valuable, while working with your hands is less attractive and less valued, even though it may pay more.

Remember, too, that your parents have been living for the past thirty years in a world dominated by talk of the end of physical work (machines will do it all), the importance of the "knowledge economy," and the surging fortunes (with a few bumps) of the digital media, finance, and government sectors. There is something in what they say. The right person with the right skills and good luck can grab a great job with a bank, a trading firm, or a high-technology company — but that same person, with lesser skills or not such good luck, can end up taking airline reservations over the telephone until she is replaced by online systems.

Understand where your parents are coming from — but if the skilled trades attract you, hold your ground. There are great opportunities as an apprentice and the investment of time can be truly rewarding.

The real reasons young Americans are not directed in large numbers to the trades are simple:

- **We tend to avoid physical labor** where we can.

- **Most of us are so urban in character** that many young people grow up without much hands-on experience with fixing cars and tractors, operating outboard motors, working on construction, and other tasks that develop facility with and interest in skilled trades.

- **We've been influenced by years of complaints and criticism from environmental groups directed at the natural resource sector.** As a result, work in that sector, once celebrated as the center of the American economy, has been undermined. Americans haven't stopped consuming huge quantities of natural resources, but we don't want to actually work to extract them.

CONSIDER THE FINANCIAL BENEFITS OF APPRENTICESHIP

As with any part of the economy, there are no guarantees with apprenticeship programs. Companies run into financial difficulties, sectors expand and contract, jobs come and go. Right now, there are terrific opportunities in the skilled trades, particularly in the western United States, and specifically in the natural resource sector. Apprenticeships are usually offered in areas where there are solid and continuing employment possibilities, thereby giving you a clear indication of future prospects. Many former apprentices go on to establish their own businesses, either as independent operators or as owners of companies. Starting as an apprentice is often an excellent way to build up practical experience and, by watching closely, to develop an understanding of how the industry operates. Many successful American businesspeople started their careers as apprentices in the skilled trades.

An apprenticeship can lead to lucrative full-time work or to lower-paid but still valuable employment. Not many bicycle mechanics and chefs make $150,000 a year, but neither do schoolteachers. A substantial number of gasfitters, crane operators, and pipefitters can pull in big bucks, particularly on western resource projects. Most people who make the transition from apprentice to journeyworker earn decent incomes, although they, too, are vulnerable to downturns in the local economy or the closure of a manufacturing plant.

Remember that income starts at the very beginning of the apprenticeship. While your college- and

---

HERE'S A QUICK TEST

Go to Google and type in "Qatar" and "pipefitter." Look at the list of employers in this small Middle Eastern country looking for tradespeople. The advantage of having a tightly controlled system is that although it can be tough to get the apprenticeship in the first instance, the credential, once earned, travels extremely well and can open doors literally around the world.

university-bound friends are spending their own or their parents' money on tuition and books, you're earning a wage from your first day of work (with breaks in earning when you take your turn in school). Apprentices often complete their program with little or no debt, which puts them quite a few steps ahead of those who took alternate routes. People in the skilled trades have the added advantage of being mobile, both in the United States and internationally.

PICK THE RIGHT APPRENTICESHIP PROGRAM

Like everything else we've discussed, apprenticeships and the skilled trades are not for everyone. Some people are simply not made to be heavy equipment repair specialists, draftspeople, arborists, or four-color sheet-fed offset press operators. It is vital that you know yourself and are familiar with the field that you are considering. Spend time investigating the various skilled trades. Companies looking for employees often attend career and job fairs. Give them a serious amount of time. Don't expect to be actively recruited. Unlike the universities that will fall over you with fancy brochures and attractive recruitment stories, the skilled trades are looking for very practical people who are not drawn by glitter.

If you see something you like, ask to visit the workplace. Spend a day or two shadowing a journeyworker in the field — they're often very keen to see a young person interested in their specialty. If you can, build an apprenticeship option into your high school program; it will provide you with a head start if you decide to go down this path and will provide you with valuable work experience if you opt for a different career. If you're keen enough, an employer might hire you for a part-time or summer job, giving you a chance to explore the sector in even greater detail.

The key here — as always — is finding the right match. Employers want young people who know how to work, have the aptitude for a skilled trade, and are interested in self-improvement. You want a position that will lead to a decent career with a solid income and some long-term flexibility. We wish more young people would consider apprenticeships. The government of the United States and several state governments are making a real effort to promote youth participation in the skilled trades through grants and other means. The companies are eager if you are.

So here's the bottom line. Skilled tradespeople really know how to work. They're proud of their abilities, have sophisticated skills, keep up with developments in their industry, and don't like being looked down upon by the white-collar brigade, especially when they have higher incomes than office workers do. They generally like their work and are good at it. Approach the skilled trades with the respect that they deserve. They can demand hard work, but it's very good work, with significant prospects for personal growth and prosperity. Reject the idea that there's something wrong with working with your hands in the trades. That is rubbish. For the right people, apprenticeships and the skilled trades are dynamite options.

11

PREPARING FOR
LIFE AFTER HIGH SCHOOL

NOW WHAT DO YOU DO?

If you've stayed with us this far, good for you! Even though we are old, we know just how frightened you are about what is ahead for you — if you still aren't at all nervous, you definitely should be, at least a little bit. Hopefully, you now have a better sense of who you are and what you should do next. In these last three chapters, we will give you the tools to make the best of the time you have left before graduation, offer you some guidelines for how to optimize the time you spend preparing yourself for whatever comes next, and, finally, present a framework in which you can situate yourself and your future.

Despite our efforts to the contrary, we know that some of you will follow the swarm to college and join those who actually should be there. For that reason — and, frankly, because that's where our experience is strongest — we are going to focus here on the ways in you can best prepare yourself for college. It is important to remember, though, that the suggestions we are making here are also relevant — in some way — to any of the paths open to you. Becoming good at math, for example, may not seem to be particularly important to you if you're setting out to travel or committing yourself to a year of volunteerism. But the disciplined, rigorous thinking needed for advanced math can help you to organize your efforts so that you achieve your desired outcome.

ARE YOU READY FOR SUCCESS?

Let's assume that you have passed the curiosity test and made the decision to go to college — a decision made alone, with your parents, or as a result of broader social pressure to attend. The next question that arises logically is this: are you ready? We are sorry to have to tell you that, for large numbers of young people, the answer is NO! Coming to college when you are not fully prepared is a really bad idea that can lead to a great deal of unhappiness. However, coming when you are keen and ready can be a real joy. Preparation helps, as does self-awareness.

Here are the top five conditions for success at college:

- **High school grades are important** (though they are not guarantees of success). The research shows that high-achieving high school students do well in college. Students who come to college with an average in the mid- to high eighties will, in general, do well — though their grades may well fall substantially. While individual circumstances vary, students who come to college with a high school average of 75 percent or lower have a fairly small chance of succeeding in their studies, and many of those with less than 80 percent will also struggle. Time and effort spent in high school do pay off.

- **English writing ability is one of the most important predictors of career success.** There are no shortcuts here. *You must be able to read and write effectively.* This is one of the greatest shortcomings of today's college students. Too many students devote great effort to their mathematical and scientific skills and much less to writing. This is a huge mistake. Learn to write well. If your mother tongue is something other than English, we are impressed with your ability to learn another language or two. But students with English as their second language often have serious problems at the college level, where tolerance for bad grammar, poor spelling, and awkward sentence construction is typically very low. Don't rush to college if you barely passed the English-language entrance standard.

- **Mathematics matters.** All high school students wanting to get into top college programs should have completed academic mathematics courses through to twelfth grade, including calculus if available. There are two major reasons for doing so. First, numeracy matters and is of fundamental importance to many of the fastest-growing, best-paying careers around — from such obvious scientifically based fields as nanotechnology to areas such as finance, accounting, and economics. Second, mathematics is a very good indication of overall intellectual ability. Math is challenging, tricky, innovative, and creative. Other courses in high school have similar qualities, but you do not require high-end skills to get top grades in many of them. If you can do well in math (and not simply by taking the same course two or three times, as in the notorious high school "victory lap"), you have demonstrated the capacity for hard, intellectually demanding work.

- **Reading (a lot) is key.** This was part of the "curiosity test" and is, we think, vitally important. An amazing number of young adults do not read newspapers, magazines, nonfiction books, high-quality literature, or serious blogs and other Internet-based commentary. Less than one quarter of all college students in the United States read as much as a single book per year above specific course requirements. We find this depressing. Literate young people are engaged and often well-informed. The best college students read a lot. If you do not read on a regular basis, the chances that you will find college interesting are quite small. Note, by the way, that reading is strongly correlated with writing ability. Good readers are typically strong

---

COLLEGE READINESS CHECKLIST

Do the following six statements apply to you?

- I am naturally curious.
- I have strong grades (above 80 percent, and 90 percent for elite college programs).
- I write well and I enjoy writing.
- I am good at math.
- I am a reader.
- I am self-motivated.

If you are six for six, you will likely have your choice of colleges and your pick of many top programs. But if you miss on one or more of these items, take a long, hard look at yourself. Are you really ready for success at college?

writers. Read. Read some more. Then keep reading. We have a longer section on this later.

- **Self-motivation is essential.** Students who rely on parents and teachers to get their work done are at risk in college. After high school, students are pretty much on their own — and some find this difficult to deal with. Professors do not often check to see if you attend classes or nag you to get your assignments done on time. If you count on your parents to get you up for school and meet your deadlines, and if you depend on teachers to make sure you stay on course in your studies, you don't have the work habits you need for college studies. This is not — by the way — a skill set that you can really wait until after high school to develop in full. Top athletes push their coaches as much as the other way around. Accomplished musicians do not need to be reminded to practice. The best students approach their studies with the same energy and commitment.

HAVE YOU PLANNED PROPERLY?

You are about to make one of the most important decision of your life. How much time have you devoted to this decision? Wealthy American families spend tens of thousands of dollars on college coaches, test-writing seminars, campus visits, and the like. The parents of an academically gifted child will incur great debts to give their child the chance to succeed at a top school — even though there is less evidence all the time that superior intellect and attendance at a top school result in brilliant careers. The struggle to get into the elite institutions is a national obsession, even if the effort is of questionable value. Do some Googling and read the debate on whether going to Harvard is a good or a bad thing — opinions vary a lot. The majority of Americans are easy-going about their choice of college — probably because, in contrast to the typical view of the American situation, the local colleges are easy to get into if you have halfway decent high school grades. Indeed, most young people just sort of fall into both the choice to attend college and the selection of the institution (typically it is the one closest to home). In contrast, families in other countries make this into a decade-long saving and planning enterprise.

Check out what happens in other countries. In China, fighting to get into the best universities (Nanjing University accepts only one of every thousand applicants), children study relentlessly for their last two years of high school in order to make top grades. Hundreds of thousands of families around the world save for years so that one or more of their children can attend a well-regarded foreign institution — like the ones that you have available to you for surprisingly little effort.

Here are eight major steps that you should take to prepare properly to make the right choices:

- **Keep your options open in high school.** Teenagers often make rash decisions in high school: dropping academic math for an extra computer class, avoiding language courses, and worrying as much about protecting spares as the content of the courses they take. Do not take the easy road. Remember that college, if you go, will be much harder and more demanding than high school. Take a full course load, take demanding and high-quality courses, and make sure that you do not close off your academic options. For example, if you do not complete the right twelfth grade math courses, you could find yourself denied access to many of the most attractive programs on many college campuses.

- **Establish a history of work.** Nowadays there is no substitute for experience. It is vital that you work during the latter stages of high school and that you find jobs that have some relationship to the kind of future that you envisage. If you are interested in becoming an entrepreneur, look into starting a summer business. If you are keen about working in construction, get a job as a handyperson's helper. Whatever you choose to do — get a job, do it well, demonstrate that you are a hard and effective worker, and earn a positive recommendation.

- **Volunteer.** While some cynical students look at volunteer work as a way of building a resumé — helpful if you expect to be competitive for law or medical school — there are many great reasons for all young adults to volunteer. First, establishing a pattern of giving and helping is good for the soul — it both builds and reflects your character. Second, volunteer activities provide leadership opportunities and can give you excellent practice in a variety of semi-professional areas. Opt for something that involves organizational responsibilities or technical work, like being a treasurer for a school club. These kinds of commitments reveal a great deal about your personality and your general abilities.

- **Explore the world of work.** It is always astonishing to talk to young adults who have decided to prepare for a career that they know only in the abstract. Learn as much as you can about the fields of endeavor you are considering. Attend career days. Go to job fairs. Read the want ads. Check the websites for government employment bureaus or the trade unions, or Monster.com. Job shadow as often as you can (your parents' friends, community members, and neighbors often provide great opportunities). If you are interested in the law, sit in the public section of a courtroom and watch the law in action (be prepared to be bored; it's not like TV). The best teachers are often those who volunteer in elementary school classes while still in high school. They at least know what they are getting into. Many professional associations or trade unions are keen to help young people learn about opportunities in their fields. Remember, as you go about this process, that eliminating options — you thought you might be a teacher, but then you decide that dealing with thirty adolescents in a class is an unattractive proposition — is as important as identifying precisely what you do want to do.

- **Be wise about money.** Universities and colleges in America, contrary to public belief, need not be a huge drain on your resources — unless you are from a low-income family, in which case they can be prohibitively expensive, or unless you follow the American swarm to brand-name colleges. Unfortunately, students and families are often ill-informed about what the actual costs are. Tuition costs are only part of the total expense, particularly if the student is living away from home. Attending college means making significant sacrifices in your standard of living. You are at college to study and improve yourself, and you cannot and should not live as though you are fully employed (i.e., no fancy car unless your parents are wealthy and indulgent). Smart young people heading to college have given careful thought to the sources of funding (parents, employment, government loans and grants, scholarships and bursaries) and the real expenses associated with going to school. Spend a lot of time planning your budget and considering the alternatives. And if you decide not to go to college, the time and effort spent on budgeting will stand you in good stead as you make the transition to the workforce.

- **Pay attention to the world around you.** Watch what is happening in our country's trading relations with China. Keep tabs on the progress of the American economy. See what is happening with the resource sector in western Canada, particularly the petroleum industry. Keep a critical eye on what people say about the future. These are not just news items of interest to your parents. They will define your future prospects and opportunities. There are patterns amid all of the noise and debates, and you have to find the part of the broader picture that works for you.

- **Explore alternatives.** Plan to devote a substantial amount of time over your last two years of high school to considering all of the options, many of which are described in this book. Consider colleges, universities, apprenticeships, the world of work, and the other alternatives that we describe. This is your life. Take charge of it.

- **Do a full accounting of the entire cost of the choices that you are considering.** First, be understanding of your parents. If they are footing the bill for your advanced education (for many students, grandparents are putting in money as well), they are making major sacrifices. Be respectful of what they are giving up, and of their commitment to you. This may help you understand why they believe that they have a major stake in your decision. Second, make sure you include lost income in your financial planning. If you headed into the workforce right after high school, you would likely get only an entry-level job, perhaps in a coffee shop or grocery store. At the national minimum wage (assume it is $7.25 an hour), you would earn about $15,000 a year. If you take five years to complete a degree (instead of working), you will have lost $75,000 in income. So, the degree, at $15,000 a year in lost income (the "opportunity cost") plus tuition and board fees (say, another $75,000), is actually going to cost you (or someone) a total of at least $150,000 and possibly twice that sum, minus whatever you earn in part-time and summer work. If you spend this money on your education and end up selling coffee or stocking shelves anyway, you will have made a major investment in your education for a small financial return.

To us, this advice seems pretty obvious, and we know from our experience with the thousands of young adults we have known over the years that following it works. It is easy to differentiate between young people with real potential and the ones marking time as they work their way through their courses and programs. Here is the key point: in the not-so-distant past, the simple fact that someone had a college degree answered an employer's most important questions about an application. In 1960, having a degree generally meant that you were intelligent, motivated, endowed with good work habits, reliable and dependable, innately curious, and well-organized. But now the college entrance gates have swung almost completely open — just see how many of your high school friends (some of whom, you will agree, were hardly stellar in class) are going to college. As the colleges have accepted a much broader range of students, the ability of an employer to assume that a degree represented all of these personal qualities has diminished. A college degree still means something: it does require persistence, a certain level of skill and — depending on the field — a good deal of ability. But this might not always be the case, and that is why you need much more in your resumé if you expect to get noticed.

If you've decided at this point that college is for you, we want to prepare you the best way we know how to make it a huge success. Remember, if you want the career you are hoping for, you must be able to stand apart from the swarm. The time to prepare for this success is now — well, actually, the time to start was several years ago, but now is still better than never.

HOW CAN YOU GET (OR SHARPEN) THESE ESSENTIAL SKILLS?

It would be nice if everything we say could be upbeat, and if we could tell you nothing but sweet thoughts: you are the greatest generation that ever lived, your education so far has been first-rate, you are fully equipped for college, where you will succeed and make your parents proud. College won't be too difficult, because you were an A student in high school, with an 80 percent average, and so on and so on. But we won't lie to you: all of this may be true, or some of it, or none of it. Only you can judge (until, of course, your college judges you).

There are, though, two things that are essential to your success in college. They also will significantly improve your chances for success in whatever you do in your life.

LEARN TO WRITE

Let's start with the conclusion to this part: there is nothing — not anything — more fundamental to success in an English-speaking college than the ability to write English prose. This is true in the sciences as well in the humanities. It's probably less true if you are aiming for a degree in physical education (more important there to have athletic ability, but you will still be surprised), but it's vital everywhere else. Allied with this is the ability to read fluently and critically. Yes, of course you can read and write. We aren't suggesting that you are illiterate. But can you read and write at a college level? A dismaying number of college students can't — a fact that illuminates one of the great failures of the contemporary American primary and secondary education system.

On the subject of writing, we have good news and bad news. The good news is that, given practice, anyone can learn to write in a manner that will be acceptable to those who grade undergraduate essays and research papers in the various disciplines. There are a number of different styles used at college: papers written for the humanities and social sciences are not the same as those written for the physical sciences, where "scientific writing" is required. But it can all be learned, if you want to learn it. Be warned, however, that universities do not want the compositions that you wrote in high school. They do not care how you spent your summer vacation, nor are they interested in what a colorful character your grandfather was. They want evidence of research and analysis, clearly and correctly put forward in prose.

We assume here that you really want to learn to write, that you are going to take writing seriously, and not just scrape through with C-grades along with the swarm, or — heaven forbid — buy your essays from some criminal Internet source. (Shame on those who do this — college and other institutions have clever ways with which to catch them, and the students deserve the heavy penalties that await them if caught.)

Before we tell you how to learn to write, we should explain why correct writing is necessary. You may have experienced some fussy teacher, a stuffy pedant who tells you silly stuff such as the "rule" that you should never end a sentence with a preposition. Someone once said that to Winston Churchill, who replied "this is the kind of nonsense up with which I will not put." (If you don't know what a preposition is, then you have a point at which to start learning.) That's not what we mean, and it's not even, contrary to what English teachers will tell you, that you have to write well to make your meaning clear. Of course you do, but you'd have to be a pretty awful writer to write in a way such that a reader couldn't tell what you were writing about, though we have read some student papers of this kind.

The harsh fact is that the way you write is a marker of your education and, to some extent, of your class background — much as Americans like to pretend that social class does not exist in their country. Example: if you write *I don't know nothing about it*, English teachers will recoil in horror (we will too), though your meaning is perfectly clear. (Some will say that *I don't know nothing* means that you do know something, but that's just pure pedantry.) The reason that it's wrong to say this is a social one: it makes you sound uneducated. Do you want to sound like a doofus when you submit a college paper, apply for a job, or write a letter or an email in the course of your employment? Do you want people to roll their eyes when they read your writing? Surely not, and that's why you want to write correctly. The rules of correct English writing are not carved in stone, and they do change over time: they are simply the usages that educated people and good writers have decided upon, and though the preposition thing is not one of them, the rule against double negatives is.

How, then, do you learn to write? It's simple, but not necessarily easy, and here is the bad news we mentioned above. The best way to learn to write is not to study the rules of English grammar — the difference between a principal and a subordinate clause, and all the others. You will want to do this, but later on. Here's the secret: to learn to write, you have to internalize the structure and rhythms of the written English language, and the best and probably the only way to do this is to read. Read, and read, and read, and read. Read good fiction, read as much as you can, read a book or two a week, not drivel like zombie novels written for adolescents, but fiction by masters of English from past years such as Jane Austen, Ernest Hemingway, and John Steinbeck, or, to pick modern American examples, Alice Walker, Kurt Vonnegut, Joyce Carol Oates, Philip Roth, Maya Angelou, Jack Kerouac, and Toni Morrison. Have you ever read *The Color Purple, To Kill a Mockingbird,* or *One Flew Over the Cuckoo's Nest?* Were they assigned high school reading? If so, you probably viewed them as a chore. But read them again, carefully, and see how the sentences and paragraphs are constructed. Listen to the rhythm of the words. You are not going to write like these people, and neither are we — nor would we want to. But they are masters of English prose, and you can learn from them. Don't try to learn from the writers of earlier generations. You want to write in a modern fashion, not like Charles Dickens. Read twentieth- and twenty-first-century fare.

Read good nonfiction. There's so much of it that it's hard to know what to recommend, but after a while you will recognize it. As the U.S. Supreme Court justice said about pornography, you will find it hard to define, but you will know it when you see it. Ask someone you respect to recommend some reading in a field that interests you. Read a book a week, two books a week, and eventually you will internalize what good English sounds like. Check out Malcolm Gladwell, an elegant writer whose books offer fascinating insights. Once you know the sound and rhythms of English, you will be able to write. After that, you can learn the rules of grammar. It's appalling that many high schools no longer teach them, but that's another story.

And then you should write. You will, of course, write all your high school assignments, but some schools don't give very many, and some go in for the composition type of thing that doesn't do you any good at college. Why not write for the school yearbook or, even better, become the school correspondent for your local newspaper? Write wherever you can: news in the bulletin of your temple, church, or mosque, something about your hockey team for the newspaper. Write letters to your elderly relatives who don't use the computer. Have someone whose literacy skills you trust look over your writing and comment on it. Yes, all this is work, but you want to stand out from the swarm, don't you?

How long will it take to learn to write? Well, a good time to start is as early as possible, as soon as you actually learn to read. Six years old is about right. Most great writers were voracious readers from their youth. But it's never too late, and if you start now and read and write consistently, you can become a decent writer, turning out essays and research papers that, if not Hemingway-esque, will at least not embarrass you.

We say again: *there is nothing, not anything, more fundamental to success in college than the ability to write English prose.* Start a serious program of reading now or, even better, yesterday. You say you don't like to read? Ah, well then ...

STUDY MATH – AND LEARN TO LIKE IT

Or at least study it. When we told you we were going to give you friendly and helpful advice, this didn't imply that it was advice you necessarily would welcome. Here it is: if you want a chance at the fullest range of careers after graduation, you must study mathematics at college, and this means taking serious math in high school, not the watered down courses. We can hear the protests and howls of rage already. American students, raised in an era of celebration of individual choice and encouragement of easy pathways to success, have learned to fear and hate mathematics. We will admit that high school math is often poorly taught. For lack of properly qualified teachers, more than one high school has assigned a physical education or English teacher to teach a math course, and this is worse in the United States than most countries. Nevertheless, math is one of the most important and foundational subjects in high school. If you intend to go to college and if you want a full chance at a wide range of careers, you must study academic math in high school. What is more, if you want a real shot at twenty-first-century success, you had better be reasonably good at it.

Let's start with the hardest sell, that math is intellectually challenging and fun. Properly taught, high school math is full of riddles, puzzles, creative formulas, and, most important, problem solving. Math teaches mental agility, builds a lifelong facility with numbers, and provides a foundation for advanced study in other academic subjects. It is not easy — but neither is English for those who don't have a natural aptitude for it — and it is a program of study that is truly incremental: what you learn in elementary school is essential for high school, which in turn is a requirement for success at college. You have to study math, stick with it, internalize its intellectual dynamics, and learn to apply its thought processes if not its formulas in many other aspects of your life.

Many American students are at a severe disadvantage compared to those of other nations (not surprisingly, the national performance on international tests suggests that, as a group, American young people are not doing very well — showing mediocre and declining results in the global race to mathematical literacy). In East Asia (where attention to mathematics is an obsession) and in Eastern Europe, there is a deep commitment to the fundamentals of mathematics. All students in these regions study math throughout their school years. They learn by rote and they work in very competitive environments, their parents working as hard to push them on as most American parents do to convince their children they are all above average. By rote we mean, for instance, that they memorize the multiplication tables, something that many American schools abandoned in favor of getting students to "understand" what eight times seven is.

The result of all this is that American students, as a rule, develop a strong aversion to mathematics. Even Barbie got into the act. A few years back, one of the talking Barbies was programmed to say "I hate math," generating widespread anger among feminists for stereotyping young girls as being anti-math. Actually, boys hate it just as much. High school students and college students alike talk about math courses as the academic equivalent of a colonoscopy (if you don't know what a colonoscopy is, look it up, and be glad you are still young). Some persist, particularly the science-oriented, because they are told that studying math is good for them or because it's a program requirement. But the majority of the students opt out. Only a minority of high school graduates have taken advanced high school math — advanced meaning the kind that all collegiate graduates took two generations ago. Many of those who take it do so more than once, struggling to get the math scores that they need to get into the most competitive programs.

This leads to the practical reason for tackling mathematics. Students who do not complete the right high school courses and who do not succeed at first-year college math will find more than half of all the programs on campus closed to them. Some of the most popular academic and professional fields — engineering, applied science, finance, accounting, economics, computer science, environmental modeling — require a high level of fluency in and comfort with math. In other areas, math is included as a barrier and test, a program requirement that does a fine job of weeding out the weak and unmotivated from the hard-working and determined. Check the program requirements across campus at the college closest to you and see what programs require high school and college math.

Equally important, those programs with high math requirements are also the programs with the greatest career opportunities and the best income levels for graduates. Without math you could be denying yourself access to some rewarding and interesting programs. Career-wise, you will be blocking access to the best-paying and highest-demand jobs in the modern economy. The message is simple. Study math. Work hard in high school and try to enjoy it, and if you can't enjoy it, work hard anyway. If you can't warm to it, then study it because it is essential to your future and will determine your options in college and, very likely, in the workforce. If you say, "But I hate it," we won't say, "Suck it up," but that's what we are thinking. . . .

HOW ELSE SHOULD YOU PREPARE?

Beyond the two major things (learning to write and studying math), the things that you need to do to succeed in college — or wherever else you may go — are largely evident through common sense and open dialogue with parents, teachers, and people working in whatever job appeals to you. Nevertheless, we'll note the following pieces of advice:

- If you're going to college, you should take the high school courses that prepare you for postsecondary education. Take the serious math courses, not the easy ones designed to make sure that every eighteen-year-old, no matter how unskilled, has a high school diploma.

Take the serious English courses, the ones in which you have to read Shakespeare (*please* tell us that your school offers them), not the so-called "applied" ones with names like "Contemporary English" or "Communications." It's true that there are some universities in the United States that will accept any twelfth-grade course for admission, but you don't want to go that route.

- Construct a resumé that will indicate what a stellar person you are, as well as giving you as much practical experience as possible. Do what interests you: coach a young kids' soccer team, be a camp counselor in the summer, teach Sunday school, win a prize at the science fair, or learn to play the bassoon. Don't just loaf around texting your friends and following Justin Bieber and the Kardashians on Twitter (people actually do this … what a waste of time and life).

Everything positive you do adds up, and when you are applying for a college program that's hard to get into, your impressive resumé will be a big help. Good luck.

12

SURVIVING AND THRIVING IN POSTSECONDARY EDUCATION

GETTING SETTLED IN NEW SURROUNDINGS

Let's assume that you have made the jump and decided to go to college (the largest group of you), community college (the second largest), or a technical school (a smaller number but growing fast). Hopefully, you've done the work necessary to determine which path is right for you and then completed the preparatory work that we outlined in the previous chapter. Now you've just been dropped off at your new residence, have boarded a bus to a campus far from home, or are setting up study space in your parents' basement. So, what's next? What do you have to look forward to? How can you best adjust to a strange and challenging environment?

The three types of institution named above are not the same, and their programs differ greatly. Small, elite programs pay a great deal more attention to you than mass-enrollment first-year courses at big universities. Small campuses are more welcoming. A community or junior college, on the other hand, is more similar to high school — particularly if you attend one close to home. Expect to see some of the high school crowd, have smallish classes, and experience much less intensity than at a four-year college. Technical institutes are like colleges, but with higher energy and much more focus on applied and practical work. You will be doing things right away at a technical school and finding your feet more slowly at a college.

The advice that follows is fairly generic — although it applies best to the college and technical school environment and less so to community colleges. The jump in standards and expectations is much greater between high school and college than it is between high school and a community college — depending, of course, on the particular program you are in. University campus life is more complex and all-encompassing than what you will find at a community college, with many more rituals, ceremonies, and traditions. But even that varies. A high-intensity technical institute, like Rensselaer Polytechnic Institute, has much more of a buzz than an access-oriented college like California State or the satellite institutions of the University of Wisconsin. If you've chosen to further your education at any of these places, dig in and have fun. Capitalize on opportunities, make new friends, participate in campus life, and absorb the intellectual and professional benefits of the place. You are off on a very different kind of adventure.

Here's a decision that will have a huge effect on your college experience: should you live at home — assuming that there is a college in your community — or should you go away somewhere and live in a college residence, or an off-campus apartment? We've had both experiences, since one of us did live at home as an undergraduate, while the other went to a university a long way from his home community. On the whole, we recommend going away, but there's no question that living at home is cheaper — assuming your parents don't charge you rent — and there's not as much of a break in your social life (something that has disadvantages too). But if you can possibly afford to do so, we think you should go to a different community and even a different state. We won't belabor this point here, since we make it in several places, but it's a decision that comes with choosing a college.

FINANCIALS

When it comes to the question of costs, you will read different estimates. Technical institutes and community colleges generally have lower fees for most programs than colleges and universities — though these, too, are changing. Our view on finances for American colleges is very simple. The cost of attending private colleges in the United States is arguably ridiculous and seriously disconnected from the benefits of the on-campus experience or the likely career benefits of attending an elite or private institution. Put bluntly, going to a high-quality, specialized professional program at a public institution will produce much better career results — but less prestige, poorer parties, and less appealing food — than a high-cost private college, and you will probably also have to do without the climbing wall and the twelve-person hot tub.

At the most expensive American universities, the cost of tuition and board alone has now passed sixty thousand dollars a year — as much as three hundred thousand dollars for your degree! This is a sum that seems out of most people's reach, and is a reason that student debt is such a crushing burden in the United States. It has to be paid, too — the university can refuse to release your transcript or let you graduate until you have paid every last penny. And, if you leave without a degree and owing money, they may put the debt collection agencies on your trail. Perhaps your parents have money set aside, but they are unlikely to have sufficient funds on hand. Ask them about their 529 — the income tax code for higher education savings plans. Find out about Pell grants. But if a family has three or four children, coming to college in two- or three-year intervals, they are facing the prospect of crippling costs, expenses that will drain the family coffers for a generation. Perhaps your parents are wealthy and can simply cut checks every year — some are, and if this is the case, you are lucky. If you live at home for free, you can save a minimum of ten thousand dollars a year, which is a big reason why so many students do this.

Of course, there are ways to lessen this financial burden. Many of the most expensive places have generous scholarship plans, a fact that is not usually mentioned in discussions of student debt. Take, for example, Duke University, where tuition, board, and fees for 2014–2015 are $60,500. Taking into account the fact that these costs go up every year, that's a quarter of a million dollars for your degree. But, in fact, half of all students at Duke get some sort of financial aid, either scholarships, bursaries (need-based aid), or athletic scholarships. The average grant is $39,200, which means that for half the students, the average cost is about $20,000 a year. The other half have rich parents, or friendly bankers.

Why, you ask, shouldn't the government pay for it? After all, your education is a benefit to society, especially if you are studying something useful and practical such as medicine or civil engineering. The traditional argument is that, even if you are studying something that is not particularly useful to society (say Latin and ancient Greek literature), your education makes you a better person, and this is to everyone's benefit. True enough, but the counter-argument is that your education also benefits you — because, on average (but only on average), it gives you a better salary than you would get without it. America isn't Cuba, where doctors make the same as street sweepers, so perhaps you should pay something up-front for your more prosperous future. Thirty years ago, state governments paid over half the cost of running universities and the federal government funded a substantial amount of the student loans portfolio. In your parents' and grandparents' generations, state colleges had low (or in a few cases no) tuition fees, mostly because state grants were generous. But then grants started to dry up, faculty members got higher pay, and the costs of running the places increased. Fees went up, and the cost burden shifted to students and their families, who now pay the lion's share of the costs, even in the so-called public universities. There is no sign that this is likely to change.

Perhaps you can get some financial help. The elite schools, like Harvard, are often what is called "needs blind," meaning that they accept students based on academic and personal qualities and not on the ability to pay the high fees. This does not mean a free ride, however. The big schools typically ask to see a student's parents' financial details and adjust the tuition fee accordingly. The very top students will get competing offers from many different schools and may get the near mythical "free ride" that is generally reserved for top athletes. The core message is this: do not assume that college is too expensive; there are solutions. Scholarships and bursaries are both money that the university or other sources give you; the difference between them is that the first are based on academic achievement, while the second are based on need. There are also in-course scholarships, and other ones donated by outside groups that give awards to the children of veterans and the like.

But unless you are an outstanding genius and win some sort of full-ride scholarship, you will still have to come up with a substantial amount of money. As the Duke example shows, this amount can be $20,000 a year (plus whatever you choose to spend on having fun). It helps to be an excellent athlete, since American colleges provide first-rate support to star players. It is not uncommon for an elite high school athlete to be offered tuition and room and board for four years, amounting to some $250,000. Not bad for an amateur athlete.

You are going to have to live on a budget. Sorry, we know that budgeting is a pain, but there's a good reason for doing it: you don't want to come out of university with a huge student debt if you can possibly avoid doing so. By 2014, total student debt in the United States had, remarkably, reached close to $1.1 trillion (6 percent of total debt in the country) — more than the total of credit card debt. Among former students who have debt — and a full one-third do not, due to scholarships, work or family contributions, and/ or because they went to low-cost colleges — the average post-graduation debt is $28,000. What is worse, many students fail to graduate, particularly from for-profit private universities, but still have a large debt dragging them down for decades. Our favorite horror story about student debt is the woman who wanted all her life to be a veterinarian, so much so that she borrowed money to take her degree at an institution in the Caribbean. Now thirty and working at the Caring Hearts Animal Clinic in Gilbert, Arizona, she owes the American government $312,000, which, unlike other debt, cannot be discharged in bankruptcy, an obligation that will dog her (sorry) all her life.[1] This won't happen to you, though, unless of course like her you take a degree at the Ross University School of Veterinary Medicine on the island of St. Kitts and borrow heavily to pay for it.

Be careful with money, or your bad decisions could drag you down for years. But you don't want to do this; it's no way to live, it's not very responsible, it's bad for your credit, and you will eventually want to borrow money to buy a house, something that's difficult to do if your credit rating is bad. Even if you pay the loan off on time, as most students do, it's no fun starting life owing twenty-eight thousand dollars or more. You could buy a pretty nice car for that amount. This is no time to suffer from the remorseless logic of compound interest. As we've mentioned above, under the law, student loans are not dischargeable in bankruptcy. This means that even if you declare bankruptcy, the loans still hang around your neck until you pay them off. You are in your thirties, your business fails, you file for bankruptcy, and your debts disappear. But not your student loan. It's possible to still be paying it back out of your Social Security in your sixties and later; this actually happens to people. So think very carefully before you take on this kind of debt.

You need to ask yourself how much you need a car, or an iPad — Android tablets are cheaper and just as good — or other consumer items.

If you have a student loan, everything you buy is essentially on credit, though admittedly at a much better rate than the credit card companies will give you. You have to have some fun —Why not a ski trip to Colorado? — but you have to consider whether it's worth adding to your debt load. If, on the other hand, you have the money and are debt-free, then, as the Cajuns say, *laissez les bons temps rouler* (as long as your assignments are in on time).

It's also possible that your parents can't afford to help much, you don't have a scholarship, you don't want to burden yourself with debt, and yet you want to go to university. How are you going to manage this? Traditionally, the answer was to get a summer job and, indeed, it used to be possible to make enough money between the end of classes in the spring and the start of courses in the fall to pay for tuition, books, and part of your room and board. Almost everyone could do this, and those with connections could get an industrial job that saw them come back to campus with a substantial amount of money. For some lucky students, summer employment still works, but not many of you are going to find a job that pays eighteen thousand dollars over the summer, let alone the more than sixty thousand dollars you will need to cover the cost of an elite private school. You could, of course, get a full-time job for a year or more and save like a beaver for university expenses. This takes a great deal of self-discipline, but some students do it, and it's a really good idea.

The usual solution to this dilemma is to take a part-time job. It used to be that poverty-stricken students would be hired by the university to wait on tables in the dining room and do similar jobs, but these positions are usually filled by outside workers nowadays. The common solution is to get a job in a restaurant or bar. The statistics on this subject are startling: in 2013 almost 80 percent of college students were working at least part-time during the school year, for an average of nineteen hours a week.[2] Some, of course, worked more. Suppose you end up working thirty hours a week in a restaurant — that's twice as many hours serving customers as spent in class for a traditional five-course lecture-based program. Are you a student working in a restaurant or a service worker taking classes in your spare time? Sometimes it's difficult to tell.

Pity the students who have to do this, who must spend thirty or even forty hours working, in the hope that this will enable them to complete their degree. For all but the superbly talented and dedicated, this is a major error. To the working time, add fifteen hours in class. College advisors say that you should plan to spend three hours working on a course for every hour of class time. For an arts program, with typically around fifteen classroom hours a week, this translates into a forty-five-hour-per-week commitment. For a heavy science program, add an extra ten to fifteen hours. And you haven't had any fun yet, to say nothing of sleep or social interaction. Somehow many students who figure that they can do a full course load and take on a full-time job wonder why things are not working out so well. This is the kind of pressure that makes students drop out of university, and is an important reason why so many take more than four years to finish their degree.

Worse still, such a work and study schedule leaves no time at all for one of the greatest things about being a college student, which is the opportunity to go off on trips of self-discovery. If you are in class or labs fifteen hours a week, and spend another thirty working on term papers, course readings, and other assignments, and if you don't have an outside job, you have a huge amount of spare time to go and hear guest speakers, play touch football, join student organizations and clubs — the choir, the Society for Creative Anachronism, political organizations, charitable and volunteer groups. Above all, you have all that wonderful time to learn things outside of the classroom and outside of your required reading and assignments.

Why not choose the debt-free route? Yeah, yeah, you're thinking — easy for you guys to say. What's the answer? Where is the money to come from? Well, we can't prescribe for you, but what we would do in a situation where we had no

LEARNING OPPORTUNITIES BEYOND THE CLASSROOM

There's the library, with hundreds of thousands or millions of books, depending on where you are, most of them unavailable on the Web. You can wander down the stacks and find interesting books that will rivet your attention.

Then there's the famous chemistry professor, Dr. Whatshisname, the Nobel Prize winner, lecturing to a class of graduate students. Perhaps you can slip into the back of the class and listen to him. Here's Randy Schekman, 2013 Nobel Prize winner, professor of molecular and cell biology at Berkeley, giving a public lecture. Go and hear it.

All this you can do if you aren't spending thirty hours a week slinging hamburgers.

money is not take out huge loans, and not kill ourselves and ruin the college experience by working ourselves ragged. What we would do is the third option suggested. We would take as much time off between high school and university as we needed to get together enough money to see us through the degree, an approach that works best at a public college. You are going to have to pay the money back eventually; why not get it up front and enjoy your college years? You may well have a better experience if you come to college at twenty-one instead of eighteen in any case. You're going to live to be eighty, statistically — what's a couple of years more in the workforce compared to getting out of college debt-free?

Give this some serious thought. You've been at school for twelve years, and you have four more to go in college. If you wait a couple of years and save your money you will have a far better experience in every respect: you will be more mature, you will have more real-world experience, and you won't have to wait on tables or serve beer in a pub during your postsecondary studies. It's surprising that more young people don't do this. Perhaps they think that if they don't go to college at eighteen they will lose the will to go, and will never do so. But if the impulse is that weak, perhaps they weren't meant to go in the first place.

WHAT IS YOUR PLAN B?

We have noted elsewhere that only a very small minority of people who express interest in medicine actually get into medical school. (Of those who do get in, almost all graduate, because the entrance standards are so high that no one who gets in is incapable of doing the work.) It must be terribly disappointing to be rejected, especially for those who have been answering "doctor" to the question "What do you want to be when you grow up?" since they were old enough to talk. Some try more than once and do eventually get in. Others go to the kind of offshore medical school that landed that poor veterinarian three hundred thousand dollars in hock to the government.

Some will go elsewhere in the medical field, into nursing or medical research, while some will go into other branches of science. Some will choose other fields entirely, and some will simply drop out. The point is that *you need a plan B.* Given the low success rate for medical school applications, it would be foolish to put yourself in a situation where you've invested two or more years in something that comes crashing down around your ears, leaving you with no idea what to do next. One solution is to take courses that will be useful in medically related fields. For instance, business courses might help if you want to make a career in the pharmaceutical industry. Perhaps you could become a high school science teacher. In any case, don't leave yourself open to disaster like a deer caught in the headlights. Plan for contingencies.

YOU'RE NOT IN HIGH SCHOOL ANYMORE

This seems obvious, but think about what it means. It means that you are now on your own in a number of ways. The most important of these is that, by and large, your instructors are not going to compel you to do anything. Most notably, very few college instructors take attendance, so if you want to skip class, there is no immediate penalty. No bad conduct marks, no going to the principal's office, no detention, no expulsion. What freedom, and what a wonderful change from high school! You will find that the absence of the police/prison guard atmosphere that is so much a part of high school life makes all the difference in the world. Being responsible for your own success (or failure) through self-discipline (or lack of it) is what distinguishes you as a young adult from the child you used to be not so many months ago.

But of course there's a corollary. If you don't come to class, and there are marks for class participation, you will get nothing. If you miss the deadline for handing in a term paper, you will be severely docked or will get nothing — unless the instructor is a pushover, as some of them are. If you skip labs, you will get nothing. There are many public schools where the standards for graduation are, to put it politely, suspect, and all students are passed along and graduated for mostly social or political reasons, even if they have done nothing at all. This won't work at any but the weakest colleges. No one is going to entice you to complete course requirements at college. There they are, do them or not, and take the consequences. A bit scary, but liberating.

You have other new freedoms too. Assuming you are living in residence, you can sleep in as long as you like, party till dawn (assuming you don't break the noise regulations), change your clothes every day or never, eat residence food (everyone complains about it), and drink and experiment with dodgy substances with no parents looking over your shoulder. Some people overdo aspects of this (see below on booze and drugs), some people make many friends, some people isolate themselves and are unhappy. It's up to you. No one will run your life for you. You're not in high school anymore.

STAY IN RESIDENCE, AND GET A ROOMMATE

Living in residence is more expensive than living with Mom and Dad, but we think that you should have the residence experience if you can possibly afford to do so. We don't think you should live in an off-campus apartment in the first couple of years; that can be a very isolating experience. In fact, some of the elite colleges, Duke for example, require all first-year students (they still call them freshmen) to live on campus in residence.

We make this recommendation for several reasons. An important one is that it gets you out of your parents' house. You are aware of the meme (an English-prof word that means an idea or belief that spreads through a culture) of the unemployed college graduate in his or her thirties still living in Mommy and Daddy's basement, an object of derision and scorn. You don't want to end up that way (so you'd better start planning your future carefully right now), and really, the sooner you cut the umbilical cord, the better. Living at home prolongs your adolescence and delays your transition into adulthood. You don't want that, do you?

Naturally there will be exceptions. There are people who for cultural reasons will be more closely bound to their families, and will live at home till marriage, and thus would not dream of going to live in a residence. There are others who for one reason or another need more family support than they will get living in residence. This advice is not directed at them.

You should get a roommate too. In fact, some colleges will not put first-year students in single rooms. Your first reaction may be to say, "But what if the roommate is loud/a drunk/annoying/a nerd/smelly, etc.?" If your roommate is truly horrible, abusive, or some sort of psycho, you can always ask to be moved — but the point is that part of your adult life is learning to get along with all kinds of people. You are a devout Christian, and your roommate is an atheist. You are an intellectual, and your room-mate is a hockey jock. You are a neat freak, and your roommate is a slob, or vice versa. How are you going to get through the year? Well, that's the whole point: you are going to have to find some way of getting through it — with patience, accommodation, or negotiation.

You really want to get away from the "helicopter parent" situation, so called because these people hover over their college-aged "children" like search-and-rescue helicopters over crash victims. They register for their children in their children's names; they phone the registrar's office to see how their kids are doing (by law the office can't give out information although there are ways around it). They phone the instructors to ask why their kids didn't get an A on their last term paper. Unbelievable, you say. But it's true, and it's getting more common all the time. After all, how many parents want to pay forty thousand dollars a year for C's and D's? Do you want to stay at home and be smothered in that way?

There are new friends to be made in residence. Some people who live with their parents while at college tend to hang around with the old high school crowd, people who are living with their own parents. In a univer-sity residence you will make not only new friends, but ones from a much greater variety of backgrounds than in your old neighborhood. This is valuable not only as a means of broadening your circle of friends and your horizons generally, but also as a great means of making contacts that will be useful to you in your later life. Imagine that you are in the busi-ness program, and down the hall in residence is a student whose father is a vice-president of JPMorgan Chase. You are interested in art, and your roommate's mother is a conservator at the Smithsonian or the Museum of Modern Art in New York. What a terrific resource! Such things happen more often than you would think, particularly at the higher-rated colleges.

Not only should you live in residence, but you should seriously con-sider asking to room with an international student. This is one of these win-win situations where you do a good deed but get a big reward in return. The good deed part is obvious: a great many international students are seriously deficient in English, especially spoken English, despite hav-ing taken English as a second language courses. They are just as adrift in the United States as you would be in Punjab with only a shaky knowledge of Punjabi. Everything about America is strange to them, save for the stereotypes created in movies and television, and some of it is frightening. Imagine coming direct from Amritsar to Norman, Oklahoma, especially if you start in January.

You can do a really good deed and get lots of good karma (as your grandparents used to say) by helping a student like this navigate a strange and new country. Some international students hang around exclusively with students from their own country, which is a really bad idea — most importantly because it reduces their chance to practice English with native speakers. If they room with you, they will have no choice but to speak English, though you may learn some Punjabi or Urdu or Cantonese as well.

But there's something in this for you, too, other than good karma. Remember why you are at university. We hope you are there to broaden your horizons and learn as much as you can about the world. Some students are, while others are just there for career reasons. Getting to know a student from another country really well is a tremendously broadening experience, especially if you are from a part of the country without a large immigrant population. But even from a more practical perspective, becoming a good friend of someone from, say, Hong Kong or Japan can have all sorts of benefits. Wouldn't it be fun to spend a year or two in a Japanese or Chinese city learning the language and working as an intern for some commercial firm, or teaching? Think of all the benefits that might flow from this. If your roommate isn't able to help you in this, he or she may know someone who can. Doesn't this sound more interesting than going back to your hometown and teaching elementary school at the same place you went to? You can always do that later if you really want to — and, in any case, there's a huge oversupply of teachers these days and it's really tough to get a job.

WHAT ABOUT FRATERNITIES AND SORORITIES?

Fraternities go back a long way in the history of American higher education, with many of them founded in the decades before the Civil War. We aren't talking here about the "professional" fraternities and sororities, aligned to particular occupations, but to the residential ones that are a familiar feature of many college campuses. Are they for you? It depends on how you feel about living in a house exclusively with other young men or women, because unlike many residences, these places are same-sex only. How do you feel about forging "strong bonds of brotherhood or sisterhood?" This is attractive to some people but not to others. Fraternities and sororities have attracted criticism, and some studies have suggested that members of Greek organizations (so called because their names are made up of Greek letters) do worse academically in their first year than other students, though the effect is apparently less after the first year. The most controversial thing about fraternities is the practice of "hazing," the initiation rituals by which newcomers are admitted to membership. Often these are harmless, but there have been incidents of serious injury and even death (typically from alcohol poisoning), and hazing has been banned or curtailed on some campuses. Some colleges, particularly small liberal arts institutions, have banned fraternities and sororities altogether, on the grounds that they are elitist and exclusionary. If Greek life attracts you, look into the fraternities and sororities on your chosen campus.

DON'T BLOW OFF ORIENTATION

American colleges know how to have fun — and it starts with the start of first year! Almost all colleges have an "orientation week," during which first-time students are given tours of the facilities, and may attend talks by academic, residence, and student activities administrators. Of course your eyes may roll at the thought of someone walking you through the library, but it's worth taking the tour. Libraries are much different than they were twenty years ago, when they were simply repositories for huge numbers of books and periodicals. The old file-card cabinets have been replaced by computer terminals, and the people behind the desks are highly computer-savvy, able to direct you to valuable online resources that you will need in your research. It's good to know where the health services office is before you need it, how the cafeteria system works, what the student government can do for you, what the residence rules are, what athletic facilities are available (some places have amazing facilities that rival those of the fanciest health clubs), and so on. All this is well worth the time you spend on it.

If you are in residence, you can use the orientation period to get to know your roommate. If he or she is truly awful, you can switch, though the residence authorities are reluctant to do this, and are likely to ask you to give the situation some time. Orientation is the time when you get to know people who may end up being your friends for life, and it is a serious mistake to skip this period and come to campus the day before classes start. We won't guarantee that every moment of orientation will be golden: the person who gives the little talk on how the university's grading system works may be a total bore. Some of the private colleges have orientation sessions that are absolute marvels of participation and integration; others are mindless beer busts. Check out Colorado College if you want to see how well an institution can do the first few days on campus. On the whole, orientation is very much worthwhile. Don't blow it off.

A word about a modern trend in college residences: Some places are now offering higher-end accommodations — luxurious facilities of various kinds, spacious rooms, better restaurant-style food, all for a price. We aren't communists by any means, but this offends our sense of social equality. You aren't there on holiday; you are there to learn. Even stranger is the new trade in boutique designer residence rooms. You, or your mommy and daddy, can spend several thousand dollars improving your dorm room with fancy curtains, furniture, carpets, and so on. Some colleges permit this, but we find the idea of a show-home residence room more than a little creepy. What's wrong with college dorm grunge? It was good enough for grandpa, and it's good enough for you. If your folks have that much money, there are more responsible things to do with it. And besides, do you really want to end up rooming with another yuppie prince or princess?

TIME MANAGEMENT: SELF-MANAGED LEARNING

You will hear about this during orientation, but it bears repeating: time management is essential for success at college, and it is vitally important that you pay attention from the first day of classes onward with regard to how you spend your time. Very few of you did this in high school, but this is another way in which college is different from what went before: you absolutely cannot afford to goof off during the academic year. The best thing to do is to get a day-timer — a calendar in which you keep track of what you are doing — so that you won't forget when your classes are and when your assignments are due. You can get paper ones, but probably a good digital one would be best. We assume everyone has a laptop or a tablet; ten years ago very few of you did, but times change, and a computer and smartphone are now essential. You should set aside a certain time of the day for study, and plan ahead for a big push for assignments of various kinds. You need to know what you are doing for the week ahead, day by day, and for the month ahead, and for the whole semester. You should allocate your time as though you were getting paid by the hour. Of course you want to socialize, but you have to set aside time for study as a priority.

We know some eyes will roll at this advice. You think it's nerdy to have a day-timer like some compulsive high school dweeb sucking up for grades. Certainly if you are at college just to party, or to kill time, and you don't care about grades, you shouldn't bother. If you are working in a restaurant forty hours a week we don't really know what to say to you, since you probably have every minute of the week allocated already. But you have to realize, and we put this in boldface, italic type, though we've said it several times already: ***American colleges are swarming with students, most of them aiming at the kind of career you want, and there are not nearly enough places in these careers for all who want them. Therefore, it is essential that you take every step possible to distinguish yourself from the swarm.***

The point of time management is to arrange your schedule so that you do your best possible work. To lose grades because you are rushed on your assignments is a great shame, and it will have a bad effect on your academic and work career. Be aware, too, that the first month is the most important one, so you need to take your studies seriously from the first day. Our favorite piece of advice for students is to make the first month of every academic year work for you. We say this for two reasons. First, because focusing on the first month generates real results. Second, because very close to 100 percent of all students ignore the suggestion. You will arrive in school in September. The first few days will be taken up with orientation. Smart students will take the academic part of it seriously and go easy on the social, boozy part. Then classes begin.

Most students take a full load of five semester-long classes, each with its own set of classes, seminars, labs, readings, and assignments. The course syllabi you collect the first week are quite daunting, but, hey, you have three months, so what's the worry? The answer is that there is a lot to worry about. Here is what most students do — they procrastinate. No one is watching and monitoring your progress. Few professors provided much scheduling advice. A few smart or lucky students will be in residences with mentor dons who can guide them through the perils of first year, but the majority will be on their own.

As you go through the course assignments, you will see a bunch of essays, projects, reports, and summaries that you have to do. Even if you were reasonably conscientious in high school, you actually have no idea of how long it takes to write a college-standard assignment, which the professor says must be three thousand words long and have at least fifteen academic sources. (By the way, it's a *very* bad idea to use Wikipedia as an academic source in university assignments. This web resource is wonderful for looking up facts, but it is unreliable for modern contentious subjects — the entry on George W. Bush used to change every day, and dueling writers wrestle over control of the Obama entry now — and using it will make your instructors think you are a lightweight.)

But those three thousand words are only for *one* paper. There is also, of course, the psychology midterm, the three English papers (each requiring you to read a novel or play first), four biology lab reports and a midterm, and the weekly assignments in first-year German. Some classes require weekly readings. One of us taught a semester at a college where senior history classes required students to read 250 pages a week, and they were quizzed and graded in class on their reading. Work stacks up — that is the bad news — but you can always put it off till the last minute — and that's the really bad news.

Most first-year students procrastinate. They put off their assignments until, in a mad rush, they struggle to cope with midterm examinations, essays and reports, and other work — all in the second half of the semester. The first half, meanwhile, has been left largely work-free. This pattern is as predictable as a Minnesota winter, with students panicking in late October and early November, requesting extensions (most profs say no, though some softies will give you one), pulling "all-nighters" in a desperate attempt to keep up with a deadline (a really bad idea: how clearly do you think at 3:00 a.m.?), and watching their grade point average plummet in a flurry of poorly written essays and mediocre projects. The library, largely empty in September, is swarming with students in mid-semester, many of them frantically searching for the same books.

The solution is so elegant and so easy that it is remarkable more students do not adopt this strategy. Well, actually, it's not that remarkable, since it runs against most people's basic instincts to put tasks off. Start your assignments early. Go through all of the work that you have to do in the semester. Determine which essays or reports can be done right away and which ones have to be done at specific times in the course. Do as many of the assignments as you can in September. The library will be largely empty. The books and materials you want will be on the shelves. Librarians and writing center staff will have lots of time to help you. You will not be otherwise busy. Get at least the first draft done right away. You can always go back and revise the papers closer to the deadlines.

Following this advice will set you on a manageable path to academic success (assuming that the essays are properly written and researched). You will avoid the post-Thanksgiving panic, your work will be more carefully presented, you will experience much less stress than your classmates, and you might even be able to enjoy the work. Ignoring this advice, and we know that the swarm will do so, will leave you with a very relaxed six-week period, followed by an intense and stressful second half of the semester. Most students never quite get the logic of this approach, continuing the pattern of coasting and crisis semester after semester.

So, take this as the first test of your ability to respond to good advice. Tackle your first-semester work like a military campaign. Plan ahead, develop a workable strategy, apply yourself early, work consistently, and capitalize on the full semester's worth of time and

THE MATHEMATICS OF FIRST-YEAR ASSIGNMENTS

You will have x number of papers to write (we are talking arts courses here, but the same applies to lab assignments). The papers will, on average, take you y number of hours (and y is about three times longer than it was in high school, because you can't just make it all up out of your head, like a story — you have to substantiate your facts through research). Make note of this and plan accordingly.

You must, therefore, find $x \times y$ hours in order to complete your assignments over the course of three months. You can spread this out over all of the period from September to early December (the smart way to operate), or you can delay starting your work and cram it all into the last six weeks of the semester — the standard modus operandi for first-year students. But these students are the swarm, and you don't want to be part of that, do you?

opportunity. But we smile as we write this. If we have learned anything from watching students over the years, it is that you do not, as a group, plan very well, are not strategic in your approach to university life, and somehow believe that a panic-stricken race to complete ten assignments in three weeks will miraculously produce top-notch work. Big sigh.

Don't skip classes, even the boring ones (and some will be so boring that you will want to drive spikes into your ears — we would be lying to you if we told you that all your instructors will be excellent). We are thinking of non-science courses now — but, of course, you won't skip labs if you are in science. In lecture courses, take notes that are as extensive as possible. They can be useful for study, and in our undergraduate days we found that if we wrote down as much as we could, it helped us to remember the material, and made studying for exams much easier. For heaven's sake, if you are going to bring a laptop to class, don't search Facebook on it. Either use it for note-taking or turn it off. If you are surfing the Web, you will annoy the instructor, and for all the good the class will do you, you might as well have stayed in bed.

MAKING THE MOST OF YOUR FIRST YEAR

In most programs you will have some choice of courses and, as well as taking the courses you will need to get into the major of your choice, you should seriously consider taking one course a semester in a field you know little about. This is a great way to decide which field you want to concentrate on for the rest of your undergraduate career. We don't mean that arts students should take organic chemistry, but they might consider a course in an area that they have never studied: sociology, psychology, natural resources, and so forth. Scope out such courses first, because you have to balance taking courses that will interest you and challenge you against the necessity of keeping your grades up. If taking a course in, say, ancient Egyptology sounds like a grade killer, you can audit it, usually for half the course fee, or just slip in and listen to some of the lectures. Maybe you will get turned on by the difference between hieroglyphic and demotic script and make it your life's work. You will never know if you don't sample.

Here are a few other ways to make the most of your first (and other) years:

- **Attend public events.** When politicians or other famous people come to campus, go and listen to their public lectures. Subscribe to a newspaper online. Hang around the library and read some magazines for free. Find out what you like. All of this is possible because you have taken our advice and are not working in a restaurant thirty or forty hours a week; you have all that free time to hear a lecture on the Rosetta Stone, listen to Malcolm Gladwell, and read *Scientific American*.

- **Get involved in intramural activities.** Because you have followed our advice, you have time for them. Intramural sports (from the Latin "within the walls" — that is, not with other colleges) exist in every conceivable form, from touch football to field hockey to fencing. Political organizations run from conservative to far-left progressive; if you want to shock your parents, you can join the Young Communist League USA if there is a chapter on your campus or in your city. Or, sign up for the Young Republicans and watch your parents' confidence in the security of their retirement soar! Join a volunteer organization; become a Big Brother or Big Sister, and do this because it's a good thing to do, not (just) because it will look good on your resumé. Just don't do all these things at once; you don't have *that* much time.

- **Be smart about your social life.** You're going to have to cut us some slack here, because we are old guys talking to young people about romance and sex (not always the same thing, by any means), alcohol, and drugs. There's a danger that anything we say on these subjects will sound hopelessly out of date or, even worse, creepy. Nonetheless, who you are as a sexual and social being — that is, establishing your sense of sexual identity, engaging in romantic relationships, choosing when and how much alcohol you consume, and deciding whether or not you will take recreational drugs — most often matures during your postsecondary years. There are two fundamental rules when it comes to sexuality and relationships. The first — especially in this time of HIV/AIDS and various STDs — is "play it safe." The second — which should be obvious and can apply to issues beyond human sexuality — is "be a decent person." Sex, love, and possibly commitment are always in the air on university campuses. Be aware of this fact and make the most of it, always remembering the two rules. When it comes to alcohol and drugs, pragmatism needs to lead the way. As you know, alcohol poisoning is a very real thing, and illicit drug use is, beyond being illegal, simply a very good way to destroy both brain cells and academic records. The philosopher Democritus (Greek, 460–370 BCE) said that "immoderate desire is the mark of a child, not a man." Good advice.

> **HOW'D YOU LIKE TO TRADE PLACES WITH US?**
>
> You know something? Talking about this with you in this way is making us a little envious.
>
> You are going to have a great time at college if you take the right steps to prepare yourself. We wish that we could follow you to campus as young students once again, especially now that we know how to make the system work.
>
> Tell you what: let's switch roles — you be old geezers, and we'll take your place, draw up a study schedule, join some clubs, go out for the track team, and yes, have a great social life (we'll get to that shortly). What do you say? Fair trade?

- **Be careful — and decent — in your sexual behavior.** Sex is a hot topic on American college campuses, with various honor codes, rules about consent for sex, and an ever-vigilant press looking for signs of sexual predation at the university level. Parents hate this conversation. Most hope you are still a virgin leaving high school (there is reason for their optimism, as the number of graduates who are still virgins is rising — between 25 and 30 percent of young people, in fact). They hope you will find your true love at college. But the reality is different — although you also need to know that campus sexual activity is much lower than movies and television suggest! Be careful. The sexual politics of American campuses are complicated and unpredictable, as you can see in the newspapers. Treat your partners/lovers with respect, make sure consent is clearly and honestly granted, and try to separate drinking, drugs, and sexual activity. Be smart. The price paid for a mistake is rising, and so are the chances of being caught.

GRADE SHOCK

You may be in for a shock when you get your first college grades, depending on where you are studying and what high school you came from. The subject of "grade inflation" in high school is a controversial one, but a 2005 study[3] suggests that high school grades inflated by 12.5 percent between 1991 and 2003, which means that the work that got a C– in the earlier year would have got a solid B twelve years later. This wouldn't matter, except that college grades generally haven't experienced the same degree of inflation; hence the shock of finding out that the effort that got you a B in twelfth grade won't do the same in college. Another study[4] points out that two-thirds of students graduate from high school "with honors," and in order to be in the top 10 percent, you have to have a 97 percent average! Colleges have suffered from grade inflation too, but not to the same extent, though it's hard to generalize. Princeton has a policy limiting the number of A's in any class to 35 percent. The University of Georgia and Auburn among others provide feedback to high schools: "You may have sent us a student with a 3.7, but that's translating to a 2.6 at Auburn." Our advice here is simply to be aware of the possibility that your high school grades may not translate at all into equivalent college grades.

Wellesley College has an interesting solution. First-year courses are taught on a pass/fail basis only. If you complete the course work satisfactorily, you pass. Otherwise, you fail. No A's or D's. Just a yes or no. Even this elegant solution has problems. Students do not know if they passed easily or almost failed — if they are the top student in the class or are an average performer. For young adults used to competition — and for parents nervous about their achievement — the pass/fail system is kind of like kissing your pet dog — friendly but unimpressive. So, Wellesley College has a solution there as well. As of 2014, students receive a "shadow grade" for each course. They are told, for example, that they passed but are also informed that they would have received a mark of 82 percent if the grades counted. The college does not record the grade officially, so the 52 percent mark is a warning rather than a permanent scar on the transcript of the would-be medical student. The top students lose out, although the professors know who they are and honors and recognition will come in due course.

Here's the bottom line on this topic: it's not that college is always more difficult intellectually than high school, though it often is. High schools vary so much in quality that it's impossible to generalize about them. The SAT is the great leveler in this respect, and although the test is highly controversial in education circles, it's safe to say that if you did very well on it, you probably won't be stymied by the intellectual demands of college, depending, of course, on the program you select. But as we mentioned earlier, the majority of colleges don't require the SAT, which leaves you little by which to judge yourself. Where the difficulty with grades comes in also is with the social and personal skills we mentioned earlier: essentially, even with a good SAT, whether you succeed or fail is largely up to you. Southern Methodist University publishes a useful chart[5] comparing high school and college, and we strongly endorse the advice they give:

HOW IS COLLEGE DIFFERENT FROM HIGH SCHOOL?

Following the Rules in High School	Choosing Responsibly in College
• High school is *mandatory* and usually *free*.	• College is *voluntary* and *expensive*.
• Your time is structured by others.	• You manage your own time.
• You need permission to participate in extracurricular activities.	• You must decide whether to participate in co-curricular activities.
• You can count on parents and teachers to remind you of your responsibilities and to guide you in setting priorities.	• *You* must balance your responsibilities and set priorities. You will face moral and ethical decisions you have never faced before.
• Each day you proceed from one class directly to another, spending 6 hours each day — 30 hours a week — in class.	• You often have hours between classes; class times vary throughout the day and evening and you spend only 12 to 16 hours each week in class.
• Most of your classes are arranged for you.	• You arrange your own schedule in consultation with your advisor. Schedules tend to look lighter than they really are.

- You are not responsible for knowing what it takes to graduate.

- **Guiding principle: You will usually be told what to do and corrected if your behavior is out of line.**

- Graduation requirements are complex, and differ from year to year. You are expected to know those that apply to you.

- **Guiding principle: You are expected to take responsibility for what you do and don't do, as well as for the consequences of your decisions.**

Going to High School Classes

- The school year is 36 weeks long; some classes extend over both semesters and some don't.
- Classes generally have no more than 35 students.
- You may study outside class as little as 0 to 2 hours a week, and this may be mostly last-minute test preparation.
- You seldom need to read anything more than once, and sometimes listening in class is enough.
- You are expected to read short assignments that are then discussed, and often re-taught, in class.
- **Guiding principle: You will usually be told in class what you need to learn from assigned readings.**

Succeeding in College Classes

- The academic year is divided into two separate 15-week semesters, plus a week after each semester for exams.
- Classes may number 100 students or more.
- You need to study at least 2 to 3 hours outside of class for each hour in class.

- You need to review class notes and text material regularly.

- You are assigned substantial amounts of reading and writing which may not be directly addressed in class.
- **Guiding principle: It's up to you to read and understand the assigned material; lectures and assignments proceed from the assumption that you've already done so.**

High School Teachers

- Teachers check your completed homework.

- Teachers remind you of your incomplete work.
- Teachers approach you if they believe you need assistance.

- Teachers are often available for conversation before, during, or after class.

College Professors

- Professors may not always check completed homework, but they will assume you can perform the same tasks on tests.
- Professors may not remind you of incomplete work.
- Professors are usually open and helpful, but most expect you to initiate contact if you need assistance.
- Professors expect and want you to attend their scheduled office hours.

- Teachers have been trained in teaching methods to assist in imparting knowledge to students.
- Teachers provide you with information you missed when you were absent.
- Teachers present material to help you understand the material in the textbook.

- Teachers often write information on the board to be copied in your notes.

- Teachers impart knowledge and facts, sometimes drawing direct connections and leading you through the thinking process.
- Teachers often take time to remind you of assignments and due dates.

- Teachers carefully monitor class attendance.

- **Guiding principle: High school is a teaching environment in which you acquire facts and skills.**

- Professors have been trained as experts in their particular areas of research.

- Professors expect you to get from classmates any notes from classes you missed.
- Professors may not follow the textbook. Instead, to amplify the text, they may give illustrations, provide background information, or discuss research about the topic you are studying. Or they may expect *you* to relate the classes to the textbook readings.
- Professors may lecture nonstop, expecting you to identify the important points in your notes. When professors write on the board, it may be to amplify the lecture, not to summarize it. Good notes are a must.
- Professors expect you to think about and synthesize seemingly unrelated topics.

- Professors expect you to read, save, and consult the course syllabus (outline); the syllabus spells out exactly what is expected of you, when it is due, and how you will be graded.
- Professors may not formally take roll, but they are still likely to know whether or not you attended.
- **Guiding principle: College is a learning environment in which you take responsibility for thinking through and applying what you have learned.**

Tests in High School

- Testing is frequent and covers small amounts of material.

Tests In College

- Testing is usually infrequent and may be cumulative, covering large amounts of material. You, not the professor, need to organize the material to prepare for the test. A particular course may have only 2 or 3 tests in a semester.

- Makeup tests are often available.

- Teachers frequently rearrange test dates to avoid conflict with school events.

- Teachers frequently conduct review sessions, pointing out the most important concepts.

- **Guiding principle: Mastery is usually seen as the ability to reproduce what you were taught in the form in which it was presented to you, or to solve the kinds of problems you were shown how to solve.**

- Makeup tests are seldom an option; if they are, you need to request them.

- Professors in different courses usually schedule tests without regard to the demands of other courses or outside activities.

- Professors rarely offer review sessions, and when they do, they expect you to be an active participant, one who comes prepared with questions.

- **Guiding principle: Mastery is often seen as the ability to apply what you've learned to new situations or to solve new kinds of problems.**

Grades in High School

- Grades are given for most assigned work.
- Consistently good homework grades may raise your overall grade when test grades are low.
- Extra credit projects are often available to help you raise your grade.

- Initial test grades, especially when they are low, may not have an adverse effect on your final grade.

- You may graduate as long as you have passed all required courses with a grade of D or higher.
- **Guiding principle: *Effort counts.* Courses are usually structured to reward a "good-faith effort."**

Grades In College

- Grades may not be provided for all assigned work.
- Grades on tests and major papers usually provide most of the course grade.

- Extra credit projects cannot, generally speaking, be used to raise a grade in a college course.
- Watch out for your *first* tests. These are usually "wake-up calls" to let you know what is expected — but they also may account for a substantial part of your course grade. You may be shocked when you get your grades.
- You may graduate only if your average in classes meets the departmental standard —typically a 2.0 or C.
- **Guiding principle: *Results count.* Though "good-faith effort" is important in regard to the professor's willingness to help you *achieve* good results, it will not *substitute* for results in the grading process.**

HOW TO MAKE THE TRANSITION TO COLLEGE

- Take control of your own education: think of yourself as a scholar.

- Get to know your professors; they are your single greatest resource.

- Be assertive. Create your own support systems, and seek help when you realize you may need it.

- Take control of your time. Plan ahead to satisfy academic obligations and make room for everything else.

- Stretch yourself: enroll in at least one course that really challenges you.

- Make thoughtful decisions: don't take a course just to satisfy a requirement, and don't drop any course too quickly.

- Think beyond the moment: set goals for the semester, the year, your college career.

So, be warned and be prepared. College is to high school as army boot camp is to summer camp at the lake. You will be treated like an adult from the outset, even though many first-year students are not ready for the challenge. Close to 30 percent of all first-year students drop out or fail out. Welcome to a tough world.

13

WHO ARE YOU AND
WHAT ARE YOUR CHOICES?

WHICH OF THESE PROFILES BEST DESCRIBES YOU?

By now you should have a pretty good idea about who you are and which of the options we have outlined in this book has the best chance of helping you achieve a prosperous and interesting life. No one ever fits exactly into a category — but there are some general patterns that do make sense. You know much of this now: if you are curious, college is a good bet. If you like to work with your hands, an apprenticeship program can be great.

So, to wind up this long lecture, here is a rough guide to various profiles of young people, with suggestions for which options might best suit them. As always, we want you to be honest with yourself as you consider where you might best belong. This definitely is no place for lying to yourself.

THE SEEKER

You are looking for a deeper meaning in life, beyond money and career, are smart, intelligent, and highly motivated but don't know what to do with your potential. Thank goodness for you. The world needs more people like you — people who care deeply about the environment, social justice, and spirituality. Take time to define your place in the United States and the world. A year of travel and volunteering could help a lot. If you are religious, bible colleges provide excellent opportunities for personal and spiritual development — and many are good academically as well. A small liberal arts college might suit you perfectly. So, take the time to explore — the world, your options, and your place in society — and give yourself the time to build the skills you need to make a difference with your life. Volunteer with a not-for-profit organization and discover some of the thousands of people out there who share your passion for making the world a better place.

THE SWARM MEMBER

You know who you are. You don't like to read, do not write much, and do not particularly like school; you plod along with average grades, lack motivation, and have no idea what you want to do in life. You are going with the flow, following your classmates into college and university prep classes, looking into the same schools as your friends, and tuning out parents and teachers when they talk about the need to raise your game. You are undeservedly confident and may be heading for a real crash. You can get into college if you decide to go, but remember that that is no great accomplishment these days. In many ways, we wrote this book for you. You are the kind of student who sits in the back of the first-year lecture hall surfing the net on your laptop, rarely does the reading, hands in mediocre assignments, and looks terminally bored by the whole college or university experience. You are — not to mince words — not ready for the big time. You need time to mature, develop a focus in life, and decide what you want to make of yourself. There is no "royal road" out there, no employers waiting to offer you jobs at sixty thousand dollars a year. You might muddle your way through university; but you can easily crash and burn on the job hunt. Your boredom and casualness are serious turnoffs to would-be employees, who have their radar set to weed out underachievers like you. You really need a reset. You need to consider all of the options we have laid out here and you need to slow down your rush through life. You need to prove yourself, through volunteering, work, or business — and you need to find your purpose in life. Trust us.

THE BRAINIAC

You are really smart and hardworking, you love to read, and you are ambitious. Head to university and consider the professions, including medicine. Realize that you will have many options in life, and be open to exploring new possibilities as they emerge throughout your studies. Remember, too, that at college you will not likely stand out from the crowd as much as you did in high school. In fact, many high-IQ students and high achievers in high school do not do well academically at college or in the workforce. Being smart in high school is no guarantee of a comfortable life. But you are also likely one of those who universities love to teach. But there is no easy route to real success, and many of you will experience two disconcerting things: your grades may drop, often substantially, and some people who finished behind you in high school will soar to the front of the class. So here's a warning. If you had to work like a beaver to get top grades in high school, you may be in for a shock. College is much harder. Students who worked moderately hard at their schoolwork and did lots of other things make the best college students. Obsessive students often have trouble adjusting to the more free-form system at university. So, turn on the afterburners.

THE THINKER

You are intelligent, love to read, have strong writing skills, but are not strong in math or science. Too bad. You should have worked harder and sooner on the math and science, for you have narrowed your college and technical school options considerably. No degree in civil engineering for you! But there are many good opportunities for you — including law, teaching, and government service. These days, too many of you are heading into business, but you should give serious thought to an arts program as well. People like you, if they are really good and willing to work hard, can succeed anywhere — in business too. You should follow your instincts about university, taking a broad first-year program and looking for a field of study that really interests you.

THE BUILDER

You are good with your hands and like to make things, but you are a nonreader — that is, you rarely pick up a book, magazine, or newspaper to read for pleasure. If you did reasonably well in high school, you are probably being pushed toward college. Pay attention to the warning signs:

nonreaders do not do well in university. There are great options out there, but you should probably focus on the technical schools, community colleges, or apprenticeships — or spend some time in the workforce before you take the plunge. Remember that there's good money in the skilled trades. Many of you will do very well in life, and could easily out-earn a lot of those heading directly to college. Surprise yourself. Surprise everyone.

THE WAFFLER

You are reasonably smart, you lack specific goals, but you like money and the good life. You are a candidate for the swarm but are academically better than most of that group. You are one of those being directed toward university, even though your heart is not really in it. If you have entrepreneurial skills you may be okay, as long as you have a strong work ethic. But you could have a difficult future, and the first year in postsecondary education could be a real shock. We are worried about you. Take some time off — volunteer, work, and get your act together. You can go to college, technical school, or university if you are really committed, but you will be wasting your time if you are not prepared to make a life change in doing so. Remember, you are in danger of becoming a swarm member, of falling into the undifferentiated mass that is heading into a career and financial desert. This is your chance to stop waffling and decide that you are going to exploit all of the talent and ability that you possess. Nothing less will do.

THE TECHIE

You are smart, reliable, hardworking, inventive, but non-bookish. You are well suited for the technical school alternative. Colleges and apprenticeship programs are other good options. But even here, know that the best opportunities will go to people who read. You have great opportunities ahead and the business world is really looking for people like you. But start reading more. Become a real specialist in areas that you find interesting and make sure you get some work experience. In the current economy, you have surprisingly good opportunities, but you have to apply yourself — harder than ever — if you want the best ones.

THE REACHER

You come from a disadvantaged family background. You have not been treated fairly in life, and have discovered that the system does not really cut you a lot of slack for poverty, family circumstances, isolation, and other challenges. You have probably faced many struggles in your youth, but you are intelligent and willing to work hard to get ahead. Many of you, particularly from single-parent families, have an inspiring parent pushing you on. You may be unaware of the real opportunities available for you and you likely underestimate your skills and options. We worry about you, mostly because you are likely to undersell yourself. Rich kids do better than you in school, but you are probably every bit as smart and talented. Seek out a trusted teacher, a counselor, or a community mentor — and pay close attention to what they tell you. They have a better sense of your potential than you do. Don't let anyone — including yourself — sell you short. We admire you for seeking to capitalize on your basic abilities. By the way, there is a fair bit of assistance, financial and otherwise, from community groups, colleges, technical schools, and universities for people in your situation.

THE RICH KID

You have enormous advantages, great social skills, and a healthy sense of entitlement. While your parents' money may buffer you from most of the realities of life, we are worried about you too. Money can get you a car and all sorts of electronic gizmos, but it cannot write your examinations, get you to work on time, or motivate you. Take the best lessons from your parents and their friends — entrepreneurship, drive, ambition, work ethic, and, yes, money — but realize that you need to be your own person. Dump the sense of entitlement; there are no easy paths to achievement. Capitalize on your privilege, and realize that you can make a difference in the world. Consider taking some time to volunteer. You could probably do with a reality check about how the rest of the world lives. We've met a lot of you at colleges over the years. You came to complain about your grades, and some of you had your parents call in to support your case. Tacky, and counterproductive. It is devastating to fail when your parents have given you so many advantages — but it is possible, and we know from experience that it's painful to watch. Buckle down and prove yourself.

THE ARMY BRAT

As a son or daughter of U.S. military personnel, you are a creation of America's deep and rich military culture that has a remarkable educational connection through military academies. Not surprisingly, this culture permeates the country as a whole. You probably signed up for one of the ROTC units that operate in thousands of American high schools or are one of thousands of young people educated in military-dominated schools. It is not surprising that you are seriously contemplating a military career, often to the exclusion of all other options. The neat thing about being an "army brat" — a term that we do not use in a derogatory manner — is that you look on the military as a backdrop to your educational and professional development and not as a specific specialization. Two "brats" from the same high school can have great lives and careers through the armed forces: one as a trained electrical technician who studies at the local college and then enters the army, and the other as a student at West Point, targeted for the officer corps, and trained as a medical doctor — both of them educated on the government's dime. We know that you army brats are not military fanatics. Instead, you are inheritors of a broad and proud American tradition of military service, looking to build a career in one of the most important sectors of the American workforce.

THE HIGH SCHOOL HERO

There are adults who see high school as the best years of their lives. You may be a high school athlete or campus leader — with great social skills and a reasonable academic record — but you feel seriously unsure about the future. You must know that very few of you are going on to become professional athletes. In our world, the best ones are marked for greatness in their early teens. Being the best athlete in a mid-sized regional high school might not even put you in the top one hundred in your state. So, what now? If you are a good athlete — and, surprisingly, the best opportunities may be in the smaller sports, such as gymnastics, golf, or diving — look into athletic scholarships. American colleges have great deals — providing as much as free tuition and room and board — for top athletes. If you truly love your sport, even if it will not be a full career, why not ride it as far as you can? If you don't know what you want to do career-wise, consider taking a year off to work, travel, or volunteer. You need to put the cheering crowds and high school heroics behind you and focus on your career and educational prospects.

THE "TIGER MOM" SURVIVOR

You have intense parents. You have done well in school and have high grades and an impressive list of accomplishments. Your parents have been on your case since elementary school, insisting on music lessons, extra-curricular homework (don't you love Kumon, Oxford, and the Sylvan Learning Centers?), volunteer activities, and a sport or two. They have driven you mercilessly, and you are tired of the lack of free time and the control exerted by your parents. Take the time to give your folks a big hug and a great "thank you." You are better prepared than most for what lies ahead. Sure they pushed you — to be ready for a harsh, competitive world where the advantages go to the most intense and highly motivated people. You have real potential to succeed at university or technical school. Don't resent what your parents did to and for you. In the years to come, you will discover how much better prepared you were for adulthood than your classmates who were coddled and spoiled by their parents. But speak frankly to them about what you want. While they often have fixed ideas about what you should do — medicine, law, accounting — many will change their minds if you show you have done your homework on a par-ticular career. If that doesn't work, consider drawing a teacher or guidance counselor into the conversation.

THE CHALLENGE SURVIVOR

An increasing number of students with serious learning difficulties and mental health issues are making it through high school and even through college and university by virtue of an enormous amount of hard work and parental devotion. These are people who, two generations ago, would have been simply sidelined — and we heartily applaud them for their achieve-ments. Only those young people wrestling with these challenges — and their parents and siblings, of course — understand in full the frustrations, difficulties, and effort required to succeed. Our elementary and secondary schools have many more supports than in the past, providing young people with a platform upon which they can build a choice of futures. Postsecondary institutions provide similar assistance, and many more students are overcoming psychological or other barriers to learning. Our country is much the better for their determination. They may face other challenges with the transition to the workplace. We think, though, that if you can master the world of postsecondary education, you can probably master anything, and we have no fears for your future. Good for you. Do not, however, assume that the next stages will be easy or automatic, as there are significant barriers to advancement still in place. The work ethic and sheer guts you needed to move forward, however, have likely prepared you well for the difficult issues of the workforce.

THE REST

These profiles cover the great majority of high school graduates. Simple categories, of course, never cover everyone. There are other groups — stoners, dropouts, juvenile delinquents — who face real challenges in the coming years. Some of you — are you reading this book? — were ill served by being kept in high school until you were seventeen or eighteen years old. You would have been far better off getting some work experience — and a jolt of reality — starting at sixteen. Too bad that our society makes it so difficult to have a good life without at least a high school education. If you are in this category, you will need to make a strong effort to succeed in life. But it can be done, and we urge you to do it. Someone in this category who reads and can write reasonably well can recover and find good opportunities down the road. Ditto those with technical skills, from car mechanics to computer programmers. Most of you, particularly those with behavioral or social issues, need time to grow into your brain. While your classmates are facing difficult choices at seventeen and eighteen, you will have your turn ten years later. When the time is right, colleges are great places to relaunch yourself, and apprenticeships can serve very nicely if you are technically minded. Like it or not, you are going to have to take time off now, probably to find a job of some sort. Life is not over at eighteen, by a long shot. Surprise yourself, your parents, and your classmates. You can make a lot of your life — but it will take hard work. You are part of a large group in the United States — and government, business, and the education system are seriously worried about you. Unless you, collectively, get your act together, this country could be in serious difficulty. But the idea that you are ready for college is, given your underperformance and lack of motivation, a serious error. Some of you will go on to college and university and will become dropout statistics. A third of those who enter college don't finish their program. What good does it do you to be one of them? You leave with no credentials and likely a sizeable debt. Don't go down this path.

A FINAL NOTE TO STUDENTS

In the end, the decision about your future is really up to you. Parents are influential, and so are teachers. They have your best interests at heart, but they are not going to live the rest of your life for you. Don't underestimate the importance of the choice you are about to make. There are tens of thousands of dollars in immediate costs involved — and a career of earning and opportunity waiting to be defined.

We know it's hard. Life is like that — awkward, complicated, unnerving, and very, very real. You are about to become an adult — and we know that the prospect is scarier than most of you are prepared to admit. There are no easy paths ahead. Hard work, curiosity, intelligence, integrity, and character will ultimately matter more than whatever credential you end up with. Welcome to the reality of the twenty-first century. It *is* a jungle out there, with no easy path and no obvious choices. If we have alerted you to the wide range of possibilities and convinced you to take this post-high school decision very seriously, we have done our job. Over to you.

A FINAL NOTE TO PARENTS

We have been rough on you. We are parents, and grandparents too. These have been hard decades to be a parent, with the pressures of economic uncertainty, popular culture, drugs, teenage sexuality, and on and on. Oh, for the easier times of our youth, right? But North American parenting has been a significant part of the problem facing our children. Many parents have been permissive, and have given their children everything they possibly could want — probably too much and too soon. We bought into the cult of self-esteem, without realizing that telling our children they can be all they want to be is hokum. (Did that work for you? Great if it did — but Ken dreamed of being a major league baseball player and that plan never made it past Babe Ruth League.) The global economy has been tough. You know this, in your own lives and in those of friends and neighbors around you. And you want what is best for your kids. We get that.

But be wary of following the crowd, of assuming that the *learning* = *earning* mantra of our age actually means something. You need to help your children get the right opportunities, not the popular ones. If they are truly ready for college, then prepare them for it, save money (and make them pay part of the cost), and support them in their exploration of campuses and programs. Try not to impose your will on them. Instead, focus on encouraging them to keep their options open rather than narrow their vision to a single degree. Make sure they keep up their math and science in high school, support a broad first-year program so that they can explore postsecondary opportunities, go with them to visit colleges, universities, or technical schools. If they are uncertain, do not rush them. A year of work, travel, or volunteering could do them a world of good.

Your greatest challenge is going to be letting go. Your children are young adults. They have to become independent-minded, even if that means making mistakes and suffering broken dreams. Congratulations on getting your sons or daughters through to high school graduation. While academically this is not the challenge it once was, socially it is a much harder task than in the past. A complex, ever-changing world awaits them. You have done your very best to get them ready.

* * *

We want to end by returning to a point we have made repeatedly. To students: try to avoid going with the flow — joining in with what we've called the swarm. In our new world, specialization and differentiation matter much more than being part of the crowd that, lemming-like, may be headed for the employment and career cliff. America's system of colleges, technical schools, universities, and apprenticeship programs provides many avenues for personal development. Work, entrepreneurship, volunteering, and travel add to the range of options. To parents: your children — your young adults — need the ability to navigate the world on their own, and on their own terms. Support them in this vital journey, even if it takes a markedly different path than you had anticipated. Their future is not going to be the same as our past. If we are lucky, it will be even better, with more opportunities and additional benefits. But, finally, *it is their world*, not yours, or ours. It is our duty to launch them on their way. From this point on, they are in control.

Ken Coates
Bill Morrison

APPENDIX

COLLEGE RANKINGS – SOME USEFUL, SOME NOT SO MUCH ...

No country in the world is as infatuated with ratings as the United States. College football and college basketball ratings are national obsessions. *Entertainment Tonight* rates the movies, and the website Rotten Tomatoes found a way to convert personal views about movies into a national rating system. Americans rate their politicians (www.congressratings.com), their restaurants (tripadvisor.com; yelp.com), college professors (ratemyprofessors.com), and doctors (www.ratemds.com). Since the release of the movie *10* in 1979, men have been using the ten-point scale to rate women (women are equally numerical in their rating of men, but they are less blatant about it). But nowhere — nothing else is even close — is this obsession with ratings as clear and intense as with colleges and universities.

Colleges are obsessively concerned about ratings that, in our opinion, are more misleading than helpful. We encourage you to ignore the ratings system entirely, and to focus instead on the match between your needs and abilities and the four thousand institutions out there. Princeton and Stanford are brilliant institutions, well-deserving of their reputations. But they are absolutely the wrong place for many students. Minot State University in North Dakota is no one's idea of an Ivy League elite institution and it is not highly regarded nationally (to use the ratings systems we abhor, it is listed as the 103rd best college in the U.S. Midwest by *U.S. News & World Report*), but it is a fine choice for small-town high school graduates of middling academic standard. Those same students would crash and burn at Yale; at Minot State, they have a much better chance of achieving their academic and professional potential.

The institutional ratings tell you next to nothing about the likely experience for an undergraduate student. A high-achieving, academically driven student would do best at Swarthmore or Middlebury, two of our favorite colleges. A more creative but committed student should look at Reed College, a brave institution that thumbs its collective nose at the ratings system. A free-thinking, innovative student should check out Evergreen State. Ratings systems reflect things like faculty research, reputation, size of the library, residence facilities, and other measurable elements. They absolutely will not tell you whether or not a particular institution is the best choice for you. So, please resist the temptation — one that drives many parents, who can become obsessed with national reputation — to focus on ratings.

Ratings can be fun, but take them as nothing more than a manifestation of America's preoccupation with relative standing. Check out the lists below — from the "best colleges and universities" to the best places for surfing, sex, drugs, libraries, residence life, and students with deafness. These ranking systems are subjective, and in some cases irrelevant or just plain stupid. Knowing the best-rated school in the United States for sex (Rutgers, in case you want to know) is meaningless if you go there and cannot get a date. Discovering — surprise! — that Brigham Young University has the most drug-free environment is of limited value if you stumble across the campus dealer the day you arrive in residence.

The best word on the subject is an article on the Salon website[1] that points out how meaningless these ratings are, and why you shouldn't base a "life-changing decision" on them. The gist of the article is that the ratings hardly ever talk about the ever-increasing cost of college, and instead talk about various amenities:

> ... the fact that Harvard University takes the time to detail the vast expanse of its amenities (70 individual libraries, a 3,000-acre forest research station, 12 teaching museums, a 265-acre arboretum making up just some of them, in case you were wondering) in the first few pages of its brochure shows just how significant they are to a college's image. What brochures don't tell you is that these extensive amenities are covered by the rising

college tuition. This is especially true for public universities, where tuition covers nearly half of their revenue.

On the other hand, perhaps you want to know the campus where people have super-high SAT scores, or the places where it's easiest to score — drugs, sex, or maybe even a good library. So for fun, and for whatever they are worth to you, we include a few of them here. If you go to the web pages listed in the endnotes associated with the lists, you can find out much more about each of the institutions listed.

TOP TWENTY SAT SCORES RANKING: WHICH COLLEGES HAVE THE BRIGHTEST KIDS?

(average critical reading and math scores)

1.	California Institute of Technology	1,545
2.	University of Chicago	1,515
3.	Harvard University	1,505
4.	Princeton University	1,505
5.	Yale University	1,500
6.	Vanderbilt University	1,490
7.	Franklin Olin College of Engineering	1,489
8.	Washington U in St. Louis	1,485
9.	Harvey Mudd College	1,480
10.	Columbia University New York	1,480
11.	Stanford University	1,475
12.	Northwestern University	1,470
13.	Pomona College	1,460
14.	Rice University	1,460
15.	Dartmouth College	1,455
16.	Duke University	1,455
17.	University of Pennsylvania	1,450
18.	Tufts University	1,445
19.	Williams College	1,445
20.	Amherst College	1,440

Source: *www.forbes.com/sites/schifrin/2014/08/04/top-100-sat-scores-ranking-which-colleges-have-the-brightest-kids*

AMERICA'S TOP TEN COLLEGES IN 2014

(according to Forbes magazine, with annual cost)

1.	Williams College	$61,850
2.	Stanford	$60,749
3.	Swarthmore	$60,671
4.	Princeton	$55,832

5.	Massachusetts Institute of Technology	$59,020
6.	Yale	$61,620
7.	Harvard	$59,950
8.	Pomona College	$59,730
9.	U.S. Military Academy	n/a
10.	Amherst	$61,544

Source: *www.forbes.com/sites/carolinehoward/2014/07/30/americas-top-colleges-2014*

TEN BIGGEST COLLEGES IN AMERICA

(by undergraduate enrollment)

1.	University of Central Florida	51,269
2.	DeVry University (IL)	48,782
3.	Liberty University (VA)	47,460
4.	Texas A&M University-College Station	44,315
5.	Ohio State University—Columbus	44,201
6.	Pennsylvania State University—University Park	40,085
7.	University of Texas-Austin	39,979
8.	Florida International University	39,045
9.	Arizona State University—Tempe	38,735
10.	Michigan State University	37,988

Source: *www.usnews.com/education/best-colleges/the-short-list-college/articles/2014/09 /09/ 10-most-least-pricey-private-colleges-and-universities*

TEN MOST EXPENSIVE PRIVATE COLLEGES 2014–15

(tuition and fees)

1.	Columbia University, NY	$51,008
2.	Sarah Lawrence College, NY	$50,780
3.	Vassar College, NY	$49,570
4.	Trinity College, CT	$49,056
5.	Carnegie Mellon University, PA	$48,786
6.	George Washington University, DC	$48,760
7.	Oberlin College, OH	$48,682
8.	Tufts University, MA	$48,643
9.	Harvey Mudd College, CA	$48,594
10.	Bard College at Simon's Rock, MA	$48,551

Source: *www.usnews.com/education/best-colleges/the-short-list-college/articles/2014/09 /09/ 10-most-least-pricey-private-colleges-and-universities*

TEN LEAST EXPENSIVE PRIVATE COLLEGES 2014–15

(tuition and fees)

1.	Berea College, KY	$870
2.	Brigham Young University-Provo, UT	$5,000
3.	LeMoyne-Owen College, TN	$5,450
4.	Rust College, MS	$9,286
5.	Tougaloo College, MS	$10,210

6.	Amridge University, AL	$10,305
7.	Philander Smith College, AR	$10,490
8.	Life University, GA	$10,500
9.	Blue Mountain College, MS	$10,534
10.	Alice Lloyd College, KY	$10,980

Source: *www.usnews.com/education/best-colleges/the-short-list-college/articles/2014/ 09 /09/10-most-least-pricey-private-colleges-and-universities*

TEN BIGGEST ONLINE COLLEGES

(student population as of 2013)

1.	University of Phoenix	442,033
2.	Ivy Tech Community College	175,313
3.	American Public University System	110,644
4.	Miami Dade College	100,855
5.	Lone Star College System	98,313
6.	Liberty University	95,639
7.	Houston Community College	93,625
8.	Arizona State University	81,789
9.	Kaplan University—Davenport Campus	77,566
10.	Northern Virginia Community College	77,552

Source: *http://collegestats.org/colleges/online/largest*

TEN BIGGEST PRIVATE COLLEGES

(student population as of 2013)

1.	New York University	38,391
2.	Brigham Young University	34,126
3.	University of Southern California	33,500
4.	Boston University	32,735
5.	Liberty University	32,222
6.	Nova Southeastern University	28,796
7.	Columbia University	25,495
8.	Northeastern University	24,752
9.	DePaul University	24,352
10.	Long Island University	24,170

Source: *www.answers.com/Q/List_the_10_largest_private_universities_in_the_US*

TOP TEN COLLEGES FOR HISPANIC STUDENTS

(percentage of Hispanic students)

1.	University of California, Santa Cruz	26%
2.	San Diego State	27%
3.	University of California, Riverside	32%
4.	Whittier College, Whittier, CA	35%
5.	St. Edwards University, Austin, TX	33%
6.	California State Polytechnic, Pomona, CA	35%
7.	University of La Verne, La Verne, CA	48%

8.	University of Houston	25%
9.	Florida International University, Miami	66%
10.	California State University, Long Beach	33%

Source: *www.bestcolleges.com/features/top-50-colleges-for-hispanic-students*

TOP TEN HISTORICALLY BLACK COLLEGES

1. Morehouse College, Atlanta
2. Howard University, Washington DC
3. Spelman College, Atlanta
4. Fisk University, Nashville
5. Florida A&M, Tallahassee
6. Tuskegee University, Tuskegee, AL
7. North Carolina A&T, Greenville
8. Xavier University, New Orleans
9. Winston-Salem State, Winston-Salem, NC
10. Tougaloo College, Tougaloo, MS

Source: *www.bestcolleges.com/features/top-30-historically-black-colleges*

TOP TEN PARTY SCHOOLS

1. Syracuse University, Syracuse, NY
2. University of Iowa, Iowa City, IA
3. University of California-Santa Barbara, Santa Barbara, CA
4. West Virginia University, Morgantown, WV
5. University of Illinois at Champaign, Champaign, IL
6. Lehigh University, Bethlehem, PA
7. Penn State University, University Park, PA
8. University of Wisconsin-Madison, Madison, WI
9. Bucknell University, Lewisburg, PA
10. University of Florida, Gainesville, FL

Source: *www.collegeatlas.org/top-party-schools.html*

TEN BEST LIBERAL ARTS COLLEGES

1. Williams College
2. Amherst College
3. Swarthmore College
4. Wellesley College
5. *Bowdoin College
6. *Pomona College
7. Middlebury College
8. **Carleton College
9. **Claremont College
10. **Haverford College

(* and ** indicate ties)

Source: *http://colleges.usnews.rankingsandreviews.com/best-colleges/rankings/national-liberal-arts-colleges*

TEN BEST COLLEGES BY REGION — NORTH

1. United States Coast Guard Academy, New London, CT
2. Cooper Union College, New York, NY
3. United States Merchant Marine Academy, Kings Point, NY
4. Elizabethtown College, Elizabethtown, PA
5. Messiah College, Mechanicsburg, PA
6. Lebanon Valley College, Annville, PA
7. Massachusetts Maritime Academy, Buzzards Bay, MA
8. Maine Maritime Academy, Castine, ME
9. *Elmira College, Elmira, NY
10. *Merrimack College, North Andover, MA

(* Tied for ninth place.)

Rankings are based on indicators of excellence such as freshman retention and graduation rates and the strength of the faculty. Focus is on undergraduate degrees.

Source: *http://colleges.usnews.rankingsandreviews.com/best-colleges/rankings/regional-colleges-north*

TEN BEST COLLEGES BY REGION — SOUTH

1. *Asbury University,Wilmore, KY
2. *High Point University, High Point, NC
3. *John Brown University, Siloam Springs, AR
4. University of the Ozarks, Clarksville, AR
5. Florida Southern College, Lakeland, FL
6. **Covenant College, Lookout Mountain, GA
7. **Meredith College, Raleigh, NC
8. Flagler College, St. Augustine, FL
9. ***Milligan College, Milligan College, TN
10. ***Tuskegee University, Tuskegee, AL

(* Tied for first place. ** Tied for sixth place. *** Tied for ninth place.)

Source: *http://colleges.usnews.rankingsandreviews.com/best-colleges/rankings/regional-colleges-south*

TEN BEST COLLEGES BY REGION — MIDWEST

1. Taylor University, Upland, IN
2. Ohio Northern University, Ada, OH
3. Augustana College, Sioux Falls, SD
4. College of the Ozarks, Point Lookout, MO
5. Dordt College, Sioux Center, IA
6. *Cedarville University, Cedarville, OH
7. *Franklin College, Franklin, IN
8. *Marietta College, Marietta, OH
9. *Northwestern College, Orange City, IA
10. University of Northwestern-St. Paul, St. Paul, MN

(* Tied for sixth place.)

Source: *http://colleges.usnews.rankingsandreviews.com/best-colleges/rankings/regional-colleges -midwest*

TEN BEST COLLEGES BY REGION — WEST

1. Carroll College, Helena, MT
2. Texas Lutheran University, Seguin, TX
3. California Maritime Academy, Vallejo, CA
4. Oklahoma Baptist University, Shawnee, OK
5. The Master's College, Santa Clarita, CA
6. Oklahoma Wesleyan University, Bartlesville, OK
7. Corban University, Salem, OR
8. *Menlo College, Atherton, CA
9. *Oregon Institute of Technology, Klamath Falls, OR
10. *Warner Pacific College, Portland, OR

(* Tied for eighth place.)

Source: *http://colleges.usnews.rankingsandreviews.com/best-colleges/rankings/regional-colleges-midwest*

TOP TEN SPORTS COLLEGES: MOST ACADEMICALLY AND ATHLETICALLY DOMINANT

1. University of Florida
2. University of Michigan
3. Ohio State University
4. University of Texas at Austin
5. Stanford University
6. University of Alabama
7. University of North Carolina at Chapel Hill
8. University of California
9. University of Southern California
10. University of Oregon

Source: *www.ranker.com/crowdranked-list/universities-with-the-best-college-sports-programs*

TWENTY HARDEST COLLEGES TO GET INTO

(undergraduate acceptance rates as a percentage, 2013)

1.	Stanford University	5.7%
2.	Harvard University	5.8%
3.	Columbia University	6.9%
4.	Yale University	6.9%
5.	Princeton University	7.4%
6.	United States Naval Academy	7.4%
7.	Cooper Union College	7.7%
8.	Massachusetts Institute of Technology	8.2%
9.	University of Chicago	8.8%
10.	United States Military Academy	9%
11.	Brown University	9.2%
12.	Alice Lloyd College	9.4%

13.	Dartmouth College	10.4%
14.	California Institute of Technology	10.6%
15.	Claremont McKenna College	11.7%
16.	College of the Ozarks	12.2%
17.	University of Pennsylvania	12.2%
18.	Duke University	12.4%
19.	Vanderbilt University	12.7%
20.	Pomono College	13.9%

Source: *http://colleges.usnews.rankingsandreviews.com/best-colleges/rankings/lowest-acceptance-rate*

TWENTY EASIEST COLLEGES TO GET INTO
(all accept 100 percent of undergraduate applications)
1. Bismarck State College, Bismarck, ND
2. City University of Seattle, Seattle, WA
3. CUNY — College of Staten Island, Staten Island, NY
4. CUNY — Medgar Evers College, Brooklyn, NY
5. Daytona State College, Daytona Beach, FL
6. Dixie State College of Utah, Saint George, UT
7. Granite State College, Concord, NH
8. Indian River State College, Fort Pierce, FL
9. Jarvis Christian College, Hawkins, TX
10. Metropolitan State University, St. Paul, MN
11. Missouri Western State University, St. Joseph, MO
12. New Mexico Highlands University, Las Vegas, NM
13. Oklahoma State University — Oklahoma City, Oklahoma City, OK
14. University of Maryland — University College, Adelphi, MD
15. University of Pikeville, Pikeville, KY
16. University of the Potomac, Washington, DC
17. Utah Valley University, Orem, UT
18. Wayne State College, Wayne, NE
19. Weber State University, Ogden, UT
20. Western International University, Tempe, AZ

Source: *http://colleges.usnews.rankingsandreviews.com/best-colleges/rankings/highest-acceptance-rate*

TEN HIGHEST GRADUATION RATES
(percentage of students entering in 2007 who graduated in four years)

1.	Franklin W. Olin College of Engineering, Needham, MA	93%
2.	Pomona College, Claremont, CA	93%
3.	Fashion Institute of Design & Merchandising, Los Angeles, CA	91%
4.	Haverford College, Haverford, PA	91%
5.	Amherst College, Amherst, MA	90%
6.	Carleton College, Northfield, MN	90%
7.	Davidson College, Davidson, NC	90%
8.	Hamilton College, Clinton, NY	90%

9.	University of Notre Dame, Notre Dame, IN	90%
10.	Vassar College, Poughkeepsie, NY	90%

Source: *http://colleges.usnews.rankingsandreviews.com/best-colleges/rankings/highest-grad-rate*

TEN CO-ED COLLEGES WITH THE HIGHEST PERCENTAGE OF FEMALE STUDENTS

1.	Pacific Oaks College, Pasadena, CA	95.95%
2.	St. Anthony College of Nursing, Rockford, IL	93.88%
3.	LIM College, New York, NY	93.43%
4.	Allen College, Waterloo, IA	93.25%
5.	University of Tennessee Health Science Center, Memphis, TN	92.94%
6.	Research College of Nursing, Kansas City, MO	92.72%
7.	Trinity College of Nursing and Health Sciences, Rock Island, IL	92.24%
8.	Cabarrus College of Health Sciences, Concord, NC	92.18%
9.	Chamberlain College of Nursing-St. Louis, St. Louis, MO	91.85%
10.	Sojourner-Douglass College, Baltimore, MD	91.52%

Source: *www.collegexpress.com/lists/list/co-ed-colleges-with-the-highest-percentage-of-women -students/370/*

TEN CO-ED COLLEGES WITH THE HIGHEST PERCENTAGE OF MALE STUDENTS

1.	The Citadel, Charleston, SC	90.38%
2.	Virginia Military Institute, Lexington, VA	89.96%
3.	Massachusetts Maritime Academy, Buzzards Bay, MA	89.94%
4.	Neumont University, South Jordan, UT	89.98%
5.	University of Advancing Technology, Tempe, AZ	89.78%
6.	Embry-Riddle Aeronautical University, Daytona Beach, FL	88.57%
7.	Vaughn College of Aeronautics and Technology, Flushing, NY	87.02%
8.	United States Merchant Marine Academy, Kings Point, NY	86.84%
9.	California Maritime Academy —Vallejo, CA	86.7%
10.	United States Military Academy, West Point, NY	83.93%

Source: *www.collegexpress.com/lists/list/co-ed-colleges-with-the-highest-percentage-of-male -students/367/*

TEN MOST ETHNICALLY DIVERSE COLLEGES

1. Rutgers, Newark, NJ
2. Andrews University, Berrien Springs, MI
3. Stanford University, Stanford, CA
4. St. John's University, Queens, NY
5. University of Houston, Houston, TX
6. University of Hawaii-Manoa, Honolulu, HI
7. University of Nevada-Las Vegas, Las Vegas, NV
8. University of San Francisco, San Francisco, CA
9. Nova Southeastern University, Fort Lauderdale, FL
10. Texas Woman's University, Denton, TX

The categories used in the calculations are black or African American, Hispanic, American Indian, Asian, Pacific Islander, white (non-Hispanic), and multiracial. Students who did not identify themselves as members of any of those demographic groups were classified as whites who are non-Hispanic for the purpose of these calculations.

Source: *http://colleges.usnews.rankingsandreviews.com/best-colleges/rankings/national-universities/campus-ethnic-diversity*

TEN BEST COLLEGE RESIDENCES
(percentage of students living on campus)

1.	Princeton University	97%
2.	Columbia University	95%
3.	Massachusetts Institute of Technology	93%
4.	California Institute of Technology	92%
5.	University of California — San Diego	92%
6.	Stanford University	91%
7.	Yale University	88%
8.	Dartmouth College	86%
9.	Stevens Institute of Technology	85%
10.	Vanderbilt University	85%

Source: *www.usnews.com/education/slideshows/top-10-colleges-for-housing/1*

TOP TEN MILITARY COLLEGES

1. U.S. Naval Academy
2. U.S. Military Academy (West Point)
3. Texas A & M University
4. U.S. Air Force Academy
5. Norwich University
6. Virginia Military Institute
7. The Citadel
8. U.S. Coast Guard Academy
9. U.S. Merchant Marine Academy
10. Valley Forge Military Academy & College

Source: *www.toptenz.net/top-10-military-schools.php*

TOP TEN COLLEGES FOR ENGINEERING AND TECHNOLOGY 2014
(global ranking provided on the right)

1.	Massachusetts Institute of Technology	1
2.	Stanford University	2
3.	University of California, Berkeley	3
4.	California Institute of Technology	4
5.	Princeton University	5
6.	University of California, Los Angeles	10
7.	Georgia Institute of Technology	11

8. Carnegie Mellon University	12
9. University of Texas at Austin	14
10. University of Michigan	16

Source: *www.timeshighereducation.co.uk/world-university-rankings/2013-14/subject-ranking/subject/engineering-and-IT*

BEST TEN COLLEGES FOR FRESHMAN RETENTION RATE

(colleges where first-year students are most likely to return in second year)

1. Columbia University, New York, NY	99%
2. University of Chicago, Chicago, IL	99%
3. Yale University, New Haven, CT	99%
4. Brown University, Providence, RI	98%
5. Dartmouth College, Hanover, NH	98%
6. Massachusetts Institute of Technology, Cambridge, MA	98%
7. Princeton University, Princeton, NJ	98%
8. Stanford University, Standford, CA	98%
9. University of Notre Dame, Notre Dame, IN	98%
10. University of Pennsylvania, Philadelphia, PA	98%

Source: *http://colleges.usnews.rankingsandreviews.com/best-colleges/rankings/national-universities/freshmen-least-most-likely-return*

TOP TEN CHRISTIAN UNIVERSITIES AND COLLEGES

1. Emmanuel College, Franklin Springs, GA
2. Indiana Wesleyan University, Marion, IN
3. Fresno Pacific University, Fresno, CA
4. Shorter University, Rome, GA
5. Asbury University, Wilmore, KY
6. Bethel College, Mishawaka, IN
7. Warner Pacific College, Portland OR
8. North Greenville University, Tigerville, SC
9. College of the Ozarks, near Branson, MO
10. Waynesburg University, Waynesburg, PA

Source: *www.christianuniversitiesonline.org/top-christian-colleges-exceeding-expectations*

FIRST THINGS' TOP TEN SCHOOLS IN AMERICA 2010

(First Things is an ecumenical religious journal)

1. Wheaton College, Wheaton, IL
2. Thomas Aquinas College, Santa Paula, CA
3. Princeton University, Princeton, NJ
4. United States Air Force Academy, Colorado Springs, CO
5. Brigham Young University, Provo, UT
6. Yeshiva University, New York, NY
7. University of Virginia, Charlottesville, VA

8. Duke University, Durham, NC
9. University of Chicago, Chicago, IL
10. Franciscan University of Steubenville, Steubenville, OH

Source: *www.firstthings.com/article/2010/11/college-rankings*. All the *First Things'* lists are taken from this source. You can read it online to see the criteria they used.

FIRST THINGS' FIVE SCHOOLS ON THE RISE, FILLED WITH EXCITEMENT

1. Belmont Abbey College, Belmont, NC
2. Wake Forest University, Winston-Salem, NC
3. Houston Baptist University, Houston, TX
4. The King's College, New York, NY
5. Concordia University Wisconsin, Mequon, WI

FIRST THINGS' FIVE SCHOOLS IN DECLINE, FILLED WITH GLOOM

1. Valparaiso University, Valparaiso, IN
2. Gonzaga University, Spokane, WA
3. Dartmouth College, Hanover, NH
4. Azusa Pacific University, Azusa, CA
5. Notre Dame of Maryland University, Baltimore, MD

FIRST THINGS' TOP SEVEN SECULAR SCHOOLS LEAST UNFRIENDLY TO FAITH

1. Princeton University, Princeton, NJ
2. Duke University, Durham, NC
3. University of Virginia, Charlottesville, VA
4. University of Chicago, Chicago, IL
5. Stanford University, Stanford, CA
6. Columbia University, New York, NY
7. California Institute of Technology, Pasadena, CA

FIRST THINGS' TOP TEN MOST CATHOLIC CATHOLIC SCHOOLS

1. Ave Maria University, Ave Maria, FL
2. Christendom College, Christendom, VA
3. Franciscan University of Steubenville, Steubenville, OH
4. Thomas Aquinas College, Santa Paula, CA
5. Benedictine College, Atchinson, KS
6. Belmont Abbey College, Belmont, NC
7. Thomas More College of Liberal Arts, Merrimack, NH
8. University of Dallas, Irving, TX
9. Providence College, Providence, RI
10. Mount St. Mary's University, Emmitsburg, MD

FIRST THINGS' TOP SIX LEAST CATHOLIC CATHOLIC SCHOOLS
(Presumably for those who want a taste of Roman Catholicism in their education, but not too much.)
1. DePaul University, Chicago, IL
2. University of Detroit Mercy, Detroit, MI
3. Seattle University, Seattle, WA
4. Niagara University, Niagara Falls, NY
5. University of San Diego, San Diego, CA
6. Lewis University, Romeoville, IL

FIRST THINGS' TEN BEST SERIOUSLY PROTESTANT SCHOOLS
1. Wheaton College, Wheaton, IL
2. Calvin College, Grand Rapids, MI
3. Taylor University, Upland, IN
4. Gordon College, Wenham, MA
5. George Fox University, Newberg, OR
6. Westmount College, Santa Barbara, CA
7. Seattle Pacific University, Seattle, WA
8. Houghton College, Houghton, NY
9. Grove City College, Grove City, PA
10. Whitworth College, Spokane, WA

AMERICA'S TWENTY DRUGGIEST COLLEGES
1. University of Colorado-Boulder, Boulder, CO
2. Denison University, Granville, OH
3. Dartmouth College, Hanover, NH
4. Bryant University, Smithfield, RI
5. Kenyon College, Gambier, OH
6. Illinois State University, Normal, IL
7. University of Oregon, Eugene, OR
8. SUNY-Purchase, Purchase, NY
9. Bates College, Lewiston, ME
10. SUNY-Fredonia, Fredonia, NY
11. Ohio Wesleyan, Delaware, OH
12. Eckerd College, St. Petersburg, FL
13. Rowan University, Glassboro, NJ
14. Grinnell College, Ginnell, IA
15. Trinity College, Hartford, CT
16. University of Rhode Island, Kingston, RI
17. Dickinson College, Carlisle, PA
18. Penn State, Erie, PA
19. University of New Hampshire, Durham, NH
20. University of Montana, Missoula, MT

Source: *www.thedailybeast.com/galleries/2011/12/01/druggiest-colleges-universities-photos.html#slide_22*

TEN LEAST VALUABLE COLLEGE MAJORS

(Starting with the least. Figures are earnings and unemployment rate of recent grads.)

1. Anthropology and Archaeology — $28,000, 10.5%
2. Film, Video, and Photographic Arts — $30,000, 12.9%
3. Fine Arts — $30,000, 12.6%
4. Philosophy and Religious Studies — $30,000, 10.8%
5. Liberal Arts — $30,000, 9.2%
6. Music — $30,000, 9.2%
7. Physical Fitness and Parks and Recreation — $30,000, 8.3%
8. Commercial Art and Graphic Design — $32,000, 11.8%
9. History — $32,000, 10.2%
10. English Language and Literature — $32,000, 9.2%

Source: *www.forbes.com/pictures/fgek45hg/the-least-valuable-college-majors/*

AMERICA'S TEN WORST COLLEGES

(Based on an equal weighting of tuition cost, graduation rate, average student debt, and default rate on debt. Worst one first.)

1. New England Institute of Art, MA (for-profit)
2. Columbia College, Hollywood, CA
3. Fountainhead College of Tech, TN (for-profit)
4. St. Augustine's University, NC
5. Platt College, Aurora, CO (for-profit)
6. Becker College, MA
7. Brooks Institute, CA (for-profit)
8. Mt. Sierra College, CA (for-profit)
9. Menlo College, CA
10. University of Advancing Technology, CA (for-profit)

Source: *www.washingtonmonthly.com/magazine/septemberoctober_2014/ features/americas_worst_colleges051752.php?page=all*

TOP TEN UNIVERSITIES FOR SKIING AND SNOWBOARDING

1. University of Colorado at Boulder
2. University of Utah
3. University of Vermont
4. Dartmouth College
5. Montana State University
6. University of Washington
7. Oregon State University
8. Boise State University
9. University of Southern California
10. University of California at Berkeley

Source: *www.theskichannel.com/news/featured/20130622/top-10-universities-for-skiing*

TEN BEST COLLEGES AND UNIVERSITIES FOR STUDENTS WITH DISABILITIES

1. Samford University, AL
2. University of Alaska, Fairbanks, AK
3. Diablo Valley College, Pleasant Hill, CA
4. Barry University, Miami Shores, FL
5. Beacon University, Leesburg, FL
6. DePaul University, Chicago, IL
7. Anderson University, Anderson, IN
8. Iowa State University, Ames, IO
9. Massachusetts International College, Springfield, MA
10. Boston University, Boston, MA

Source: *http://disability.about.com/od/ChoosingCaregiversAndSchools/tp/Best-Colleges-And-Universities-For-Disabled-Students.htm*

TEN BEST COLLEGES FOR OLDER STUDENTS

1. University of Texas at Dallas, TX
2. University of Utah, Salt Lake City, UT
3. University of Massachusetts, Lowell, MA
4. Regis University, Denver, CO
5. Ohio University, Athens, OH
6. Florida International University, Miami, FL
7. University of Alabama at Birmingham, AL
8. Northwest Nazarene University, Nampa, ID
9. Augsburg College, Minneapolis, MN
10. St. Joseph's College, Brooklyn, NY

Source: *www.bestcolleges.com/features/50-best-colleges-for-older-students*

TOP TEN SURF COLLEGES

1. University of California, Santa Barbara, CA
2. Point Loma Nazarene University, San Diego, CA
3. University of California San Diego, San Diego, CA
4. University of California Santa Cruz, Santa Cruz, CA
5. New York University, New York, NY
6. Pepperdine University, Malibu, CA
7. California Polytechnic State University, San Luis Obispo, CA
8. University of Hawaii Manoa, Honolulu, HI
9. San Diego State University, San Diego, CA
10. University of North Carolina Wilmington, Wilmington, CA

Source: *www.surfermag.com/features/top-10-surf-colleges*

TEN MOST DTF COLLEGES IN AMERICA

(We are not going to tell you what DTF stands for; you can look it up online on Urban Dictionary. We include this cringe-making list simply as an example of how vulgar, stupid, and in this case sexist, some of these lists are.)

1. Rutgers
2. Arizona State
3. Harvard
4. University of Oregon
5. University of Connecticut
6. East Carolina University, Greenville
7. Colorado State
8. University of Texas, Austin
9. University of Wisconsin
10. University of Syracuse

Source: *www.brobible.com/college/article/the-most-dtf-colleges-in-america*

NOTES

CHAPTER 1

1. "Education Longitudinal Study of 2002 (ELS:2002): A First Look at 2002 High School Sophomores 10 Years Later," *NCES 2014-363*. U.S. Department of Education (January 2014).

2. http://education-portal.com/articles/How_Much_More_Do_College_Graduates_Earn_Than_Non-College_Graduates.html.

3. Zach Weiner, *Saturday Morning Breakfast Cereal*, www.smbc-comics.com/index.php?db=comics&id=2729#comic.

4. *Forbes* magazine publishes a list.

CHAPTER 2

1. "Fewer U.S. Graduates Opt for College after High School," *New York Times*, April 25, 2014.

2. http://nces.ed.gov/fastfacts/display.asp?id=16 .

3. U.S. Department of Education, cited in www.usnews.com/opinion/articles/2011/04/19/average-high-school-gpas-increased-since-1990.

4. The figure is from the *Christian Science Monitor*, www.csmonitor.com/Business/2013/0128/Have-degree-driving-cab-Nearly-half-of-college-grads-are-overqualified. In 1970 it was 1 percent.

5. On the subject of postsecondary education for firefighters in the United States, see www.insidehighered.com/news/2011/10/27/college-degrees-increasingly-help-firefighters-get-ahead.

6. The American National Retail Federation says that 49.5 percent of retail workers "have college degrees, are currently in college, or have attended college." Accessed November 15, 2014. www.nrf.com/modules. php?name=Pages&sp_id=1245.

CHAPTER 3

1. www.deepsprings.edu.

2. www.youtube.com/watch?v=eLdU7uts4ws.

3. Its 2010 reports says 470,000. www.phoenix.edu/about_us/publications/academic-annual-report/2010.html.

4. http://collegesofdistinction.com.

5. A serious proposal to build the Nixon presidential library on campus was narrowly turned down by a faculty vote. http://dukemagazine. duke.edu/article/nixon-library-wasnt.

6. www.collegechoice.net/posts/colleges-with-happiest-freshman.

7. http://wagner.edu/academics/undergraduate/fyp.

8. http://auabroad.american.edu/index.cfm?FuseAction=programs. ViewProgram&Program_ID=10500.

9. www.bc.edu/offices/fye/cornerstone.html; http://colleges.usnews. rankingsandreviews.com/best-colleges/rankings/first-year-experience-programs; www.hollywoodreporter.com/news/top-25-film-schools-united-721649.

10. www.pewhispanic.org/2013/05/09/hispanic-high-school-graduates-pass-whites-in-rate-of-college-enrollment.

11. Regents of the University of California v. Bakke 438 U.S. 265.

CHAPTER 4

1. www.aacc.nche.edu/aboutcc/21stcenturyreport_old/index.html.

2. A full list is at www.hfcc.edu/catalog/programs.

CHAPTER 10

1. U.S. Department of Labor, Registered Apprenticeship Program, www. doleta.gov/oa/pdf/fsback.pdf.

2. U.S. Department of Labor, Registered Apprenticeship Program, www. doleta.gov/oa/pdf/fsback.pdf.

3. The information is provided by the U.S. Department of Labor, on their registered apprenticeship website, www.doleta.gov/oa/pdf/fsfront.pdf.

4. www.doleta.gov/OA/occupations.cfm.

CHAPTER 12

1. http://learning.blogs.nytimes.com/2013/02/25/what-investment-are-you-willing-to-make-to-get-your-dream-job/?

2. www.marketwatch.com/story/nearly-4-out-of-5-students-work-2013 -08-07.

3. www.act.org/research/policymakers/pdf/issues.pdf.

4. https://www.applerouth.com/blog/2013/10/23/when-a-is-for-average-the-high-cost-of-grade-inflation.

5. www.smu.edu/Provost/ALEC/NeatStuffforNewStudents/HowIs CollegeDifferentfromHighSchool.

APPENDIX

1. www.salon.com/2014/09/15/the_big_college_ranking_sham_why_ you_must_ignore_u_s_news_and_worlds_report_list.

INDEX